Film Lighting

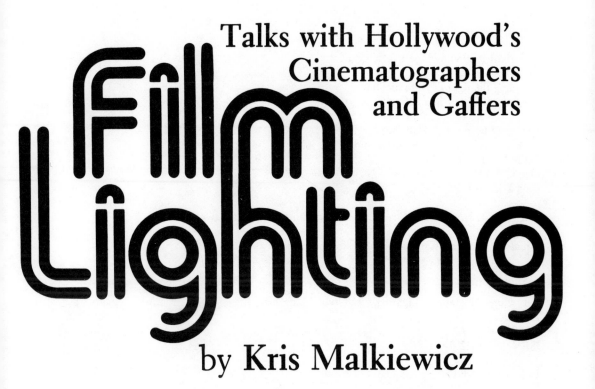

Talks with Hollywood's Cinematographers and Gaffers

Film Lighting

by Kris Malkiewicz

assisted by Barbara J. Gryboski

drawings by Leonard Konopelski

PRENTICE HALL PRESS · NEW YORK

Published by Prentice Hall Press
A Division of Simon & Schuster, Inc.
Gulf+Western Building
One Gulf+Western Plaza
New York, NY 10023

PRENTICE HALL PRESS is a trademark of Simon & Schuster, Inc.

Library of Congress Cataloging-in-Publication Data

Malkiewicz, Kris.
  Film lighting.

  1. Cinematography—Lighting. I. Gryboski, Barbara. J.
II. Title.
TR891.M35 1986   778.5′343   85-31177
ISBN 0-671-62271-4

Designed by Irv Perkins Associates

Manufactured in the United States of America

10 9 8 7 6 5 4 3 2

Acknowledgments

I AM GREATLY indebted to a large group of marvelous people who generously contributed with their expertise and their time: Richmond ("Aggie") Aguilar; John Alonzo, ASC; Bruce Berman; Bill Butler, ASC; James Crabe, ASC; Jordan Cronenweth, ASC; Nancy Cushing-Jones; Allen Daviau, ASC; Thomas Denove; Caleb Deschanel, ASC; Robert Hahn; Conrad Hall, ASC; Richard Hart; Adam Holender, ASC; Gary Holt; the late James Wong Howe, ASC; Philip Lathrop, ASC; Frank Leonetti; Richard Kline, ASC; Alexander Mackendrick; Michael D. Margulies, ASC; Sven Nykvist, ASC; James Plannette; Howard Prouty; Owen Roizman, ASC; Dr. Roderick T. Ryan; Douglas Slocombe, BSC; Haskell Wexler, ASC; Robert Wise; Harry Wolf, ASC; Ralph Woolsey, ASC; Vilmos Zsigmond, ASC.

There are others, too numerous to mention by name, who over the years shared with me their knowledge, either directly or as the authors of books and articles. *American Cinematographer* magazine was a particularly rich and inspiring source of information.

Contents

Preface

FILM LIGHTING is a living, changing art. Ever more sensitive film emulsions influence the choice of lighting equipment; advanced lamp design dictates new ways of lighting. To capture the essence of these new methods, I approached several cinematographers and gaffers to discuss their work and concepts. This led to many hours of interviews and many days on film sets in the studio and on location. It was a very rewarding experience. These innovative professionals proved to be very generous in sharing their techniques and ideas. I found the legendary closely guarded boxes of personal filters to be memories from the past. Today, there is a camaraderie of camera people freely exchanging their inventions with each other.

After transcribing the interviews I realized that preserving the voices of these people in the form of extensive quotations would bring the reader closer to this wealth of experience and advice. As a result, the same lighting problem is often discussed by four or five experts. In this way the state of the art film lighting emerges.

I feel most fortunate in securing the editorial help of Barbara Gryboski and in having the line drawings done by Leonard Konopelski. On the publisher's side of this venture I was greatly helped by senior editor Susan Gies.

Last but not least I am grateful to Alexis Krasilovsky for her creative typing of the manuscript.

CHAPTER One

The Cinematographer as Collaborator

"FILMS ARE light." This statement by Federico Fellini brings us to the essence of the cinematographer's art and function. One of the most important abilities of a cinematographer is to see light and to remember it. The "light memory" for the lighting cameraman is similar to the musical memory necessary for a musician.

Light is the most changing element in our daily life. We move among solid objects and among people who do not change drastically during a day or a week. But visually the appearance of our environment and of people around us may change from one hour to the next due to the time of day, the weather, or the particular source of the light. The best cinematographers are very aware of these changes and store in their memory the impact different types of light have on our emotions and our subconscious. Most people see the change in the quality of light as the day goes by, but a cinematographer must be as observant as the French impressionist painter Claude Monet, who painted the cathedral at Rouen from the same angle at various times of the day. When Sven Nykvist (ASC) and Ingmar Bergman prepared to shoot *Winter Light*, they spent an entire day observing the changes in light in a country church in Northern Sweden in order to be able to reproduce that winter light on a sound stage.

For a cinematographer, watching the light becomes second nature. Whether in a city hall, a restaurant, a night club, or in the woods, the cinematographer will file it away in his memory to be recalled when lighting a similar situation on a movie set. This will help in the final task of a cinematographer, which is to contribute to the visual character of the film.

Light will enhance or diminish the efforts of all the people who create the sets, the costumes and the makeup.

Filmmaking is a collaborative art. It would

be misleading to insist that the cinematographer is totally responsible for the visual character of the picture. Even in terms of the camera moves and framing, the creative process involves the director, the cinematographer and the camera operator, and it depends very much on their individual talents and personalities as to whose ideas are decisive in the final outcome. Yet lighting is the sole domain of the cinematographer. This is his most obvious contribution. Light can fall on the scene in a variety of ways. It can create a great many moods, but the task of the cinematographer is to choose the type of lighting that will best help to tell the story. The angle of light, its intensity, its quality (hard or soft), its color, these are some of the paints on the cinematographer's palette. The dark areas and shadows are of equal value. It was said by more than one cinematographer: "What you do *not* see is equally important as what you *do* see." The light is there to direct the viewer's attention, the darkness to stimulate his imagination.

As in all arts there are styles in lighting which characterize certain periods or certain film studios. For example the glossy Hollywood pictures of the thirties were followed by the stylized low-key lighting of film noir in the forties, and the Italian stark neorealism of the late forties and fifties.

Styles are also influenced by the personalities of the cinematographers and the technical progress in film stocks, lenses and the lighting equipment. Very sensitive emulsions and faster lenses require less light intensity. This allows for much greater use of soft, bounced or diffused light and of practical light sources that constitute part of the set. It also facilitates greater use of the available light, especially in backgrounds, such as in the streets at night. Collaboration between the cinematographer and the set designer who provides some of the lighting becomes essential.

In this chapter we will look at the various aspects of the collaboration between the cinematographer and the other vital members of the filmmaking team. Working with the director is one of the most exciting artistic relationships in this medium.

WORKING WITH THE DIRECTOR

Ideally the cinematographer's relationship with the director is a symbiotic one. The cinematographer embraces the director's vision and uses his visual talent and technical knowledge to capture the director's inner thoughts and put them on the screen. Needless to say, the process of choosing a cinematographer is of no small importance to the director.

THE HIRING PROCESS

Many directors choose a cinematographer much as they would cast an actor. They look at his body of work to evaluate his style and experience.

Alexander Mackendrick

It is my impression that most of the cameramen I know have developed a highly personal style. They have an individual character that becomes their stock in trade. During the planning for Sweet Smell of Success, *the producer, Harold Hecht, suggested James Wong Howe. I remembered Jimmy as extremely good with strong, melodramatic material and* felt his hard-edged approach would be ideal for this particular subject, so I was delighted.

Often a director will screen several films shot by a prospective cinematographer.

Alexander Mackendrick

In effect, I believe you have to trust the taste and temperament of the cameraman as you see it in his previous work. Obviously, you should take care to see a number of his films to see how he handles different genres; to see what range he has. Wong Howe had considerable range: I looked at both Body and Soul and Picnic which was in color and much more sentimental. But what I asked Jimmy for was the black-and-white harshness I'd seen in his melodramatic movies.

Once the director finds a cinematographer who interests him, he sends him a script.

Robert Wise

When you start to zero in on somebody that you think might be the candidate, you want his reaction to the script. So I usually have him read it and then, without guiding him too much, I get his input in a chat about how he sees it, what kind of texture and quality he feels the picture should have.

Sometimes we may run other films, or I might refer to some films of his that I have seen, and certain sequences that I liked. Depending on the kind of story, I may refer to some painters. I did that in pictures that were period pieces. When working on Mademoiselle Fifi we turned to Daumier and his caricatures, not only for the cameraman but also for the clothes and the props. In current films you might look at photographs of contemporary things, of something with a striking look to it.

In paintings I look for lighting and composition. Very often for lighting. There is much to be gained from the examples of lighting and effects.

TAKING ON THE PROJECT

The process of selection is not one-sided. Cinematographers pick and choose among the scripts which are offered to them to find the stories which, for whatever reason, they would like to shoot. Cinematographers who are in great demand can, naturally, be more selective. As we all know, truly great scripts surface not too often and sometimes wonderful scripts can turn out to be mediocre movies.

British cinematographer Douglas Slocombe (BSC), who photographed some 100 feature films, admits to reading close to 1000 scripts. Out of this volume of work he feels that the truly memorable films could be counted on the fingers of one, perhaps two hands.

The script is certainly a useful blueprint the cinematographer can use to judge the worth of the project.

Allen Daviau, ASC

The first time I see the script I try to read it strictly as a film viewer. Not as a cinematographer. I really just sit there and say: Tell me a story. I try to be as open as possible. And you read some scripts that are good, good movies; you would enjoy seeing them, but would you enjoy shooting the movie, and would it really be fulfilling to you? What is it that you like to do? Sometimes it is the subject that just strikes you, that you would like to say something about. So I look on the basis of an overall thing: How would I enjoy seeing this film? Would I enjoy having my name connected with it? Would I be proud being part of this film? The second time through, reading as a cinematographer, I ask myself: What are the problems here? What are the challenges? What are the things that I would really enjoy working on in this picture? Does it offer me a unique challenge? Someone said, The day you go to work and you are not slightly scared, is the day you better get out of this business, because there is no challenge left for you. If you really know all the answers going in, then I do not think that you will do very good work on the picture. Because you should never stop having that fear of the unknown.

And I think that is one of the things in the script: Does it offer me something I haven't done before? Maybe it offers me something I have done before and I know I can do better than I did last time, and that is intriguing to me. But perhaps it is truly the unknown. Maybe it is something that I don't really like to do, and maybe I can get past that. I know that I do not like to shoot dialogue scenes in cars. And I read a script that was an excellent, very funny script, and 25 percent of the movie is four guys running around in a car on real location. When you think that for that much time the camera is basically rigged on the car when you can never really see what is going on and you are lighting people in the back seat as well as in the front seat, and you are balancing all different times of a day. Well, it is a real challenge if you like to do that sort of thing. But I don't know anybody who likes to shoot dialogue scenes inside cars.

In this case Daviau turned down the job although he liked the script. Since one fourth of the film took place inside a car there was no chance that the car scenes could be eliminated. In situations that are not so extreme it is better to hold off final judgment on a project until you meet with the director.

STYLE

Once a cameraman has committed himself to a project, he and the director have to agree on the style of the film. Describing a visual style with words is no small task. Directors and cinematographers have developed many ways to reach an understanding with each other. A creative cinematographer will analyze the structure of the script and will try to see it from the audience's point of view. At this early stage much time will be devoted to discussions concerning the concept.

The right atmosphere, style and visual interpretation will evolve from this process. The cameraman and director will discuss the philosophical premise of the movie; how it should look, what structure it should have, what style of framing, lighting and color.

Caleb Deschanel, ASC

Style starts to emerge when reading the script. I always read the script three or four or five times. Generally, along the way, I discuss it with the director, and then start to come up with an overall visual concept that I seek for the film. It does not mean that this concept is ironclad. Just the way an actor comes up with his character, I think, the cameraman comes up with his way of seeing a movie. Then hopefully you are in sync with the director. It is important to develop an idea about the story early enough, so that at least you will find out whether you think the same way as the director. Otherwise you get yourself in a situation where you are at odds with each other all the time. You use whatever method you can. With Hal Ashby we started out on Being There by looking at a lot of movies together and discussing the script, and then I would also take a lot of still photographs of locations and look at them with Mike Haller who was an art director and with Hal.

Viewing movies together is the most immediate way of having some common points of reference when discussing style. Good knowledge of a wide range of painters and photographers is the next important step in facilitating the communication between the director and the cinematographer. Being able to describe a certain style as one resembling a given painter, or knowing where to look for examples of a palette of desired colors helps immensely in arriving at the mutually understandable visual look of the film.

John Alonzo, ASC

Every situation is different. For pictures like Sounder or Conrack or for a picture like Norma Rae I did look at some paintings and some books and drawings of the South to get an idea of a kind of look. I would show them to the director and I would say, "What do you think of this Andrew Wyeth or these Shrimpton paintings, does this give you any thoughts, is this the kind of look that you are thinking about?" He says yes or no. So I use those. In pictures like Blue Thunder or Black Sunday there is really no artistic or aesthetic design to those pictures. It is a matter of recording what actually happens.

There is a wide spectrum of directors with diverse background and experience. Therefore the collaboration with the cameraman will take various forms. Some directors will need more help in developing the visual sense of a scene.

Conrad Hall, ASC

So many directors don't know anything about film. They are wonderful writers, they know a lot about life and the human equation and people have given them the opportunity to translate that into a film. And they don't know what to do. They are so insecure. They wander around the set and a lot of them don't pretend, and then some of them pretend. It depends on the director you get. Others are people who are knowledgeable visual artists as well as artists in every other sense. You work with them differently. They know exactly what they want. They need you less.

The directors who require the most from cinematographers are the first-time directors.

Adam Holender (ASC), who often works with first-time directors, puts them in two basic categories. The literary ones who write their own scripts and often do not quite know how to translate their ideas into a visual form and the new directors who come from other technical positions such as assistant directors, producers or editors. People in this second group are usually more experienced technicians.

Adam Holender, ASC

Like every other collaboration, working with first-time directors depends a lot on the personalities involved. But one typical problem to be aware of is the degree to which the cameraman assists the director in matters other than cinematography. At a certain point in the production the invitation to offer suggestions may not exist anymore, but the cameraman may not know when to stop. The director grows weary of advice and such help may start to annoy him.

Another potential problem lies in the director not understanding that certain visual concepts require certain disciplines, bring certain limitations. The first-time director may see these limitations as shackles. He may also have to be convinced that certain risks should be shared. If the director does not take advantage of the cinematographer's knowledge and judgment, the result may be a mediocre product. This is sometimes referred to as "television mentality", where the range of artistic possibilities on the scale of one to ten, becomes, say, four to six.

Most cinematographers are very much aware of the creative discipline necessary to maintain the established style and to serve the story in the best possible way.

SERVING THE STORY

Serving the story usually comes down to serving the director's concept. Though the cinematographer has an important role in the production, the principal storyteller at this stage is the director.

John Alonzo, ASC

I make it a rule of thumb that I am to interpret the director's concept. It is a very strict rule with me that I do not allow myself to get so in love with the frame and the lighting, that it subordinates what the director is trying to do. And if I spend six hours lighting a set that looks beautiful to another cameraman but does not mean anything to the story, then I am not doing my job for the director.

The power of cinematography lies in the immense possibilities of interpreting reality even within a given concept. The cinematographer's function is to transform an artificial environment into film reality. Lighting, optical image manipulation, choice of film emulsion, film manipulation in the laboratory, color manipulation at various stages are all tools the cameraman uses to create the photographed reality.

Caleb Deschanel, ASC

You need a certain sense of reality, but in fact you are doing a movie and you are making a statement with the light and with the composition and camera movements and all those things at your disposal as a cameraman. Your first impression should be that it is real for the story. But you can get away with an awful lot. What Vittorio Storaro did in One from the Heart with colored light was incredible. To an extent, it was a reality but it really was hyperreality. It carried beyond conventional reality, but you accept it because of the nature of the story. There is no reason why you cannot carry that sort of thinking to even more realistic settings. Obviously as an audience you do not want to be taken out of a scene by some extreme photographic element, but you certainly want it to carry you along. There are things you can do, where you exaggerate reality and create a sense of life which, if you would truly study it, you would realize that it is not real and yet your mind accepts it as being real. I think that is really what you are going for. You are going for a way of taking the greatest advantage of all the tools that you have at your disposal to create the drama, to amplify the drama. Sometimes it means exaggerating things enormously and getting away with it because the audience is carried away by the scene. You can switch key lights and you can change the level of lights and you can dial one light off and one light on when someone moves and you can do things that if you were to analyze them you would realize they don't make sense at all. But if you are telling a story and you are in sync with the story, then you can get away with an awful lot. I think that the best camerawork does that. It will make these judgments, it will stretch its 'reality' for the sake of telling the story.

Often the sets or the location will dictate the visual approach to the story. Or it may even come from the cinematographer's aesthetic taste at the given time.

Haskell Wexler, ASC

What happens photographically springs a lot from what is demanded of the photographer:

What kind of films are being made, how much time it takes to make them, what the sets look like, what the subject matter is.

Style comes from where you are personally. Right now as I am talking to you I would love to shoot a scene where there is a real bright hard sunlight just cutting through on the furniture and on the clothes. The faces are almost dark. If you are in this kind of mood when you read a script, you may actually talk yourself into believing that this particular script would look best this way. It may or may not coincide. You have to bear in mind that you are not the total maker of the film. You will have to talk to the director and the art director, and anyone else who has invested in it.

Cinematographer Conrad Hall dealt with two very different visual concepts when photographing *Fat City* directed by John Huston and *The Day of the Locust* directed by John Schlesinger.

Conrad Hall, ASC

In Fat City the idea of extraordinary tonal variations was like a style for a picture. The interiors, bars and places like that were very, very dark, so you have a sense of blackness. And then when you come outside I made the exteriors all very bright and glaring, like a lizard who comes from underneath a rock, a salamander that is blond because it has been hiding underneath a rock, it has not seen the light of day. I wanted it to be harsh and strong and abusive. And so, you go for the range, you go for the contrast. You go for the soft, dark, muted effect inside and then when you come outside you go for the bright, brilliant harsh tones. And when those things are cut together they create a kind of emotional sense which is productive for the storytelling.

You approach every project from the spirit of the film. Once you get the spirit of the film, then that determines everything for me.

On The Day of the Locust the decision to have it all shot in a warm, golden tone was made right away. Those are the broad strokes. You decide whether you are going to make this a gritty, documentary kind of look for the film about ninety percent of failed people in Hollywood, which is what The Day of the Locust is about: people who approach the flame and never get anything to do but get burned by it occasionally. Just ten percent are working and doing good and thriving in the heat of the flame. So that is a hard story. You could do it gritty. Black and white would be wonderful, because it is a period piece. Sometimes I think that is what we should have done, now that I look at it. That is not what we decided to do. The decision to make it golden was to create not their reality but their dream. In other words I wanted to posture [sic] their dream upon their reality. So you saw them living in their little apartments and they were happy living in their golden dream of maybe making it one day.

John Alonzo describes another example of lighting in opposition to the subject matter, for stronger impact.

John Alonzo, ASC

We are going to try to do Scarface in soft light because Brian (De Palma) wants it this way. It is a drama, a melodrama. It is violent and very dramatic, but he does not want to light it that way. He wants to light it soft and pretty. As he said to me, I don't want to telegraph that I am going to do something violent. I want the frame to look pretty, and the people to look pretty. And then we see that they are violent people.

Another extremely important aspect which Alonzo brings up is the consistency of a visual look.

John Alonzo, ASC

You have an overall picture, an overall script and then you go from A to Z. Very few pictures are shot in chronological order. The hardest thing is for you to keep a certain style going, so that when you put the picture in chronological order it has a nice even flow, in lighting, in composition and in the camera moves. This is my realm, my jurisdiction. If you do not pay attention to that, if you are just lighting each scene as if you are lighting a Rembrandt each time, you are going to have a checkerboard effect. You will not have a consistently smooth picture. It may be totally acceptable but it definitely influences the audiences. The audience will think that something is not quite right. This is a brightly lit shot, this a soft light and this is harsh light, this is flat light and so on. Every scene should be approached as to what part it plays overall. Simple things—you are inside a room and the sunlight is coming from a certain side, over this man's shoulder. If you take him outside, three, four days later and the sun happens to be on the other side and it is a direct cut, then you say, wait a minute, what do I do? Now you have to work with the director and the operator, try to angle him so that the sun comes from the correct side, or you duplicate the sunlight from another direction. Put a silk over the scene and shove in an arc to make the sun come from the side that will match the previous shot. These are the things that sometimes people do not think about and you have an amateurish way of handling it.

BLACK-AND-WHITE AND COLOR

A cinematographer cannot separate the problem of light from the problem of color. Through the film stock he is using, through the filters on lights and lenses, and through the printing in the lab, he cooperates with the art director in the orchestration of colors or in the modulation of the gray scale in the black-and-white films.

Alexander Mackendrick

I've always felt that melodrama and satire have characteristics in common. Ideally, I would prefer to shoot both of these genres in black and white. Distributors nowadays declare that black-and-white movies are unsalable. A compromise may be the kind of cinematography where there is a very emphatic range of tonal values, black to white, at the expense of hue values; strong directional lighting of chiaroscuro which underlines the architectural structures at the expense of the local colors of the surfaces.

When the first Japanese color features arrived in Britain, I remember well their impact on British filmmakers. Accustomed to the brilliance of Californian light, the bright hues and crisp shadows, we marvelled at the subtleties of shade and tone produced by the mists of the Japanese scenery. With the coming of color and more sensitive film stocks the sunlight which was the original incentive for a migration to the Californian West Coast is no longer quite such an essential.

There are personal idiosyncrasies when it comes to particular colors, for both aesthetic and practical reasons.

Conrad Hall, ASC

I used to hate blue on the screen, but I am changing my mind a little about that. There is a new wave of colors that you see on television, that sort of thirties blue like those real strong colors used on the orange crate labels.

The vibrant blues and pinks and oranges together which is the new thing that I begin to see happening a lot nowadays.

In certain kinds of stories these colors can be effective, although it is not a realistic look on life by any means. I basically hated blue because I shot so many exterior pictures in which the sky must match from scene to scene and I hated it because it became almost like an enemy to me, confusing my attempts to match the scenes. And to cut from one blue to another blue is terribly distracting. That is why by overexposure I eliminated the blue to make it easier for the cutter to match shots. And the fact that I appreciated how white or gray reveals color. Color is so exquisite against a neutral background. Whereas color against another color creates an emotional equation. Colors are terribly emotional kinds of elements.

The emotional meaning of colors became an object of in-depth study by the Italian cinematographer, Vittorio Storaro. Earlier in this chapter Caleb Deschanel discussed Storaro's use of color in *One from the Heart*. When beginning work on a film, Storaro writes a treatment on the psychological meaning of the color scheme. In such a conceptual statement prepared for *One from the Heart* (*American Cinematographer*, January 1982), he approaches this film as a conflict of colors representing certain states of the human nervous system and metabolism during the day and night. In his concept the green and blue are the colors of dusk and night. They represent the regenerative need for rest. Yet this natural rhythm is violated by the aggressive reds, oranges and yellows of the Las Vegas night. These colors stimulate the nervous system and raise the heartbeat. Storaro's conceptual conclusion is that through the desire for love, the opposites in the human nature, the distinction between man and woman, like the complementary colors and like the opposites of light and shadow, all unite in one energy of light ". . . that comprises them all."

It is not often that the cameraman would prepare such a highly conceptual approach to his visual understanding of the script. But it certainly points toward the potential depth of the intellectual penetration of the material. And the consistently high quality of Vittorio Storaro's work tells us that this method serves him well.

WORKING WITH THE ART DIRECTOR

Ideally all the major contributing people should be brought in early on the project. Those fortunate enough to work on Ingmar Bergman's films have the luxury of a two-month intensive dialogue with the director, actors and other members of the crew. As well as watching rehearsals, Bergman's cameraman Sven Nykvist (ASC) has the opportunity to shoot extensive tests and discuss the sets and costumes with the art director. This relationship with the art director cannot be stressed too much. He is an invaluable partner because he supervises the designers of sets and costumes.

The positioning and intensity of the practicals on the set is something the cinematographer should establish with the art director. These visible light sources of various kinds serve to visually enrich the scene, to justify the directions of studio lighting and to contribute to the level of illumination on the set. They may even serve as the major modelling lights for the scene.

The shape of the set and certain architectural components such as beams or moldings help the cinematographer to hide his lamps, stands and cables. The shape, texture and color of the walls and furniture have understandable impact on the visual organization of the frame. The way in which the set is positioned on the studio floor, for example, how much space there is outside the windows, will also influence the lighting directions and angles. For these reasons the production designer, art director and all the people involved in shaping and dressing the sets, or in choosing locations should work hand-in-hand with the cinematographer. He, in turn, can either enhance their efforts or diminish them with his lighting.

Haskell Wexler, ASC

Any work which the cameraman can do with an art director is money in the bank, because basically an art director is giving you what you photograph. You will be asking for practicals, you two will be deciding where the windows are, whether certain walls are wild, whether ceilings are wild, how high the walls are, and what color they are painted.

Today's sets, particularly in the special effects films, have very intricate lighting built into the set, like lighting through the frosted glass floors or illuminated table tops. Sometimes the instrument panels will practically light the set for you. On occasions the lighting that comes with the set or with an event which is part of the scene may have tricky exposure values.

It is evident that a wise producer should bring the cinematographer and the art director together as early as possible. However, some producers do not see it this way.

Conrad Hall, ASC

Hopefully you work a lot with the art director. There are very many producers who try to keep the two of you separated; for financial reasons, they say. What a mistake! We should be the closest of collaborators. After we hear what the director has to say, the two of us should collaborate very strongly to provide what he wants.

This unfortunately is not always the case.

Robert Wise

I found that some cinematographers are not too inclined to be overly receptive to designers' set sketches that might indicate certain kind of lighting, sources of lighting. I had one cinematographer on a major film, and the designer would come up and show the sketch of the set coming down the line and the cameraman would look at it and go his own way. He would never really turn to the designer for any thoughts that he had in his head about how it might look. And a few years later I had just the opposite experience with Ted McCord on Sound of Music.

Much depends upon the personalities involved and also on how much the cinematographer is in tune with the aesthetics of the art director. Avoiding personality clashes saves both the producer's and director's sanity.

Alexander Mackendrick

If the casting of key talents has not been done wisely, there can be misunderstandings between the production designer and the director of photography. An assertive designer may hanker after lighting that is diffused, general and unobtrusive, so that tone and color values in the settings and costumes retain their pic-

torial values. An equally assertive cinematographer may prefer the set, costumes and furniture to be neutral in color and tone so that the scene is left for him to "paint with light." If there is discord between the production designer and director of photography, the director and producer should resolve the disagreement at the earliest stage of production planning.

Filmmaking is not only teamwork but the team is composed of people with strong creative egos. This makes it doubly difficult to keep on an even keel.

Conrad Hall, ASC

You have to get the right chemistry of the people involved. One important ingredient to the filming chemistry by which it will succeed or fail is the handling of ego. When ego gets involved it destroys. Now, that does not mean that you do not have an ego. And it does not mean that your ego is not manifesting your artistic decisions, but like being in the army there is definitely a law of involvement that should be respected. When it is maligned by the ego it destroys the chemistry by which the film can be made. The director should direct, the cameraman should shoot, the art director should art direct. As soon as we start introducing our egos to take over our jobs from one another, we malign the chemistry by which the films are made. The ego out of line is a bad ingredient, but a strong ego is a wonderful thing for an artist to have.

Richard Brooks once said to me, "Would you ever like to direct, Conrad?" I was just a brand new cinematographer at the time and I said, "Well, I think so, but I am not sure yet, I will see," and he said, "Everybody should direct a film. You probably want to direct one, but, direct your own damn film, don't direct mine!" And I respect that attitude and I want it respected when I am directing. I am an aide to that man. I am not anybody who is trying to take anything away from him.

WORKING WITH THE DESIGNERS

The costume designer and the makeup artist should also consult closely with the cinematographer. It is particularly essential in black-and-white film where two colors, like certain hues of red and green, may look exactly the same on the screen, or where a light blue shirt may be preferable to a white one that could create too much contrast. For the same reason light blue or green bedsheets will be more suitable than white.

In color film production, white fabrics may still need to be "teched" down. This is often accomplished by rinsing them in weak tea. Certain dark velvets may be avoided because in a low-key lighting situation they will look black. Makeup artists will consult the cinematographer about the red sensitivity of a given black-and-white emulsion. With color stock they may be more interested in skin textures.

At the preproduction stage many of these elements will be examined in a series of tests. John Alonzo describes them as helping him to establish the visual character of the picture.

John Alonzo, ASC

I do a lot of tests in different kinds of lighting. Makeup and hair tests, wardrobe tests, and so forth. In those tests I have them moving around in five or six different types of lighting, so that the director can look at it and say, I like that, I don't like that. We try different lenses, different sizes for close-ups; a 50mm or a 150mm, to see how the perspective changes. We don't just stand an actor and say, turn three different ways and that's it. We choreograph moves for all these tests.

For more elaborate productions these tests will also include sets.

REHEARSALS

Once the production starts the relationship between the director and his cinematographer becomes almost symbiotic. There are many variations of this relationship. On one end of the spectrum you will have veteran directors who know exactly what type of staging and what camera moves they want. On the other end there will be newcomers, perhaps from the theater or from screenwriting, who will depend on the cinematographer in these areas. Even the most experienced directors are usually open to suggestions. They recognize that staging and camera movements are inherently connected with lighting and that all these elements create the picture.

The first days of shooting are crucial. You almost have to read the director's mind. You have to be physically close to him during the rehearsals, especially if he is not too good at expressing his ideas. Production time on the set is so expensive that you do not want to spend too much time on theoretical discussions. You try to discuss the scene early in the morning or after watching the dailies the night before.

Robert Wise

If you get into any kind of special shows, you make endless tests. You test the sets for color, you test your costumes and you test the labs. You get a difference in the values of your colors from the different labs. You have to test all the way around. And sometimes if you have a big set and you are going to have some prelighting, try to have it done while you are shooting something else. You will test the lighting of the set and you will see how it is coming off. On anything other than a subject that is simple and straightforward, it is very advisable to test to the extent that you can.

A storyboard provides a good frame of reference and indicates the coverage needed for the given scene. It can be an important time-saving device. The cameraman should treat the storyboard for what it is: a guide to the scenes, only a guide useful in prerigging the lights.

Robert Wise

I storyboard most of the time. The storyboard usually starts before the cameraman is on. Of course you discuss it with him when he is around. Before we start to shoot he is involved in the storyboard. I like to have a storyboard so that when you walk on the set you know where you are going to start, where you want to start, where you will put the camera, and where the actors are going to make an entrance. You discuss it with your cameraman in advance. I think that you must know where you are going. But, in developing the scene with the actors, in getting the scene on its feet, if it wants to move away from the storyboard, if the actors find additional things that you cannot anticipate sitting in your office, if you find new values, new dimensions, and if that means moving away from the storyboard, you make the adjustments.

On the set, staying close to the director and watching rehearsals allows the cinematographer to understand what the director is trying to do with the scene in terms of the dramatic rhythm of punches and pauses. Only then does it become apparent how the composition, the camera movements, and the lighting can visually emphasize the dramatic structure. At this point a cinematographer's instinct comes into play. He will be influenced by his own background, consciousness and subconscious. Films and paintings he's seen, music he's heard, books he's read will all have an effect on his visual interpretation of the scene.

This is how several cameramen see what is happening on the set at this stage.

Caleb Deschanel, ASC

An ideal situation is one where the camera angle or movement never becomes a matter of discussion, when you and the director are very much in sync and he suggests something and you concur, or you suggest something and he says, "Yes, of course," or you both say, "What if we did this?" At its best it is a process that evolves. Hopefully no one's ego becomes involved and you say, "Gee, that was my idea and that was someone else's idea."

I believe in waiting for a scene to develop. When you start to see a scene evolve, when actors are rehearsing, there is a point early on when it seems very chaotic and it seems almost impossible to put on film. But eventually the scene starts to have a certain continuity to it, you eventually start discovering that there is a way to put it on film. And the way I really like to work is that you resolve

the whole scene from beginning to end before you start shooting. Some directors don't like to work that way and inevitably you will get into a situation where you carry the scene halfway through and you are in a position where you have to make certain compromises because you have not figured the whole thing out. Compromises in lighting, in camera moves, in positions where you will put the camera, etc. I like to figure out how the scene should play all by itself, which usually means that you have to make a judgment about what the rhythm of a scene is, while you are filming it. And where the camera should be. And then usually everything will fall into place.

Planning scene coverage in advance is the most essential element in an effective lighting design.

Allen Daviau, ASC

A big thing for a cinematographer is to get into the habit of asking, "How are you going to cover the situation?" Work with your director on the coverage because we all can fall into the trap of making a beautiful master scene that is absolutely horrible for the coverage. Particularly when you are working on a TV movie, where you are really moving fast, you better be able to get in there, get your master shot and know exactly how you are going to proceed with your coverage.

All too often we fall in love with our master and then we find that in editing the scene plays mostly in the close-ups. It will happen that way and it is terrible if you have sloughed off the detail in your close-up.

You get to know how a director likes to work. Many times you get the basic gist of it and you start lighting before the rehearsal is even completed. The official procedure is to have the rehearsal, mark the positions without the camera, then start lighting the scene. The operator starts working with the camera and we have full rehearsal before shooting. What happens more and more is that if I wait till the director stops staging a complicated master I will be out of time. So often I have to start lighting when he is blocking. If suddenly he says, "This does not work, let's go over here and change it all"—well I have to tear it out and it is gone. But more often than not I will be well ahead of the game by starting to light during the blocking of the scene.

Sometimes the scene is so sensitive that only essential people are present. But most of the time it is desirable for the whole crew to watch the rehearsal.

Conrad Hall, ASC

I try to get the director to rehearse the whole scene. I like to have everybody connected with the scene: props, wardrobe, everybody, watching at that time. Camera, lighting, grips, the whole lot just sitting around, watching the director work with the actors, and the cinematographer kind of tagging along behind.

And sometimes directors like to have the editor on the scene at that point. Schlesinger is a man like that. He loves to have his editor down there, because eventually the editor is going to have to put it together. So he likes to have the whole team down there. And you rehearse the whole scene, ten pages, five pages, three pages, whatever. It might be several days' or weeks' work, depending on the schedule you have. That way everybody knows what is to be expected and can contribute more effectively.

When working with the director on a scene you digest like a cow. You chew all day long, you go out and graze in the fields and you get your belly full. And then you pick a nice tree to sit under and you burp the grass up again. It is like that when you are working. You digest the scene with the director, imbuing yourself with every possible rhythm and every piece of information that you possibly can, to be ready for the moment. Filming is the moment of many factors coming together in that special way which at another moment would be different.

Other cinematographers prefer to have only the essential people present during the rehearsals.

Richard Kline, ASC

The way I like to work on the set is to have it cleared at the beginning of all but just a few necessary people. And I have a complete rehearsal of the scene, to see where we are. Prior to that I have a rough idea of how the scene might look, and I might prerig some lights just to set a mood. After rehearsing the entire scene we may find that the mood is not right and might be totally changed.

When the director works with actors I hover and observe and I walk various positions and see what the sets are. It will probably take only 15 minutes but it is well worth it. It also gives the actors a chance to develop in the scene and to discuss it. Then after that rehearsal the director and I decide how we are going to attack it.

There is no rule with which shot we will start first. We may start with a close-up first. It is possible. And work your way back to a long shot. It is a rarity when someone will go for that, but there could be an emotional impact which you will lose going from a long shot and a medium shot to a close-up. You might drain the actor of the key moment which you would need in a close-up. So there would be this rare case when you may want to start with a close-up and work your way back. I compare filming setups to tennis. You have a serve which could be a long shot that gets you into play. Usually you start with a long shot and in a serve you have maybe an ace, which is an equivalent to staying on long shot. But the idea in tennis is to work your way to the net basically. You have better control if you work your way to the net.

Rehearsals add another dynamic to the evolution of a scene from the script and storyboard stage. The action has become three dimensional and this quality must be captured now on film.

COMPOSITION

The basic need to represent a three dimensional reality on a two dimensional surface is certainly not new in the visual arts. What separates film from the other visual arts is that it is kinetic. The filmmaker is composing motion.

Composition of movement in time can be broken down into several dynamics. Movement of the camera and/or of subjects in front of the camera is called *intraframe* movement. Screen sizes and angles of view can be manipulated in this way. *Interframe* movement is created by editing, cutting from one angle to another or from long shot to close-up. The combination of camera movements and editing becomes a truly powerful system for manipulating the film reality. Whether static or moving, the frame represents spatial depth, or three dimensions, on a two dimensional screen.

Alexander Mackendrick

We're told by those who have studied the psychology of perception that shadows are one of the clues by which the brain recognizes spatial depth. The fact that the projected image is always seen as a window into a three-dimensional world is one reason for the filmmaker's use of these dark and light areas for "designing in depth."

The figurative painters and engravers of graphic illustrations in the nineteenth century are worth study by filmmakers. Gustav Doré's work is an example. He used a formula enormously effective in emphasizing design in depth. In the foreground a subject might be lit strongly, with an emphatic key light and strong modelling. But behind this would be figures more or less in silhouette, in shadow and two-dimensional. These, in turn, would be outlined against a brighter area in middle distance, a part of light illuminating features of architecture or figures in an area of light. These were again silhouetted, light against dark, against a further background of shadow, gray but still dark. Each recessive plane contrasts with the one beyond it or in front.

The Spanish painter Francisco Goya wrote some 200 years ago, "I see (in nature) only forms that advance, forms that recede, masses in light and shadow."

Conrad Hall, ASC

In soft lighting you build depth by contrast. In other words you put the person in light and you take the light off the background. Or you put the light on the background and you take the light off the person. Or you do it with color like for example, putting a person against a blue wall. Creating the reality requires a sense of everything—of movement, of color, of value in terms of contrast, of drama, of cutting. To be good you better know everything.

It becomes obvious that a thorough knowledge of composition is an absolutely essential skill for a cinematographer. He needs it not only to create meaningful visuals on the screen but also to communicate with the director.

Alexander Mackendrick

Composing in depth isn't simply a matter of pictorial richness. It has value in the narrative of the action, the pacing of the scene. Within the same frame, the director can organize the action so that preparation for what will happen next is seen in the background of what is happening now. While our attention is concentrated on what we see nearest to us, we are simultaneously aware of secondary activities that lie beyond, and sometimes even of a third plane of distant activity: the dramatic density of the scene is much greater.

Design the blocking of the actors, the framing of the shot, with this sort of thing in mind and the cinematographer with a grain of sense will instantly realize your intention. He will use light to assist the eye path of the audience and to give dramatic depth to the scene. Most cameramen I've worked with have been very intelligent, quick to pick up on the director's intentions without the need for explanation.

Composition, both in framing and lighting, directs the viewer's eye to the appropriate part of the scene.

Jordan Cronenweth, ASC

First of all, the composition has to tell the story and create the mood. If there are a lot of elements in the composition besides the subject, you may need to lead the eye to the subject. You can do that with light. You can create certain selectivity within the composition with lighting or as an element of the composition. A lot of composition is just plain feel—how you feel.

The criterion is really the story. If you have somebody coming out of a dark building through the doorway you can have the camera way back and show the whole building and a little bit of the sky, you can have that camera closer to the door and show nothing but black and then a sliver of sky, and you can have the camera move with the guy from the door back, or you can have a close-up of him. I mean, you can interpret it in a thousand ways. But if you are just going for the composition, you are abandoning the story.

Lighting composition not only directs the audience's attention to the particular subject, but it also brings certain emotional responses to a scene.

Haskell Wexler, ASC

I do not think that the director and the cameraman should be at odds as far as framing is concerned. They are two creative people looking at the scene. And part of the framing is where the light is in the frame. If, for example, a person seated at a table has a little bright window sharply behind the right ear it would tell a different story than if that bright window were more over his right shoulder, out a little bit. It has a different emotional response, and so where this little window in the background appears in the frame, is part of the framing. So the lighting and the framing are the same thing and they have to be joint.

There are basically four popular screen ratios: Academy (1.33:1), Wide Screen (1.85:1 and 1.65:1), and Anamorphic (2.35:1). With such a variety of screen ratios, in the words of Robert Wise, "You cast your screen size to the subject matter."

Robert Wise

When I did The Hindenberg a few years ago, it was perfect for the anamorphic format. But one thing that I deplore about the anamorphic is its lack of depth. I love to be able to rake the foreground and to carry somebody back in the distance and keep that in focus. Split diopters help in these situations.

Among the visual artists the filmmaker has a rather unenviable position of not being in full control when his work is being presented to the audience. For people who rely heavily on composition to tell their stories this can be very frustrating.

Alexander Mackendrick

In the 1950s a real problem cropped up when the framing of the image became ambiguous, unpredictable. Were we working just for the cinema screen or for television? When the framing has to be a compromise the result is often disastrous.

When any of my films were reframed—the film image rephotographed for television broadcast—I could not help feeling a sense of outrage. If I remember rightly, Augustus John, a well-known British portrait painter, discovered that after he had sold a portrait, the new owner cut nine inches off the bottom of the painting so that it would fit a space on his wall. John sued for damages, even though the painting was no longer his, and, as I recall, won his case. I feel the same way about screen images. And it's not just aesthetics; it affects the narrative. In A High Wind in Jamaica one of the key shots was a wide screen shot of seven children sitting in a row as they are interrogated by the lawyer; the point of the scene was the silent reaction of two children who happened to be on each end; neither of them appeared in the television version.

It is the unfortunate lot of filmmakers that they are not in charge when their work is being projected. A visit to a local theater can at times be a heartbreaking experience, let alone seeing one's film on television.

In spite of this uncertain future, the film crew puts all its talents and skills into producing a well-composed picture.

WORKING WITH THE CREW

There are three people on the crew ultimately concerned with the composition of the frame: the director, the cinematographer, and the camera operator. The balance of power among these three individuals is affected by many factors: personal experience, the subject matter or genre of the story, the individual background and national tradition. An American cinematographer who also directs discusses his interpretation of the balance of power.

Haskell Wexler, ASC

I do not think of the director of photography as only the lighting cameraman. I think of him as the cameraman who sets the frame, the camera movement and the lighting. He does it in service to the director. If the director says, "I want to play this scene very static," then the cameraman does it this way. The cameraman may suggest, "I understand what you mean but I think that if we make a very small move toward her when she says such and such line we will be on the medium shot. It will keep the static quality and maybe help what you are trying to say." And the director may say, "I said I want this thing static, I don't want any dolly move." At this point you may doubt the aesthetic wisdom of his judgment, but you do the static shot. What I am saying is that a good director of photography feeds the director what he thinks about the scene after he gets the idea from the director what the scene is all about. If he is just trying to make what he calls a good shot, then he has no right to say anything because making films is not just making good shots. Making films is making films. The best world is one where there is mutual respect and there is a give and take; an acceptance of the fact that the director is the boss but recognizing that he is just a human being who sometimes can be right and sometimes can be wrong.

Traditionally, the cinematographer's role is perceived differently in Britain.

Alexander Mackendrick

I distinguish between the way I work with the lighting cameraman and the way I work with the operator. As Director of Photography, and boss of the whole camera crew, some cinematographers will probably challenge me on this, insisting that they are responsible for all of it. However, my temperament has been to feel that I have to design every camera angle, every screen size, every camera move. I have to work directly with the camera operator on this and cannot afford to go through the Director of Photography, though, of course, he will be present as the decisions are made. This is because, as director, I am, above all things, concerned with narrative content, the story. Other values are very important, but they come later. Since the story is told through the positioning of the actors in relation to the camera, since the blocking of actors' moves within the scene is inseparable from the design of camera moves in relation to the performer, the camera operator and I are concerned with narrative. He is the director's right hand and he is my man.

Mackendrick's description of the role of the operator stems from the heyday of the British studio system. In this tradition the cinematographer is known as the Lighting Cameraman and his role is predominantly to light the set. The operator is more concerned with the narrative. Hollywood tradition is different.

Vilmos Zsigmond, ASC

Sometimes the director will set up the composition but he will leave it up to me to finalize it. If my operator is very good I will give him a lot of freedom, I will let him decide certain things, let him be involved with it. But I certainly will work with the operator a lot because I have certain compositional feelings which the operator has to learn. For example I do not like too much headroom. It depends on the picture, but I usually like tight composition. If an operator that I work with does not have the same taste, then he has to learn to please my taste. That takes a little time but usually by the middle of the picture he can guess how I would compose it.

Since the operator is the link between the cameraman's visual concept and the composition on the screen, this relationship is very symbiotic. An operator should read the script and understand the style worked out by the director and the cinematographer.

Allen Daviau, ASC

This relation depends on where one's strengths lie. I always would have something to say about the composition. Operators I like to work with are very good detail people in terms of moving props and setting things around to make the frame really work. And they have to do it in concert with continuity people and the prop department, so that everybody is aware when you are cheating something on the mantelpiece or over on the bookcase, just to make a better composition. You get very good in doing this and in terms of knowing what will get by.

You need to know whether for the next piece of coverage it should go back or should you move it even more this way. These are all details dealt with principally by the camera operator. I like to see what they are doing, I like to ride the rehearsal if it is possible time-wise, so I can see that the composition is working, that the shot is working. There is this need of having the picture in my mind all day long, particularly in a scene I know that I will be coming back to. Just having looked in the finder makes a great difference for me, particularly if I have been able to ride the rehearsal. Of course some directors, like Steve Spielberg, like to ride the rehearsal too. Spielberg loves to stage the scene through the camera. And you see it happening, and it is marvellous because he has the sense of moving camera to people and people to camera that is just priceless. He comes into a room and many times before he even starts the rehearsal he will say, Camera here, 29mm, and he will start blocking the scene that way.

I like all my key people reading the script. Like the operator, the first assistant, the gaffer, the key grip, and others as well, if possible. It is absolutely essential that they all read it. I like everybody to know the story they are telling. So they are not just showing up in the morning as mechanics. Because the more people on the crew are involved in telling the story and coming up with ideas, the better off you are and the more sense of participation they have. I like everybody to come to the dailies. I do not believe in closed dailies. I just think that people should see the fruit of the work they are doing. And many times you will get tremendous ideas from somebody who is the third grip or the second electrician because they are looking at it from an unprejudiced point of view. It is also the sense of involvement of the unit. It is one of the best things about filmmaking and it is particularly true of a film that shoots on location; the sense of family that forms in the film crew. You are living in the same crummy motel and you are eating in the same restaurants every night and when you see these dailies together in some little room or in the neighborhood theater, it provides a reason for all these people with these diverse backgrounds being out in some strange place shooting a movie. It is one of the best things about it. At the end of a long shoot, when people are saying good-bye to each other, it is very touching a lot of times because you have been through many difficulties together.

The collaborative effort, often under adverse conditions, creates intense relationships among crew members. In a very natural way the cinematographer often becomes the nucleus of this instant family with crew members looking to his leadership.

His second-in-command in the area of lighting is the gaffer. He is not only the chief electrician but also a close collaborator with the cinematographer in shaping the look of the film.

James Crabe, ASC

I worked with several gaffers who had decidedly distinctive style in themselves. You often learn from the people that are working for you. I worked with Aggie Aguilar quite often. He works a lot with those soft lights with the egg crate grid and then he has that honeycomb that he puts on lamps, so you get the directionality of light and you are able to control the soft light.

Gaffer Richmond ("Aggie") Aguilar, whom James Crabe mentions, feels that the cameraman and the gaffer work as a team. With today's complicated camera movements occupying cinematographer's attention, lighting becomes too much work for one person. The gaffer communicates with the operator as well, regarding the frame lines of the shot. The Best Boy, who is next in line on the electrical team, runs the crew, takes care of equipment and makes the power connections. Most often cameramen leave it to the gaffer to decide on the particular lighting instruments to be used.

Michael D. Margulies, ASC

I will discuss with the gaffer what I want, where I want the light coming from, what I want the light to hit, and usually let him decide on the units he uses. Nine out of ten times he will make the decision on the unit. If I want something specific I will ask for a specific unit, but generally that is his department. I want the set looking in a certain way and I want so many footcandles and that is what he gives me.

When the gaffer and his electricians are setting the lights, the chief grip with his crew is responsible for handling all the reflective boards and the diffusion materials used in front of the lamps. They also set all the black gobos, flags and teasers to control the light spread.

James Crabe, ASC

It takes a new kind of grip nowadays. In the old days the grip was always there with a C-stand and a little flag, but when you deal with large sources you have to be quite ingenious in stringing up black cloth to keep light out of the lens.

A person who should become the cinematographer's close ally is the script supervisor. Some cinematographers plan their lighting of a given scene on the basis of the script. Others consider that you can bury your instincts by preconceiving the shots. They rely on their gut feeling. Conrad Hall confesses that he "attacks each day with absolutely no foreknowledge of what he is going to do." He knows the script, but asks the script supervisor to read the scenes for a given day, to hear it coming from somebody else. Often this reading gives him an idea. Hall also believes that the script supervisor is his ally when it comes to matching the shots.

Conrad Hall, ASC

It is very important to pay attention to matching, and it is one of the things where you work most closely with a script supervisor. You have to get together beforehand and come up with a system by which to remember how to reproduce weeks later what you had started out weeks before. You make notes on your lighting, you make notes that a given scene which was incomplete was shot at a certain time of day, what type of light there was, what kind of weather. When you are dealing with close-ups, there are means to reproduce the atmosphere, but if it is a large scope then only nature can reproduce atmosphere effectively and you have to let the production department know that this cannot be done at this time.

The problem of matching constitutes the major difference between still photography and film. It is one of the most difficult and demanding tasks for the cinematographer; matching from shot to shot and from scene to scene. It requires the ability to constantly think in terms of three consecutive shots: the one we are lighting, the one before it and the one after it. Of course, the final editing will not necessarily follow the same order and this has to be taken into consideration as well. Within one shot, lighting balance is the chief objective.

I started this chapter by stating that filmmaking is a collaborative art. The members of the crew contribute their skills to translate the story from the script onto the screen. But no one should forget that this is a make-believe world and that the safety of the crew is of paramount importance. As Haskell Wexler (ASC) eloquently states:

The problem of the health and safety of the crew as it relates to the quality of the image is an important issue for the filmmakers to address themselves to. There is a tendency among some new filmmakers to forget that we are indeed in a make-believe business, that we are creating dreams and not dealing in true reality. Some directors think that they will reach some pinnacle of honesty if indeed they will hit an actor with a real hunk of wood and bruise him. And that psychology taken one step further has to do with how risky a place we will put a camera in. If the camera and the camera crew are lying on the ground in front of a skidding automobile and it is going to be dangerous, some directors believe that the image is going to be that much more exciting. That the adrenalin that will come from the camera crew, will somehow spread itself onto the emulsion of the film and make the director a better shot. Some directors feel that they are gods and forget that they are engaged in making theater, that they are engaged in making drama, that they are making images which in a manner are used to sell Coca-Cola and automobiles, and that to risk the crew members' lives under those conditions is folly. And that is why I see the use of toxic smoke as endangering people's lives not as immediately as being run over by a car or dropped out of a helicopter, but as hurting their health. Because this smoke is toxic. I think that these are moral, ethical issues which people who are making films should think about.

A cinematographer on the job is engaged in a complex venture involving several key figures, usually with well-developed egos. It is therefore small wonder that one of the talents often mentioned as absolutely necessary for a cinematographer to have is the ability to get along with other people. Without this quality even an otherwise brilliant cinematographer can, and will, remain unemployable.

CHAPTER TWO

Lighting Equipment

OVER THE years a great variety of lighting instruments have been developed for use in the motion picture industry. As techniques of lighting change, so do the requirements of the lights. The faster film stocks allow for smaller, less powerful lights. Modern technology offers further sophistication such as fiber optics for lighting inside cars and cooler light sources for more comfortable shooting, especially on cramped locations.

Many of the new lighting systems that exist now and that will be developed over the years are actually invented on the set by ingenious cinematographers and gaffers. The prototype of the Croniecone or of the Flying Moon were born of necessity and then won general acceptance. A thorough knowledge of the currently available technology allows the cinematographer and his gaffer to choose the equipment that will best serve the specific problems of the film they are working on.

The first thing to understand about the lu-

minaire is the type of light source it employs. The two principal sources used in film lighting are the tungsten incandescent bulb and the arc lamp. The first group takes its name from the tungsten filament made incandescent by the electric current. In older kinds of bulbs this tungsten filament slowly evaporates and deposits itself on the inside of the bulb, thus darkening the globe and lowering the color temperature over the life of the bulb. To circumvent this process quartz halogen bulbs were designed. Halogen gas combines with the evaporating tungsten and deposits it back onto the filament. This self-cleaning process requires a high temperature that would melt ordinary glass. To withstand such heat quartz bulbs were developed, hence the name quartz lamps for such globes. Quartz bulbs not only retain steady color temperature but show other advantages such as longer life, smaller size and quieter operation. There is some confusion concerning the nomenclature of

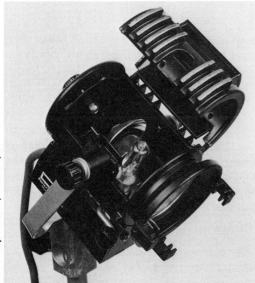

Pepper 100. One of the smallest Fresnel lights, equipped with a 100-watt quartz bulb.

these two types of bulbs. The older bulbs are often referred to as tungsten or incandescent, as opposed to the newer quartz bulbs. The truth is that quartz bulbs also have a tungsten filament that becomes incandescent. Perhaps the correct way to differentiate between these types would be to distinguish between the old incandescent globes and the quartz globes.

Arc lamps can be categorized as direct current arcs, such as carbon arcs, and alternating current arcs, such as HMI globes.

The carbon arc works on the principle of a gaseous arc that is formed between two carbon rods connected to a DC supply, such as a generator or a powerful battery.

The other type of arc lamp, operating on AC, is the gas discharge metal halide light. It employs an enclosed mercury arc with metal halide additives. HMI, which stands for hydrargyum medium arc-length iodide, is a widely used lamp of this type.

Apart from the light source type lights are

also categorized by their housing. In this respect we can distinguish between lights furnished with a lens and the so-called open-ended or open reflector luminaires. A lamp that may be viewed as a hybrid of these two types is the sealed beam globe with the lens constituting its integral part. In such a lamp the distance between the filament and the lens remains constant, unlike the focusable Fresnel lights.

Since certain luminaires have survived the test of time, we will begin our discussion of lighting equipment with lights that were designed several decades ago.

600-watt Molequartz® Tweenie-Mole Solarspot®. This Fresnel luminaire is popular among cinematographers and gaffers due to its wide range of focusing, from spot to a very wide flood.

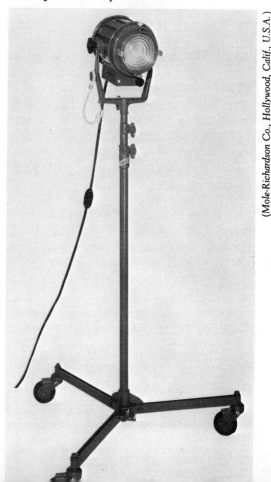

FRESNEL LIGHTS

The Fresnel lens is still the best tool for condensing light. It creates reasonably even illumination across the beam of light it forms. The light beam falls off gradually enough to allow for soft blending of two lamps lighting adjacent areas.

The smallest lamp with a Fresnel lens is tiny "Inky Dink," which houses bulbs from 20–250 watts. In recent years 600-watt Fresnel lights have become very popular with cinematographers and gaffers. With ever-increasing film speeds, smaller units of various designs are appearing continually. Such lights can often be equipped with a 30-volt globe powered by a 30-volt battery pack or belt.

For years the 1000-watt Baby, 2000-watt Junior, 5000-watt Senior and the 10,000-watt Tener were the workhorses of the film industry. With today's fast emulsions, less light is required. At the same time indiscriminate miniaturization of the luminaires would deprive us of the softer light character provided by larger lenses. Frequently a Tener will be lamped with a 5000-watt globe to cut down on light while utilizing the larger size Fresnel lens for a softer light. Often a 10,000 will be used mainly for its wide spread.

Richard Hart

I use a 10K because of the broad area that it covers. I need the spread, and I can control the light using one unit over a broad area. That gets you around having to use four or five units in four or five different places. You save the time it takes to set four lights as opposed to one.

When tungsten halide quartz bulbs, which keep the same color temperature throughout their lives, started replacing the old tungsten incandescent globes, some cinematographers questioned the light pattern produced by the quartz filament. It was considered to be less sharp, producing multiple shadows.

Richmond Aguilar

The old incandescent Baby is slightly sharper than a Baby quartz, but not enough to refuse the new lamp. Lamps will differ among themselves because of the reflectors being out of place, etc. We like the Baby Baby [1000-watt]; it has a little more spread. When you put the barndoor on, it does not cut the spread. It is lighter and smaller and therefore easier to use on location.

A Fresnel light is at flood position when the bulb is moved closest to the lens. Quartz bulbs, being smaller than the old incandescents, can be moved closer to the lens, creating a wider spread of light beam.

A lamp in a flood position gives harder light than when it is spotted. The closer the filament is to the lens the stronger the hot spot in the middle of the lens, which in turn produces harder shadows. The relationship of the light source to the quality of light is discussed later.

OPEN-ENDED LIGHTS

Whereas Fresnel lights provide well-controlled directional sources, open-ended lights are valued for their high light output and small size.

Richmond Aguilar

Open-end quartz lamps like the Mighty Mole are very good for bouncing. They are very good in small rooms because a Mighty Mole will cover a four-by-four-foot sheet of the Foam-core at a very close range. Neither a Baby nor a Junior will do it. Mighty Moles have a lot of punch and put out as much light as some of the Seniors. You do get a slight double shadow with them because the filament provides one light and the reflection from the mirror creates another. When you put a barndoor on you will see a definite double shadow.

The Mighty Mole represents a focusable light; there is also a variety of open-ended lamps giving broad illumination at a constant angle. Several manufacturers produce Broads, used for the general fill light. Cyc-Strips are mainly used for an even illumination of a cyclorama, to create a white or colored limbo effect in the studio. Cycloramas and backings are also lit with 1000–2000-watt Scoops and powerful 5000-watt dish-shaped lamps known as Skypans or Skylites.

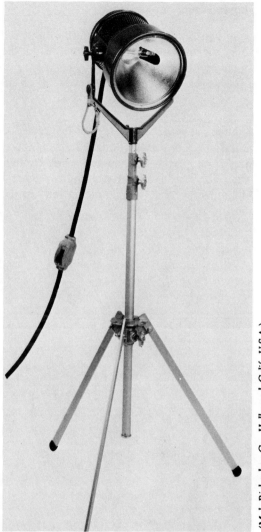

2000-watt Molequartz® Mighty-Mole. An open-ended quartz light particularly useful for bounced light application.

Six-light Molorama® Quartz Cyc-strip, for lighting cyclorama backgrounds.

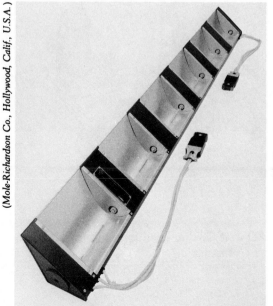

James Plannette

Cyc lights are all along the bottom and the Skypans are on top. You balance it to the foreground. Evenness you can judge by eye. The way to do it is to overexpose it, so all small problems disappear.

Similar in shape to the Cyc-Strip units is a Nooklite. Compactly designed to be positioned in places that do not offer enough room for other lamps, it is useful for general illumination and for bouncing off cards, boards, walls, and ceilings.

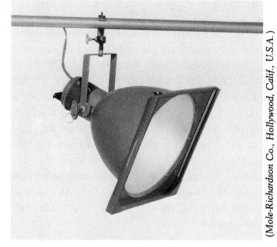

2000-watt Molequartz® 18″ Fixed Focus Scoop for lighting backings and cycloramas.

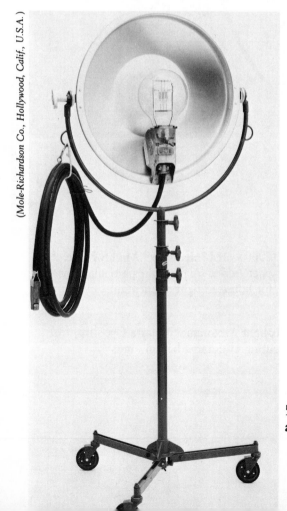

Nooklite. Primarily designed for confined locations, often used for bounced light application.

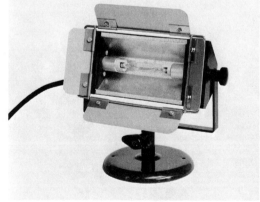

5000-watt Skylite. Used for lighting backings and cycloramas.

The family of lensless lights also includes soft lights. These boxlike fixtures vary in size and light power over a wide range of luminaires, from a 750-watt, 8″ x 8″ Baby Softlite to an 8K Super-Softlite in 36″ x 36″ size (both by Mole-Richardson Co.). For certain low ceiling locations a 2000 watt "Zip" Softlite was designed in 8″ x 17½″ by the same manufacturer.

Some gaffers build their own soft lights to fit the particular needs of size and shape.

Soft lights need periodic maintenance to provide the proper color temperature of light.

Haskell Wexler, ASC

Most soft lights after a few weeks of use tend to get warmer and lose about 200°K. I used to take some aluminum foil, crinkle it up and put it inside Mole-Richardson soft lights when I wanted a really correct color temperature. The white paint used in these lights is fairly good, but in aging it always goes toward yellow and to the warmer tones. Mixing blue paint with white helps to bring it back to where it should be.

"Coffin" light using Photo flood bulbs mounted on a frame 18 inches above the diffusion. One Nooklite is also employed.

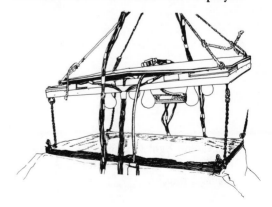

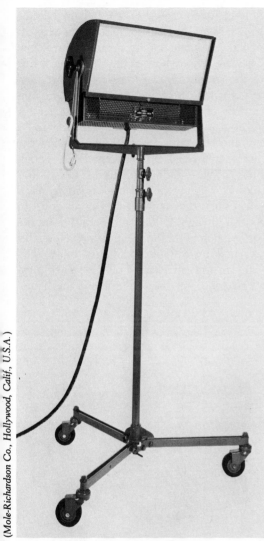

2000-watt Molequartz® Baby 2K "Zip" Softlite. The horizontal shape makes this light particularly useful on interior locations with low ceilings.

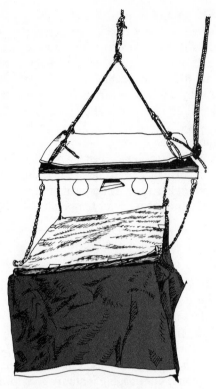

A homemade variety of a soft light became known as a *coffin* light. These lights were designed to create an overhead illumination. They are usually built at the studio according to the specifications of the cinematographer or his gaffer. A typical coffin soft light unit consists of a frame four feet by four feet or larger with a few rows of Photoflood bulbs and another frame 14 to 20 inches below the first one, covered with stretched silk, Tough Frost, or other diffusing material. On all four sides of this overhead lamp are hung black velvet skirts that can be rolled up or down to control the light falling on the walls or on the particular areas of the scene. When Nooklites are used instead of Photoflood bulbs they point up and are reflected off a bleached muslin stretched on the frame above the lights.

The black velvet skirt controls the light pattern of the Coffin light.

A fully assembled Coffin light. Its design should allow for good ventilation to avoid fire hazards.

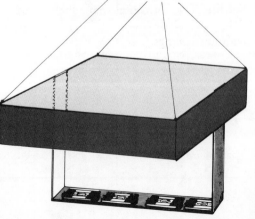

This Coffin light design makes use of IK Nooklites bounced off white card or white bleached muslin.

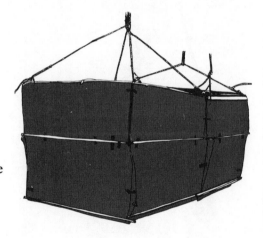

Utmost care is required to make coffin lights well ventilated in order to prevent fires.

The closest manufactured version of this kind of light is the Chicken Coop, which was a predecessor of the coffin light. It consists of a large troughlike case housing six globes sometimes with internal silver reflectors covering the filaments from direct view. It provides a high level of light that is usually softened by a diffusing material spread underneath the lamp.

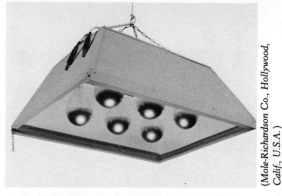

A six-light overhead cluster, traditionally known as a Chicken Coop. A soft overhead light that can be further softened by a diffuser screen.

SEALED BEAM LAMPS

It was inevitable in the development of film lighting equipment that the light focusing function of the lens and the compactness and light weight of open-ended lights should be brought together. Thus a very important and widely used family of lamps was developed. Their general designation is PAR, which stands for Parabolic Aluminized Reflector, and they are also referred to as *sealed beam lamps*, because both the lens and the reflector are built into the globe. (Car headlights are an example of such a combination.) This means that the angle of light for a given bulb is constant. To change this angle, the PAR has to be changed for one with a different beam.

Within the PAR grouping there are many subtypes, each described by a three letter designation that specifies the variable characteristics, for example, beam width, voltage, wattage, color temperature.

The 1000-watt PAR 64 (3200° K) became a favorite lamp for situations requiring a far-reaching, punching beam like street scenes at night.

Thomas Denove

A trick that I learned years ago is that the apparent intensity of the light bounced off at a sharp angle to you is much higher than the actual intensity of the light source. At night, if you take a PAR light at the end of the block and put it in the middle of the street and aim it back towards the camera, with a flag to hide the actual lamp, you can light the whole block, all of the buildings on one side of the block, with that one light. One PAR light can do it.

One of the most successful lights using the PAR 64 bulb is the Master Light.® It is actually a combination of a luminaire and a voltage converter called a controller, designed by Charles Beckett and Frank Leonetti. It is an autotransformer facilitating the boosting of voltage, for example, from 110 to 160 volts. This change of voltage causes the globe to be 100 percent brighter without a significant change of the color temperature. A slight increase in voltage also allows correction for the voltage discrepancies of a power company. One such converter can serve four 1000 watt Master Lights. Master Lights make use of PAR 64 lamps in spot, medium and wide flood lens designs. By changing the bulbs one can get the equivalent in the spread area of a 2000 watt, 5000 watt, or even a 10,000 watt and by raising the voltage the light intensity

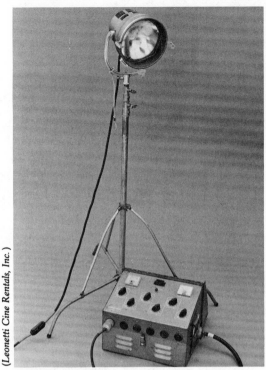

Master Light® using the PAR 64 bulb and an autotransformer which facilitates the boosting of voltage.

can be changed without changing the pattern. This avoids upgrading to a larger unit. A 10,-000 watt performance is obtained by using a spot beam globe at a longer distance. At 100 feet this unit should be able to give from 75 to 100 footcandles depending on the voltage. The beam pattern of PAR 64 is oval in shape. By turning it in the Master Light housing, this pattern can be adjusted from horizontal to vertical. The PAR globe is extremely efficient because the filament is completely reflected in the mirror and there is not much light loss on the edges. The only disadvantage of this lamp is that a light pattern with a sharp edge cannot be had, because of the structure of the lens.

The Master Light works well in combination with a diffusion screen for producing soft light. Increasing the light intensity by boosting the voltage allows us to retain the same light coverage on the diffusion screen. A Fresnel light in the same situation would have to be spotted, which would change the beam coverage.

An important fact to remember when planning to use the Master Light system is that the voltage can only be boosted when using AC. With DC power an increase in voltage over 10–15 volts would blow the filament of a globe.

PAR globes became great favorites with many cinematographers and gaffers for use on night exteriors.

Richard Hart

I like to use Master Lights for the punch, primarily. They are small, easily hidden in the background. I only use them for background lighting, like night exteriors. They are small enough in amperage that you can plug into somebody's house down the street, or a storefront or something of that nature, and be able to give your night scenes a little more depth. I am very disappointed when I see a night scene that is well lit for 200 or 300 feet and after that it is just gone. So it is always nice to be able to pick out points that are little further away. I don't use a Master Light for a key. We always carry a complement of different units, so I prefer using a more controllable light. I like my equipment to be as versatile as possible. If I am stuck with a Master Light as my key, I have to use it as bounce light or it is so spotty that you don't have the coverage that you have using a Fresnel light or something of that nature. Using a Fresnel light with focusing capabilities you still have all the diffusion materials and you also have the bounce capability.

Cameramen and gaffers can always cite several instances when the PAR lights gave excellent service on night exterior location.

James Plannette

I think that PARs are absolutely ideal for night shooting. They come as medium flat, wide flat, spot and narrow spot, whether you use them with a step-up transformer or with the normal 110 volts. They are very directional. In Chinatown they did the whole end sequence with a dozen PAR lights on roofs, etc. John Alonzo did the same on Black Sunday. Shooting night-for-night in San Pedro

5,850 watt Molequartz® Nine-light Molefay® with daylight FAY globes.

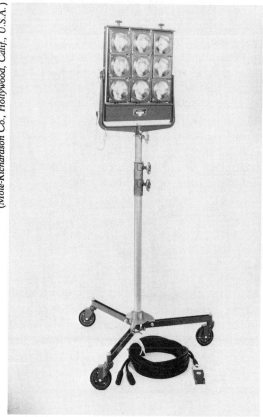

(Mole-Richardson Co., Hollywood, Calif., U.S.A.)

harbor they arranged clusters of PAR lights on boats. Each boat had a generator. Three or four boats, with maybe 10 PARs on each, moved around like light units.

For daylight use there are PAR 64 lights in 5600°K with 1000-watt and even 1200-watt lamps, like the Sylvania Brite Beam. In the PAR 36 family of lights the FAY lamp (5000°K) became best known for its use as daylight fill for exteriors or as a key light in day interior locations.

The most popular instrument using FAY globes is the Nine-Light luminaire. The dichroic coating of the globes, providing the daylight color temperature, used to fade with time, necessitating the use of booster blue gelatines as correction. Nowadays the dichroic coating is applied on the inside of the lens and it tends to be more stable. Some gaffers design their own configuration of these globes.

Richmond Aguilar

I would like to give you a little perspective on the daylight lamps. We did Five Easy Pieces with Laszlo Kovacs. We did a lot of natural locations, a lot of lighting in small houses and small locations, lighting through the windows. Those FAY lights that were available at that time were limited in that the whole light would tip down, but you could not control the individual globes. You could only twist the whole bank of globes, but this was not enough control to do the principal lighting. They were designed primarily as a fill light, more or less straight from the camera. That prompted us to make our own FAY light, a twelve light in which each globe moves, each light is on a gimbal, adjustable. So you could put the Twelve Light at the window and you could tip one globe down to light the couch in front of the window, you could swing some globes to the left to light the wall, swing others to the right to hit the doorway. You could reach across the room to the desk, tip some down to the floor. We had twelve globes to play with. It not only gave you the directional control but you could also control the intensity by using a certain number of globes. You did all control on the lamp so you did not have to go with flags and nets and so forth. We used those Twelve Lights for ten years, doing principal lighting with it on films like What's Up, Doc? and New York, New York. With diffusion in front of them, these lights gave us a nice controllable day light with a punch. That was unique at the time. And then came the HMIs. The FAY lights were not, by any means, the best to use inside, because the light would spill. The HMIs have more control and they give out less heat too. You can do what you want with them. They can be hard, semi-hard, you can put diffusion in front of them or you can bounce them off a board.

A new concept in PAR lights was introduced with the advent of *cool lights*. Here the bulb, the lens and the reflector are separate units held together by the housing. The reflector is interchangeable. When a dichroic coated reflector is used, the color temperature of the lamp is changed to daylight. At the same time the heat absorbing reflector allows for a cooler, more comfortable temperature in front of the lamp.

Richmond Aguilar

The cool light does not burn your actors, but if you use them in a room it does not make that much difference whether the heat goes up in the front or in the back of the light. You still have so many watts burning that the room eventually gets the same temperature. The color temperature falls off from the center on these lights, so you have to control the sides with flags. Only in the center is cool light a true daylight.

All the PAR type globes, including the cool lights, offer a range of lenses with narrower and wider beams.

With faster film emulsions, cameramen and gaffers are looking for less powerful globes that will still produce the color temperature of 3200°K. Next to the always popular Photofloods they are using photographic enlarger bulbs of relatively low wattage (*PH211 bulb = 75 watts, PH212 = 150 watts), which can be utilized in the practical lights and other applications.*

ARCS

Hydrargyum Medium Arc-Length Iodide (HMI) globes represent the most advanced concept in modern lighting technology. Basically it is a mercury arc between tungsten electrodes sealed in a glass bulb. The HMI housing also holds a striker unit to ignite the HMI arc. The initial jump of the arc takes a tremendous amount of power—in the range of 20 to 60 thousand volts for a one-second surge; because of this the HMI needs a warm-up time of three minutes. HMI lamps operate on alternating current (AC) only. Between the AC power supply and the HMI light a "ballast" unit is required. Thomas Denove explains the system.

Thomas Denove

The ballast serves a number of functions for an HMI light. Half of the ballast is a step-up transformer from 110 to 220 volts. Basically it works like a policeman, it is a governor. First of all the HMI light after the initial start-up and warm-up time does not run at 220 volts. Each light runs at a specific voltage. The ballast will adjust the voltage while the light is burning. Also as the HMI bulb gets older, the electrodes burn down enough to change the gap. This changes the relationship of volts and amps for the arc to jump the gap. The ballast keeps that relationship consistent regardless of how the bulb is burning. HMIs increase in color temperature about 1°K per hour of the bulb's life. The Kelvin temperature also goes up when there is a voltage drop. All HMI lights operate only on AC and therefore must be grounded for a safe operation.

When you use HMI from a battery, you need a converter to AC. There is an inverter specifically designed for use in a car, so you can run two 200-watt HMIs from a car battery. It needs an inverter to change it from DC to AC. We have a 500 watt inverter, so you can run two 200-watt lights. For camera cars that are equipped with DC-only generators, a 1200-watt inverter is available.

HMI light pulses at twice the frequency of AC. In the U.S. we have 60 cycles, so any HMI light used here is going to pulse at 120 beats per second. In this pulsation there is a discharge of light followed by a decay. And that happens 120 times per second. If you film without taking that decay time into consideration it can cause a problem which is known as flicker. It is a wave of higher and lower intensity light on the screen. In essence, every frame of film is not receiving the same amount of light. There is about one-third of a stop difference, which is more than noticeable on the screen.

If the camera is running 24 frames-per-second crystal regulated, and the supply of electricity is coming either from your main source (the power company), which is locked at 60 cycles, or an AC generator that is also locked at 60 cycles and crystal controlled, there is no flicker. It does not matter if the shutter is 90°, 142° or 205°, if there is crystal on the camera and crystal on the generator, or if you are coming out of the mains. There will be no flicker problem.

If you shoot with a 144° shutter at 24 f.p.s., each frame of film is receiving 2½ beats. This allows you a certain amount of tolerance for the frequency. If your generator is running slightly off speed, you have a safety margin at 144° shutter. You cannot change the shutter angle during the shot. At present, Panavision has a crystal controlled variable speed motor that can be used without a flicker problem. This opens a lot of new areas for HMI photography.

At the time of this writing most HMIs are rated at 5600°K plus or minus 400°. But 3200°K HMI globes are already appearing on the market. Unfortunately, the variation of 400°K will not be acceptable in a 3200°K light. In a daylight globe such a change is less disturbing, but the more critical cameramen are concerned even with these variations.

Ralph Woolsey, ASC

One of the characteristics of an HMI lamp is that when its voltage increases, the color temperature decreases, and vice versa. When public power supplies drop under peak loads, the HMI won't suffer any losses, but on the contrary its light will become more blue. However, there is a constant drop in color temperature during the life of an HMI globe at the approximate rate of 1° Kelvin per hour of burning. And there may be a significant difference among new HMI globes, some having much higher color temperatures than specified. It is a good routine to check all important key lights where consistency is essential, using a color meter, and to label them regarding filters required for correction to a standard. An old HMI can be down to 4800° K as opposed to a brand-new one, which can be sometimes close to 6000° K. We usually correct them all to about 5200° K, using regular light-balancing materials.

For daylight applications HMI lights compete both with Nine Lights and with arcs.

LTM Luxarc 12,000-watt HMI light.

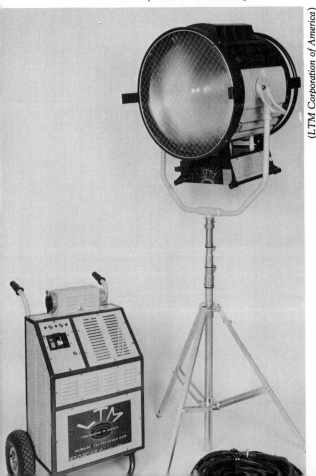

Thomas Denove

For productions that did not go out with an arc, the Nine Light was really the only source of exterior fill light we had besides the shiny boards. When the HMI came out, one of the first things you could compare it to was a Nine Light because HMIs were initially designed as an exterior light source. The cost of operation differs radically. A Nine Light without a dichroic bulb is very inefficient, because the minute you put a tough blue 50 gel in front of it, the output of light turns almost nil, which means that you have to put this Nine Light very close to your subject.

With the expensive dichroic bulbs, the cost of operating Nine Lights could be forty times higher than the HMIs.

Thomas Denove

Another advantage to HMIs is the single shadow compared to nine shadows from a Nine Light. Also the heat from a Nine Light is tremendous. A Nine Light will draw almost 6000 watts of power, and a 1200-watt HMI draws only 1200. So the efficiency is 5:1.

The 12,000-watt HMI outperforms the carbon arc. Considering all the negatives, there is very little reason to use an arc. A 12,-000-watt HMI pulls about 125 amps of current [at 120 volt] and an arc pulls 225 amps. Cabling to an arc is very heavy, as well as the tremendous amount of heat, the tremendous amount of smoke generated. It also takes a man to operate, to adjust the carbons. The whole purpose of a 12,000-watt HMI is to compete with an arc. On the 12,000-watt Luxarc from LTM, the size of the Fresnel lens is the same as on a carbon arc. The HMI bulb is tremendously resistant to shock. Very durable.

CARBON ARCS

In spite of the advantages offered by the HMI lamps the carbon arc is still widely used. In simple terms it is the hardest light source, best at imitating sunlight, and the most powerful single source luminaire for a large area. However, the new HMI 12,000-watt lamp may replace the carbon arc.

Harry Wolf, ASC

I like an arc better for an exterior than an HMI, because it has a bigger spread and it has a farther throw. I can depend on an arc. I know what it can do. I find arcs indispensable for lighting street scenes. I can rake a complete row of buildings with one arc.

Caleb Deschanel, ASC

If you can just get back with an arc and create the sense of the sun at a great distance, why use anything else? It really is a great light. It will do things that you cannot do in any other way.

The Brute remains the most widely used carbon arc. It is a 225 amp light operating at 115–120 volts DC. Today's Brutes are considerably more lightweight and they come in two sizes: Standard with a 24¾-inch diameter lens and the Baby Brute (Mole-Richardson Co.) with a 14-inch lens.

A choice of carbons is available for use with arcs. White carbons, with corrective filters, match the daylight, and yellow carbons match 3200°K tungsten illumination.

The following are the filter gel and carbon combinations: White flame carbon correction to better match daylight: Y1; White flame carbon conversion to 3200°K: Y1+MT2 or MTY; Yellow flame carbon correction to bet-

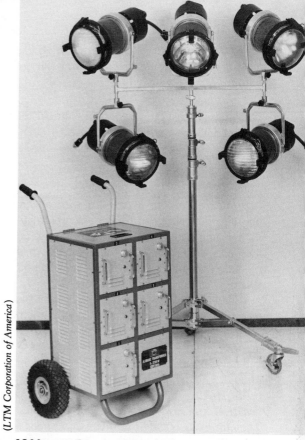

(LTM Corporation of America)

1200-watt Cinepar HMI lights with ballast unit for five lights.

ter match 3200°K: YF101. Yellow flame carbons are more apt to flicker and therefore less widely used.

It is important to keep in mind that an arc is a powerful source of ultraviolet radiation. To protect actors and crew from burns, an arc should never be used without a protective glass. Therefore, when the Fresnel lens is removed to obtain a harder light source, a Pyrex glass should be put in its place.

Richard Hart

I do not like to work without a Fresnel unless I have clear Pyrex glass for an open arc. The Pyrex holds back the UV so the actors are somehow protected. *Without it, it is like looking into a welding machine, you can get burned.*

The arc is also, so far, the best instrument for creating lightning effects.

James Plannette

Lightning effect can be created with an arc hooked up incorrectly. You reverse the polarity and you attempt to strike it. Usually, on most arcs, an indicator light will stay on when the polarity is wrong. In this position it won't strike, it will never really connect.

When the polarity is correct you touch the two carbons together and you release them and they make this little arc from positive to negative. But when the polarity is incorrect, it will never make that arc, but it will make a lot of light. So when you just keep touching them [striking] on wrong polarity, positive to negative, you will get these bright flashes. The film today is so fast that you don't need a tremendous amount of light to overpower the lighting that you already have. Years ago they used a 36-inch mirror, and they had a bunch of carbons, ten to twelve pieces, in so-called scissors, both bunches were positive, I think, so they created reverse polarity and gave a tremendous amount of power.

Richmond Aguilar comments on the same effect.

Richmond Aguilar

For lightning effect we take the lens out of an arc and reverse the polarity and let it fizzle. It is not too good for the generator, but if you do it briefly and with only one arc, it should work. Or for a lightning effect inside a room you can use window louvers covered with Messanite to make them opaque. They are wiggled in front of an arc for this effect.

Another, less powerful lightning effect can be produced using PAR Nine Lights. Many units will be connected together and then one or more breakers will be switched on and off in a random pattern.

Master Lights connected to the converter make it possible to create lightning effects coming from few directions and varied in intensity. It all depends on the area involved and the required intensity of this effect. Certainly the most powerful lightning will be provided by the arc.

Direct current (DC) to operate an arc is usually provided by a generator but for short periods an arc can be operated from a battery.

Vilmos Zsigmond, ASC

You can operate any Brute on batteries. We used a battery powered Brute in a helicopter in Close Encounters. We only needed the big light source for five minutes. You can also use batteries for a running shot in a pickup truck. You are only limited by the duration of the batteries' charge.

For all the advantages of an arc as a powerful directional source there are several factors limiting its use. It is rather heavy. It needs an operator who must change the carbons every forty minutes, and it requires a DC generator. There are outdoor situations where other lamps will actually serve better. For example, arcs are not very good when it comes to lighting the woods. Smaller units are much more versatile for lighting between the trees. PAR lamps like Master Lights are particularly useful in such circumstances. Nine Lights are also good because you can twist the vertical three lamp clusters in different directions.

COMPACT LIGHTS

Small and efficient quartz bulbs stimulated the development of portable location lights. Among the variety of such instruments, the Lowel-Light Mfg. company is a leader in sophistication of design.

For example, an instant change of reflectors on Lowel DP Light allows a choice from a smooth flood pattern to a narrow intense beam punching for several hundred feet. At the same time the parabolic design of these reflectors provides much better shadow quality than is generally expected from the open-ended quartz luminaires.

Simpler but enormously efficient on location is the Lowel-Light system. It makes use of the R-40 bulb. A lightweight barndoor attaches directly on this reflector lamp and the ingenious base plate can be easily mounted on walls, pipes, and furniture.

"R" type reflector lamps come in a wide range of sizes. The small size bulbs, like R-14 (25 watt) and R-20 (30 watt and 50 watt), are easy to hide and often very useful for low light level situations. Even smaller are the so-called peanut bulbs like the 6-watt #6S6 bulb, 1⅞ inches long, or the 10-watt #10C7, 2⅛ inches long. Peanut bulbs are often used in practical lanterns or inside cars.

It is quite useful to have the newest catalogs of the lamp manufacturers such as General Electric and Sylvania on hand.

Certain situations require a battery operated light. These are often referred to as Sun Guns, the brand name of the Sylvania light that has gained wide popularity. Usually such lights are equipped with a 30-volt lamp of 150 or 250 watts. A nickel cadmium battery provides up to fifty minutes of shooting time, depending on the globe.

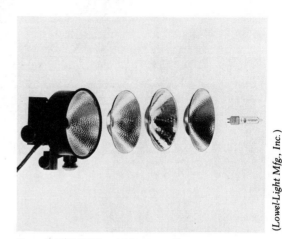

(Lowel-Light Mfg., Inc.)

Lowel DP Light with interchangeable reflectors.

Lowel Omni-Light.

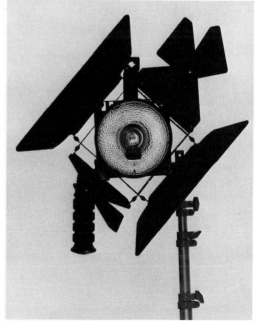

(Lowel-Light Mfg., Inc.)

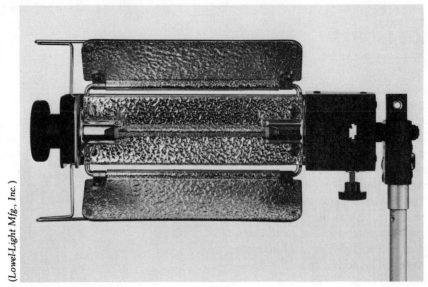

(Lowel-Light Mfg., Inc.)

Lowel Tota-Light.

Lowel Light.

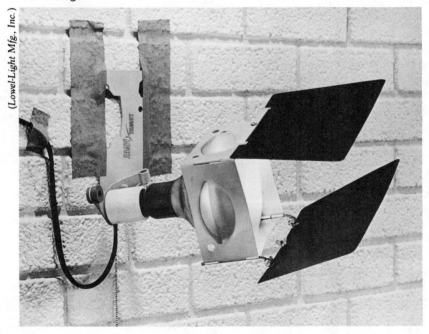

(Lowel-Light Mfg., Inc.)

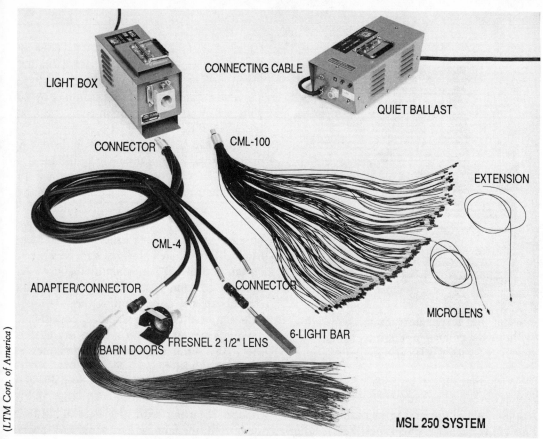

LIGHT BOX

CONNECTING CABLE

QUIET BALLAST

CONNECTOR

CML-100

EXTENSION

CML-4

ADAPTER/CONNECTOR

CONNECTOR

MICRO LENS

BARN DOORS

FRESNEL 2 1/2" LENS

6-LIGHT BAR

MSL 250 SYSTEM

(LTM Corp. of America)

Fiber optics. Micro Set Lighting system by LTM. The HMI lamp contained in the box emits light that travels through fiber strands or cables to lenses which provide cool illumination and can be submerged in water.

Today, portable battery-operated lights are available with HMI heads. Because of their efficiency, a 200-watt HMI provides an equivalent of 1000 watts of light, balanced to daylight. The HMI head is also used in an ingeniously designed LTM system which uses fiber optics to provide light in confined spaces, such as a car interior or a scale model set. For example, the power supply and the light box can be placed in the trunk of a car and from there the glass fibers are run to wherever the light beams are required.

ACCESSORIES TO LUMINAIRES

In the art and craft of lighting, next to the lights themselves, the accessories to control light in its intensity, character and pattern are most important.

Intensity of light can be gradually diminished either electrically using dimmers, or mechanically by such devices as shutters or floating scrims.

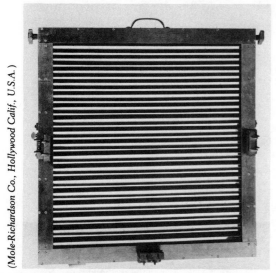

(Mole-Richardson Co., Hollywood Calif., U.S.A.)

Shutter. For mechanical dimming of lights, without the color temperature change associated with electrical dimmers.

With the advent of color, dimmers lost much of their popularity because of the color temperature drop during dimming. Today this phenomenon is sometimes used as an in-teresting effect for modulating the color of light. Modern dimmers also have a booster function. They are able to raise the voltage above the standard level, for example, by 20 volts, which results in a rise in color temperature of 200°K.

Lights can be set on dimmers individually or in groups. For simultaneously dimming a large set, a generator dim may be executed. In this method the generator operator drops the voltage to a preset level on a given cue.

Shutters work like venetian blinds and have no effect on the color quality of light. Electronically controlled shutters can be worked on cue on several lamps simultaneously. As the voltage cannot be lowered on arcs, the shutters are the only dimming method used. The simplest dimming method consists of moving a net in front of a lamp during the shot. Any scrim used in such a manner is known as a floater.

A vast array of accessories is available for controlling light without "in the shot" changes. Starting with the lighting instrument itself, the familiar barndoors and snoots

Funnels and barndoors limit the spread of light. Their function can be further modified with gaffer tape.

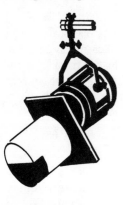
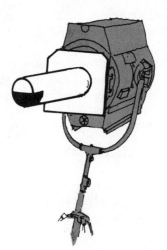
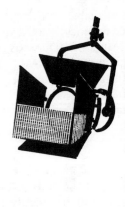

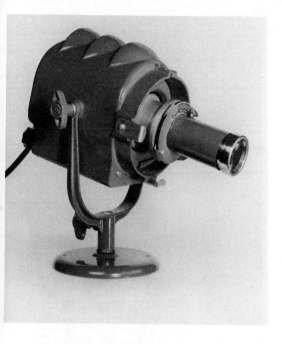

Mole Focal Spot allows for the sharply cutoff shapes of the light beam and the projection of various light patterns, such as church windows or French doors.

Cloth Flag and a Century-stand with the double arm assembly.

(funnels) limit the spread of light. They provide a sharper cutoff pattern in the flood position of the globe and a softer pattern in the spot configuration. A snoot designed with a lens at the end is called a Focal Spot (Mole-Richardson). It has several apertures and patterns that can be projected as sharp silhouettes to imitate window shadows, and so on.

Ingenious snoots can be shaped from kitchen aluminum foil. Foil is also quite useful in shielding any unwanted light leaking from the lamp housing. But care must be taken not to obstruct the ventilation of the fixture.

In front of the lens a small rectangular French flag or any other small device can be positioned on an articulated arm (flexarm) attached to the light itself. Such a flag is farther away from the lamp than the barndoor and is therefore more effective in limiting the light

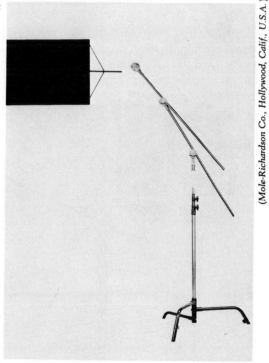

(Mole-Richardson Co., Hollywood, Calif., U.S.A.)

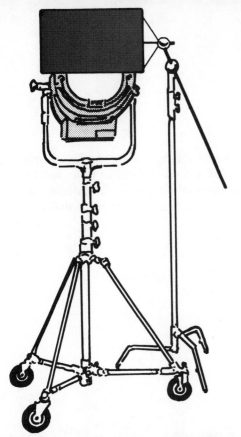

Depending on their position in relation to
the light, flags are referred to as the Topper,
the Bottomer, and the Sider.

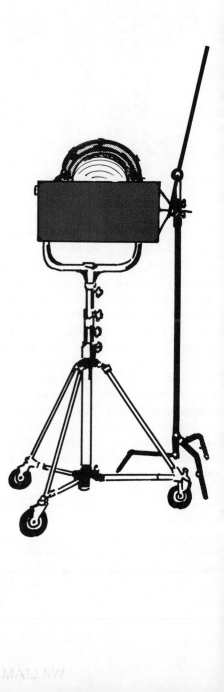

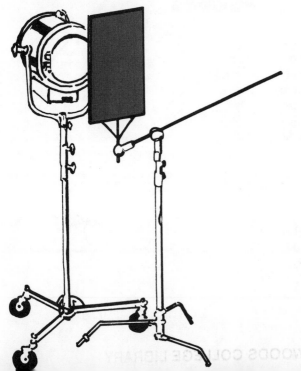

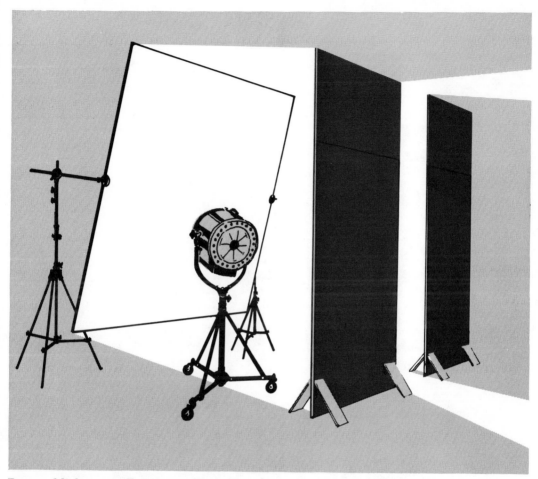

Bounced light controlled by two black Teasers.

beam. More effective yet are flags (gobos) put up on stands farther from the light source. The flags are named depending on their respective positions in relation to the light. And so we have a topper, a bottomer and a sider. Narrow flags are called cutters, fingers and sticks and round flags are known as solid dots. To control soft lights much larger flags are needed. For example teasers are large frames covered with black material. They are put up on stands or hung over a set to cut off unwanted light. Some grips design their own improvements, such as extending a flag with flap-down material to save on an additional stand.

Whereas flags cut off the light, scrims limit its intensity. Sometimes scrims are erroneously called diffusers. This is not the case. The optical principle here is that where the gaps between the wires or threads are larger

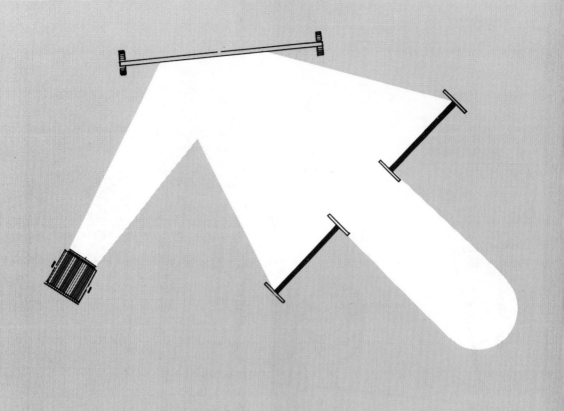

Light pattern modulated by the Teasers.

Wire net scrims and half scrims.

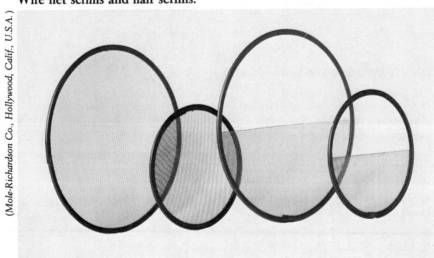

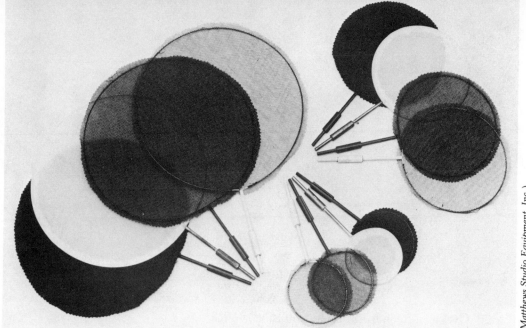

Dots and Targets.

than the thickness of the wires themselves, the scrim does not diffuse light. It only cuts down its intensity.

Round scrims which are mounted directly on the lights come as singles and doubles. A single cuts the light by one quarter, which is equal to one half an f/stop. A double cuts the light by one half, or one f/stop. Round scrims come also as half scrims with the other half of the circle open, letting all the light through.

Where the round scrims exposed to high temperature of the lamp are made of a wire mesh, the scrims to be used on stands are made of a net stretched on a metal frame. They come in the same shapes as the flags. Rectangular scrims are made with one side open, without a wire frame, to allow for a soft blending of the shadow cast.

Long narrow scrims are called fingers, small round ones are dots and larger round ones are targets. All these scrims come in single and double densities. A very fine net is known as a lavender, because of its color. When a true diffusion is needed, any of these scrims can be made of silk.

The soft lighting technique popular today requires diffusion screens which can be as large as twelve by fifteen feet. There is a wide choice of materials available. However, not all the materials can be placed safely near the lamp. Tough Spun and Tough Frost in half and full densities can be used on hot lights. The Soft Frost diffusion needs to be kept farther away from the lamp. The same pertains to tracing paper, which is a favorite with many cinematographers. Among these materials the Tough Spun stops the light most severely. On the other hand Light Grid Cloth made by Rosco cuts down the light by only one quarter of a stop, yet diffuses it very well.

Cinematographers and gaffers often test several diffusion materials before production.

Richard Hart

We tested Lee's 216 and 220, Vinalite, Velveteen [similar to Soft Frost], Hard Frost, ½ Hard Frost, Tracing Paper 1000H, which is the heavy, and the #141 which is the lighter. On Best Friends we limited it to 1000H, 141

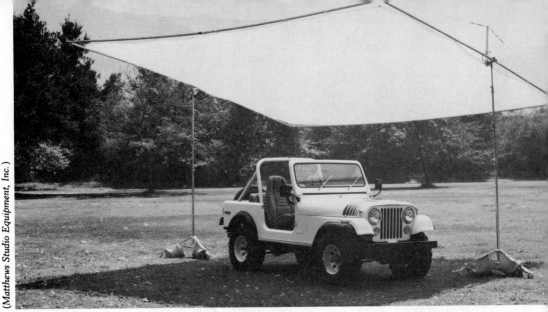

20′ x 20′ Overhead frame with silk for diffusing sunlight.

and Lee 216 Frost. And that was it. The tracing paper is made by one of the big paper companies that makes drafting papers. Actually, they are drafting papers.

Silk, which was mentioned as an alternative material for scrims, is also used for large screens and for a diffusing ceiling over the sets. Bleached muslin is another such material. Before diffusion in such sizes was used in the interiors, silk was traditionally used, stretched on frames or hung on ropes, to soften the direct sunlight on exteriors, as *overheads* or *butterflies.* These two terms are sometimes confused. Overhead is supported from two or more points; butterfly from only one.

Frames with diffusion are often preferable to commercially manufactured soft lights.

Butterfly on a reflector stand.

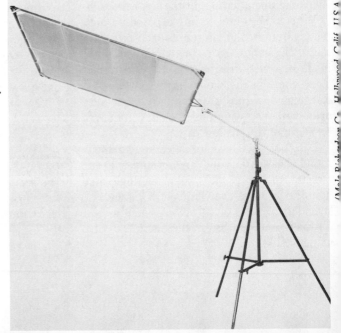

Jordan Cronenweth, ASC

Commercial soft lights are all right but they are big and bulky. They are all right for stage work, but to haul them around in a truck when you are doing a lot of practical interiors, they take up a lot of room and they don't put out much light. I can take a quartz 10K, put it through a diffusion material and I will have

five times as much light. Or you can use a Croniecone.

The Croniecone, named after its developer, Cronenweth, is a device for mounting a diffusion screen directly onto the light. It protrudes from the lamp on a widening cone so that light will not spill to the sides. The screen is close enough to the Fresnel lens to

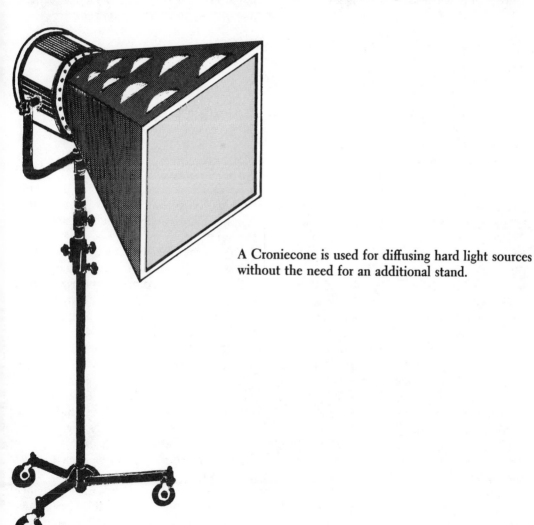

A Croniecone is used for diffusing hard light sources without the need for an additional stand.

be of a reasonable size, like four by four feet on a 5K or 10K light.

Diffusing materials are also used in the construction of a soft light source called a Japanese lantern. This round paper shade houses a bulb of required wattage and color temperature. Japanese lanterns are very light and can be positioned at the end of a stick or hung from a wire. If reflected in some glass surface on the set it will look like a practical lamp.

Gaffer Richard Hart describes a similar lighting device.

Richard Hart

For Jordan Cronenweth, I built regular lamp shades. They were made of China silk and white crepe on the outside. It does the same thing as the Japanese lantern, but it is not made out of paper. Crepe is a white washable material, more durable than silk.

POWER SUPPLY

Power supply and its distribution on the set are the responsibility of the gaffer and his best boy. Although it will not be covered in depth in this book, a general understanding of these problems is important enough for the cinematographer to merit a few general observations. For a more detailed description of power distribution, I recommend, *Lighting for Location Motion Pictures* by Alan J. Ritsko (Van Nostrand Reinhold) and *Motion Picture Camera and Lighting Equipment* by David W. Samuelson (Hastings House).

We will start by reviewing a few basic facts and equations about the electricity on which our lights operate.

Most lamps can be powered by either direct current (DC) or alternating current (AC). The main exceptions are carbon arcs, which require DC, and HMI lights, which work only on AC.

AC alternates at a specific rate (cycles). In the U.S. it is 60 cycles/second, whereas Europe operates at 50 cycles/second. Irrespective of the kind of current it is always measurable in amperes (amps). The potential of electricity is expressed in volts. Amps multiplied by volts equals the power in watts. The equation $w = v \cdot a$ is often remembered as

West Virginia. This gives us the other equations:

$$v = \frac{w}{a} \text{ and } a = \frac{w}{v}.$$

In practical terms it tells us how much light can be generated from a given electrical supply, or how much current is needed for the lights.

Adding all the watt designations of the lamps to be used and dividing them by 100 will yield the approximate amperage required. For the exact figure one would have to divide them by 120v (if such is the voltage). Simplifying it to 100 provides a certain safety margin. For example, if we are going to use five 2Ks and six 1Ks in a house on location, the total required power will be 16,000 watts. Dividing this by 100 will indicate the need for 160 amps. If the house service panel is fused for 200 amps, we are obviously in good shape.

A typical modern 20-amp fuse for one of the household circuits will be sufficient for a 2000-watt (2K) light because 2000w ÷ 120v = 16.6 amp. It even gives us a margin of safety which may be needed if long cables will add resistance and cause a voltage drop.

In Europe the voltage is usually 220 to 240

volts. In this case 2000 watts divided by 240 volts would equal a little over 8 amps. With the greater voltage the same lamps will require less amperage. For this reason European houses generally have lower total amperage, and a 13-amp fuse per circuit is common.

Fuses and breakers are designed to safeguard against overloading the wiring designed for certain amperage. Therefore replacing a fuse with a larger one is extremely dangerous. It will cause the wiring to heat up and may cause an electrical fire. For professional filming the generator is the most commonly used source of power. The direct current produced is much safer for the crew. As Richard Hart puts it: "What happens with DC is that it hits you and throws you away. It literally kicks you back. The AC holds you."

Today, because of HMI lights, many generators can produce both DC and AC currents with a 60-cycles governor. Generators come in a variety of sizes from a 2000-amp giant to a typical 1000 amp, a 250 amp, and down to a tiny Honda generator of approximately 40 amps.

On a location where a generator is not available, one has to depend on the power coming to the house from the power company supply system. If the household circuits do not provide enough amperage it is often necessary to draw it from the power main. Tapping in to such a source is known as making a tie-in, or a clip-on. This operation should be done by a certified electrician, as it is hazardous both to the person and to the system. On the film crew, the gaffer and his best boy should be qualified to do this job. If they are not, another electrician should handle this procedure. State laws can be more restrictive. It would be wise to familiarize yourself with local laws.

The tie-in is done at the service panel of the building. Before tieing-in, the other ends of the cables should be connected to a sec-

ondary location panel (fused distribution box), so that there are no loose cables with "hot" ends. The placement of a secondary fused panel, or switchboard, between the service panel and the lights is required by the safety commissions in many states. When all the connections are completed, the switchboard may be used as a general switch for the lights in one area. This way the main service panel is protected from excessive surges of electricity because the fuses in the switchboard will be the first ones to blow.

Richard Hart

A lot of times on natural interiors, small rooms and so forth, what we like to do is to put in a remote switchboard so that we can cut the power to save the heat. In between shots you just flick the switch and all lights go off. When you are in the studio a lot of times the wall is unfused, so you must use one of those remote boards, or a switchboard of some sort that is fused.

For the proper connecting and distributing of the power we should be familiar with cable sizes. They are rated in AWG (American Wire Gauge) numbers, which are usually marked on the insulation. The heaviest cable is rated as 0000, and a typical gauge to handle a 5K light at up to 100-feet extension, or a 2K light up to 200 feet, is #8. A 10K will require cable sizes #4 and #2 for 100 and 200 feet respectively. On the other end of the power demand, a 500-watt bulb can be used with a 100-foot cable gauge 16.

Cable with an inadequate capacity will warm up from overloading and eventually melt or crack the insulation, the plug, or the switch.

There is a variety of cable connectors and they should be always checked for compatibility with each other and with all the distribution equipment, such as plugging boxes, splicing blocks and spiders.

Working with lights, especially on location, requires constant alertness and common sense. The cables should be secured with gaffer tape and/or ropes so that people do not trip on them and pull down the lights. Especially cables tied-in to the service panel should be protected from an inadvertent disconnection at this point. A C-clamp attached to some structural element above the service panel can act as a support for ropes securing the cables. The location light stands should have no wheels so they are less subject to unintentional movement.

On wet locations, the use of AC should be ruled out as much as possible, unless all the necessary grounding of lights is rigorously observed. To protect cable connections from dampness they should be sealed with a silicon gel. For your personal safety, avoid holding a lighting fixture in each hand. Faulty wiring inside the light may cause the current to travel across your body. It would be particularly dangerous if these lights were drawing power from two separate phases. The potential between them would read 240 volts instead of 120. It is, therefore, an essential safety rule that in a situation where the original 3-phase, 240-volt, electrical supply is divided into two 120-volt legs, the cable distribution is arranged in such a way that lights on one phase are at a safe distance from the lamps powered by the other phase.

Be alert and be careful!

CHAPTER Three

Image Manipulation

THERE ARE many variables that affect the quality of the image that is finally projected in the theater. The more control the cinematographer has over these variables, the better chance he has to capture the precise visual effect he and the director desire for the movie.

There are three stages of the filmmaking process where the cinematographer can manipulate the image. His choice of film stock is the first stage. The characteristics of the stock he chooses will affect the color or tonal rendition of the image and the exposure levels he will use. The second stage is the shoot itself. The cinematographer's decisions about the range of brightness within the frame (which he will create through his lighting) will profoundly affect the "look" of the picture. Filters, nets of Lightflex® on the camera, or manipulation of the environment through the use, for example, of fog or rain machines, are other ways the cinematographer can control the appearance of the framed image. The last stage for manipulating the image is in the lab. The film can be processed normally, it can be forced processed, flashed, or otherwise manipulated to achieve a desired result. Once the film has been developed, the timing of the print is the final, and some feel most important, stage in the lab.

FILM STOCK

Although the majority of important commercial films made in the Western world at this writing are shot on Eastman Kodak color negative, increasing numbers of filmmakers are also using Fuji color negative to obtain a more pastel color quality. There have been cases where both stocks were used on a film, for example, to indicate a separation between two time periods. Black and white film can also be intercut with color film for similar effect. There are also good reasons for mixing films of the same brand but at different speeds. Fast films are recommended for night exteriors to take best advantage of the available light. Using the same film on a day exterior would require neutral density filters to work at an acceptable f/stop. Although rever-sal film is rarely used in 35mm it offers econ-omy for 16mm projects, due to much lower timing costs for the prints. Unfortunately, prints from the reversal (positive) films, can-not be timed as precisely as from the negative film.

BRIGHTNESS RANGE MANIPULATION

The character of a picture will be profoundly affected by the range of tone values from light to dark and by their distribution within the frame. Light falling on reflective surfaces, or shining through translucent materials, pro-duces various brightnesses. In black and white cinematography they are reproduced as gray values. In color cinematography, the bright-ness is greatly influenced by the hue and satu-ration of the colors but the final outcome is still a range of light values.

John Alonzo, ASC

The prettiest use of any color film is when you have a sort of a step-by-step scale of color value, of light and dark, so if your entire frame has 30 percent black and 30 percent white, then you want to take the other 40 percent somewhere between these two ratios of bright and dark. It is a matter of taste, but it does give you the best reproduction for color. Step all the values in the frame with your eye. Say that 20 percent of it is white hot

sky and the rest is various gray values till you get to black.

In low key lighting the frame will be predom-inantly dark, whereas in high key it is predom-inantly light. The brightness range of a scene can be measured in several ways. A spot meter will give absolute values for various small areas in the frame. The contrast viewing glass gives an overall impression of how the film will interpret the brightness range, as does a Polaroid of the scene. The experienced cine-matographer, however, comes to be able to judge the range by eye. We must understand that the brightness range is related only in-directly to the intensity of the key light. It is more the direct outcome of the colors, the textures and the luminance of the scene. The whitest white can be three stops, or more, brighter than medium gray, and the darkest black may be 3½ stops darker than medium gray. That is why a reflected light meter, pref-erably a spot meter, is used to analyze these values. It is essential to think in terms of the brightness range to be able to intelligently in-terpret the light measurements.

MEASURING AND EVALUATING LIGHT

Generally there are two types of instruments used to evaluate exposure: the incident-light meter and the reflected-light meter. The incident-light meter is the basic tool for meas-uring the light value of the sources, mainly the key lights. It is impartial as to the brightness of the subject itself. The reflected-light meter, on the other hand, indicates how much light is reflected by a given surface. It also measures the brightness of translucent surfaces such as stained glass windows, lamp shades and other light sources visible in the photographed scene. A reflected-light meter with a narrow angle of acceptance is known as a spot meter.

It is essential to remember that reflected-light meters are calibrated for medium gray of 16 percent reflectance. This medium gray standard ensures that all the reflected-light meters will react to brightness in the same manner. Remembering this basic norm allows intelligent interpretation of the reflective readings. For example, a Caucasian face has about 35 percent reflectance but a black face reflects less than 16 percent. By blindly following the reflected-light reading, both of these faces would show similar brightness values. The Caucasian face would appear a bit dark and the black face a bit light. For a more faithful representation, the white face should be given half a stop to one stop more exposure and the black face should be exposed at about one half to one stop less than indicated by the reflected-light meter. One way to make the reflected-light meter become as impartial to the subject brightness as the incident-light meter is to measure a gray card instead of the subject. Thus the reading is not biased by the lightness or darkness of the objects in the scene. When measuring a medium gray card, the card should be angled halfway between the light direction and the camera (and meter) to get the most accurate reading.

Let's look at the particular applications of the incident-light meters first.

The incident-light meter measures the intensity in footcandles of light falling on the subject. Once we decide on the footcandle level of a scene we will establish the continu-

ity of our key light values. Therefore we will be able to work at the same f/stop throughout the scene, keeping a uniform depth of field.

Incident light meters have a choice of light-accepting surfaces. The hemispherical plastic "light collector" in front of the light sensitive cell roughly resembles the shape of a human face. When held in front of a person and pointed at the camera it collects all the light and evaluates the exposure. Some cinematographers prefer using the flat disc, which makes it easier to measure one light at a time. For this purpose it is pointed at the light itself. Which method is better remains a personal choice.

Harry Wolf, ASC

Outdoors I use the Spectra with the ball. It is a great meter because it has this ball, and the way the sun hits it at an angle, that is your exposure. Inside the set I use the flat disc. If you put the ball on, you are measuring your top light, you are measuring your kicker, you are measuring everything. With the flat disc I get the directional reading and I know what I am getting. Say I am shooting at 50 FC. We will set the key at 50 FC and I will add my fill. When it looks good to me I will go up and measure it. Now let's say it is 65 FC. So I will say, all right, throw a single [scrim] in the key light. So I will bring the key light down a little bit and then I will look at it and I may bring my fill down, just a touch. Then I will measure and it will be 50 FC overall. That is the way I work. Everybody works differently.

Richard Hart

In the studio when I am working in footcandles I always use the flat disc, because I want to find out what the individual light is doing. If I am working in f/stops, most of the time I use the ball and then shade off any hot back light. I still read the key light from the key light direction as opposed to reading it from the camera. I put the ball toward the light and isolate the other lights, then I read that and then I read toward the camera which combines everything and see how it compares. I have three Spectras: one that goes from 0–f/22, one that goes from 0–f/16, and one that goes from 0–f/8. My low level footcandle meter goes from 0–50 FC.

From the moment we start using a meter on the set we have to make technical and artistic decisions. Say we are shooting on a film which is rated by the manufacturer at 100 ASA. This rating requires 100 footcandles for an exposure at f/2.8. Right away we have several options. We can use the manufacturer's rating of ASA 100. Or we may decide to rate it at ASA 125, 150, or even 200. If we do that our negative will be a bit thinner and the lab will have to print it at a lower printer light. Some cameramen will rate this film at 100 ASA for the day scenes and 200 ASA for the night, but they will have it all printed as if it had been all shot at 100 ASA. As a result, the night will look darker, which in this case is the intention of the cameraman. Another way to use the film is to rate the negative at ASA 200 and push it one stop in development. As a result the negative has a density recommended by the manufacturer but the light level was one half lower, for example, for f/2.8 we needed only 50 footcandles. The price we pay is a slightly larger grain resulting from the longer development.

Exposing the film is not only a science but an art as well. How to expose different parts of a scene becomes a creative decision.

When two actors are facing each other in a scene and one of them is a stop darker than the other, who can say which is "correctly" exposed? After all, in real life four people in a room can have four different levels of illumination on their faces. One of them standing near the window in a shaft of strong sunlight will be from a purist point of view overexposed, yet this is a very realistic rendition. Another, in a dark corner, will be underexposed two stops, and still the whole scene may be perfectly acceptable.

The majority of experienced cinematographers usually measure their key lights but set all the other lights by eye. Late in the evening when the eyes get tired, it is sometimes necessary to check a few other lights as well, in order to match shots filmed earlier to create visually uniform scenes. For this purpose, the incident light meter became a standard tool for interior cinematography.

James Crabe, ASC

For the establishing of a key light, the meter is handy. It is not a bad idea to shoot the whole sequence at f/4, for example, because lenses have a certain look at f/4, there is a certain consistency of depth of field, and all that stuff. Oftentimes no one had measured the first light and you end up balancing to f/8 stop, or something a lot more than what you really need. So I like a gaffer that uses a meter to measure these areas. But the rest is done by eye. I have a contrast filter but I do not use it a lot. What I sometimes do is have a pair of sunglasses with me, with a kind of neutral density. I don't wear them a lot, because if you do your eye adapts to that. Once in a while I just throw them on and look around and maybe I will catch something that needs adjusting.

Reading the key and establishing how different picture areas should relate to the key exposure is the interpretive way of lighting the scene. Much of it is done by the eye.

Caleb Deschanel, ASC

Basically I use the meter after I have finished lighting. As long as I know that I have got somewhere around the overall level that I am working for. If I want to shoot at f/2.5 I sort of shackle that, and then I light just by eye and then I go back and figure out where my exposure should be. You are much better by using your eye. Your eye is so much more sensitive. All viewing glasses are interpolated anyway. It is not as if you trust it overall. For me, I use it to make a judgment about my relationship between shadows and highlights. I don't use it for contrast ratios. I squint to see that.

Reading the key is the most important thing to me. I read the key and then I interpolate what it means. Generally I would say I want that to be hotter than what I am reading, say it is f/5.6 and I want to overexpose that a stop or so. I make a judgment of what I see with my eyes, is the light hot on his face or is it dark, what is my overall impression? Is it overall dark? My impression in looking at you is that it is hot, so I want that to burn out. Everybody has a different way of making judgments about things. If you have something that is within a really limited range, like shooting in the fog, when the things are pretty much evened out then generally you try to get into the medium gray area or a little hot.

Students of cinematography are often unsure of how to use the incident meter. They frequently ask where to point the meter when the key light comes from the side or from three-quarters back, or when one person is in a very bright light and the other is in shadow. Here are a few more suggestions to clarify this issue:

Vilmos Zsigmond, ASC

One way to use an incident meter is to read the shadows on the face and then determine how dark you want this face to be in relation to medium gray (one stop darker or two stops darker) and then expose accordingly. With negative stock I would not expose for highlights, unless highlights are in a large percentage of the frame. But if only 10 percent of the face is in the highlights I would allow them to bloom out, rather than lose details in the remaining areas because you cannot go much darker than two stops on the face. Say that I read f/2 on the darker part of the face. When I expose at f/4 I will retain details in the face and still the highlights will blow out three or more stops. But if sixty percent of the face is lit by the sun, you will not expose for the shadows. You will let the shadows go black. You always have to consider what is the important part of your picture if you cannot bring it into balance with your lighting. You just have to expose for the part which you want to see correctly exposed and allow the rest to go either white or black. You have no choice.

Other ways to improve the balance of a high contrast scene are flashing or using Lightflex, which we will discuss in more detail later in this chapter.

Establishing exposure becomes an interpretative process. This is the reason why it does not make sense to have an automatic exposure system built into a professional motion picture camera.

Richard Kline, ASC

I think that photography is basically the eye. You might need some sort of technical device such as a meter to get an overall reading, just to know where you are, but if you start lighting by meter then you become a slave. When I use the meter, I use Luna-Pro for exterior, or the Spectra. On an interior set, only the Spectra because I am used to that meter. But I rarely use the meter. I think you have to decide what you want to expose for in the set. It could be the wall behind the actor, and you want the face to go down. So you decide and that is what you expose for, and you take a reading on that. If it is a long shot and there is a face cross-lit, hot on one side only, and if it is just a small item in the set, then the face is not quite the place to take the exposure. Maybe you will rather expose for the body if the whole body is in the side light. If you are doing a close-up, then your considerations are easier, you may want to go in between, or you might want to go for the bright side of the face with nothing on the other side. So obviously you would expose for the light. But you may want to put a little bit of light in the shadow, just a reference light, so that you can get a shape of some sort.

Caleb Deschanel, ASC

As a general rule, depending on the size of what is in frame, I usually figure that the whitest white is about four stops overexposed and the blackest black is somewhere around 3 to 3½ stops underexposed, depending of course on the background. I can take someone and underexpose his face 2 stops and put him against the black background and you would see his face really well. I could then light the background to 4 stops over, and have the front of his face exposed exactly the same way, and you would hardly be able to see any detail in his face, because your eye cuts down that front detail. It is a realy psychological thing that happens. One of the things that I did in Being There is, that in order to create

the blacks that I wanted I actually overexposed the film, so the highlights were actually hotter in order to create the illusion of the blacks being blacker. It is part of the nature of contrast. If you show absolute black on the screen it is milky. I don't care how good the lab, there is no such thing as absolute black. Whereas, if I put a spot of white light in the middle of the black, that black will appear much blacker. Certainly one of the reasons we used a lot of practical lights in Being There was to create that sense of black.

Our exposure considerations will also be conditioned by the decision on the overall light levels to indicate the mood and the time of day.

Harry Wolf, ASC

If you are shooting night interior, naturally your key is going to be a little lower. I don't work in the same high key as I do in daylight. Day interior naturally is a little more up, it is a little more fill, you have a little more light on the walls, but on your night shooting you make it look like night.

I expose 5247 [Eastman Color Negative] with 100 FC at f/4, that is normal, so I would go to 75 FC at night interior. I expose 5294 [Eastman Color High Speed Negative] with 50 FC at f/4, which gives me a rich negative. For effect lighting I shoot anywhere from 20 to 30 FC at f/4. Whatever film I use I find that f/4 gives me the depth of field I want. Only in extreme light conditions will I break this rule. I have used T/1.4 lenses in this respect.

Many cinematographers work at an f/stop that would facilitate the use of a zoom when needed, without changing the light levels. Others like to work at very low light levels and at the corresponding wider apertures. Their reasoning is that it is better to judge lighting contrast at low levels and that the more one stops down, the more half tones and quarter tones of brightness are lost. However, films shot with a wide open lens can be very annoying with so much of the frame intentionally out of focus.

For the fine analysis of the various brightness ratios in the scene, a spot meter with a 1° acceptance angle is a very useful instrument. The spot meter represents a reflected light metering system, which measures the brightness of the subject, whereas the incident meter measures the light falling on the subject. A spot meter is especially useful when there are translucent objects like stained glass windows in the scene, or practical sources of light, whether windows or lamps.

Caleb Deschanel, ASC

I almost always use a spot meter for highlights, for windows, for light sources that are in the frame and occasionally to judge shadow details. They are much more sensitive now. It used to be that you could not read 4 stops underexposed if you were shooting at f/4 or f/2. They just weren't accurate at a lower range. Now Minolta is completely accurate down to 1/10 of an f/stop. [Some spot meters can be misleading.] Despite the fact that they say that they are reading one degree, every spot meter is affected by what is around the measured spot. They do not totally isolate what they are reading. You really have to be careful about how much you believe it. You have to know when to believe it and when not to believe it.

Generally spot meters are used more for analyzing the brightness range of the scene than for measuring exposure.

James Crabe, ASC

I use a spot meter mostly in commercials when I am dealing with translucent things, like a glass of beer. A typical case of measuring transmitted light would be taking a reading of a stained glass window. They always used that example when talking about reflected light meter readings, because if you go with an incident meter, there is nothing there. I don't use the spot meter for determining exposure usually, but it is a very handy tool.

One should be very careful when using the spot meter to determine the exposure because it reads a very small portion of the subject. Yet, for the purposes described here it is an extremely valuable tool.

Ralph Woolsey, ASC

I use a spot meter a great deal. There are definite situations where only this meter gives a fast and accurate answer; for instance, in a church when photographing inaccessible stained glass windows. You often start by asking yourself, "What am I going to read to get the basic exposure?" You might measure the widest range of significant tones with a spot meter and take the average. As with any subjects which are transilluminated, including signs, video displays, transparencies, and so forth, you are really measuring the brightness range. Some extreme situations might require an ND filter in front of your spot meter when reading targets like a blast furnace.

All new meters are calibrated with EV numbers. The maximum range is from −4EV to about 26EV, and each succeeding number equals a difference of one stop. In the Minolta digital meter, once you release the trigger a spot reading is displayed for at least 30 seconds, and the outside readout gives you the stop without computation. EV numbers are displayed inside the meter in 1/10-stop increments. Here is an example of using the meter to learn how much light is lost by the neutral density tint of a glass door: Maybe the door will be opened during a shot, so we want to know how much lighter the exterior is going to be. First, I read a specific target through the open door and note the EV number. Then I close the door and read the same target again. If it read #7 when open and it dropped to #5½ when closed, the change would be 1½ stops. The Minolta meter reads 1/10-stop differences very accurately. Here is another situation for use of a spot meter: Some of my students were using a camera inside a car, photographing through the windshield, but also seeing the rearview mirror in the frame. They got a larger-than-normal mirror in order to see a motorcycle officer approaching behind the car. Their exposure through the windshield was good, but the reflection in the rearview mirror was very dark. The mirror had a neutral density tint that absorbed a lot of the light and the rear window of the car also had some tint. By taking a spot meter reading—through the rear window—of a target like a piece of paper, and then turning around and reading it again in the rearview mirror, they could have the exposure difference, which was at least a stop and a half. One way to balance the difference would be to replace the original ND mirror with a clear one. Another way to make this shot could utilize some neutral density material on the windshield in order to balance its brightness to the rearview image as desired. And don't forget that the apparent density of an ND material increases as you look through it at oblique angles. A spot meter will measure such differences quickly.

Another area where the spot meter proved to be a valuable tool is in evaluating the brightness of the sky.

Vilmos Zsigmond, ASC

Basically I use a spot meter to control the sky, that is, to control the balance between the sky and the faces. During the day the relationship between the sky and the sun stays the same but when you are doing dusk shots the density of the sky should be maintained throughout the scene. As it gets darker you have to reduce your lights on each take to maintain balance. You can extend your dusk this way. Dusk is the only way to shoot day-for-night that doesn't look phony.

This brings us to the subject of light measurement on the exteriors. Here many cinematographers will use a regular angle reflected light meter such as a Luna-Pro or Weston, as well as an incident one. The spot meter, which also belongs to the reflected meter category, is used for specific tasks, such as the evaluation of the sky for sunsets and dusks.

Ralph Woolsey, ASC

Reflected-light meters are calibrated for 16 percent reflectance and this value fits into the standard ⅓ stop sequence of light value intervals. Eastman based its Neutral Test Card on 18 percent, which is not significantly different.

To set an exposure for the sky after the sun has set, I read the sky near the horizon where it is brightest. Previously I have decided the reflectance value I want that area to reproduce on the screen, and have preset my spot meter for that value. Remember that "normal" exposures set with a reflected-light meter will reproduce the target area as a 16 percent value. A 65 percent value would look 2 stops brighter; 80 percent looks white, etc. So to give your target a 65 percent screen value you must compensate two stops wider than the meter reading. On the Minolta digi-

tal spot meter I preset my value by shifting the shutter-speed number. If it is normally 24 fps, and I shift to 96 fps, which is four times faster, this gets me up to 65 percent reflectance from the normal 16 percent for which the meter is calibrated at 24 fps. If preferred, you can shift your normal ASA to a lower index and get proportionally brighter target values. Now, if you are doing "magic hour" and waiting for lights to come on in the buildings, you can judge this visually. When you get the right look, you can then read the sky for, say, a 65 percent value and immediately read out the stop. Using this method gives one confidence in exposing right down to the last usable sky glow with the fastest lens/film combination. There have been occasions where I doubted the meter, but I was invariably wrong. A note of caution: As a good practice, check your meter settings frequently, especially if you shift values as above for special exposure problems.

With the exception of the spot meter, reflected meters have a rather wide angle of acceptance. This means that in a long shot an actor standing before a large white wall will end up underexposed; the same actor in front of a black wall will be overexposed. The reason for these variations is the reflected light meter trying to average the picture so that it would be rendered close to medium gray. Therefore it indicates a high f/stop number for a shot with the predominance of white, and it designates more exposure for the predominantly black frame to bring it up to the medium gray. Obviously if an optimal exposure of the face is important we would walk up to an actor to take the reading, or we would approximate it by reading our own hand if the light levels and the flesh tones were similar. In a situation like this a spot meter would prove to be a very convenient tool.

Remembering that reflected-light meters

are calibrated to give the correct exposure for medium gray we would compare the flesh tones to medium gray and make the necessary adjustment.

The reflected light meter is a highly interpretative tool. Yet it is frequently used by cinematographers, mainly on exteriors. Large vistas in long shots represent color and contrast over which a cinematographer has little control. If he uses his incident light meter, the reading for a desert or for a glen in a forest may be the same, but the subject matter is totally different. He can interpret it to decide on the required exposure, or he can help himself by using a reflecting light meter, which will react to the brightness of the background. In a situation where the foreground action is lit by lamps, a combined reading of incident meter for the foreground and reflected meter for the background may be used.

A combination of an incident meter and spot meter is used for a triple light measuring technique for some difficult exteriors. Adam Holender suggests the following:

1. Measure with incident meter pointed toward the camera.
2. Measure with incident meter pointed first toward the sky, then toward the ground and split the difference.
3. Measure with a spot meter to evaluate the subject selectively.
4. Decide the exposure in relation to what is important in the frame.

As we see, on an exterior location where a cinematographer has less control over the lighting, his measuring methods have to be much more exact than in the studio. Backlit scenes silhouetted against the sky require especially careful interpretation. A spot meter can read the highlights and the shadows. There will be a few stops difference between the two. If we are not using any fill light we have to interpolate the best exposure for the mood we wish to create: how much to overexpose the sky and how much to underexpose the face, and where the background will be in the exposure, for example, hills silhouetted against the sky.

Besides using an incident meter and a reflected-light meter, some cinematographers like to test their contrast ratios by taking a black-and-white Polaroid picture, even when filming in color.

Jordan Cronenweth, ASC

A Polaroid is an effective way to judge balance. For instance when you have to balance between an exterior and interior. A spot meter serves a similar function.

There are inherent problems with Polaroids, though. Neither the lens nor the film latitude is identical to the lens and the film used in the movie camera. Therefore it serves only as a rough guide.

Caleb Deschanel, ASC

The limitation of a Polaroid is that you have only one lens. That is, for me, the hardest part. So many things are affected by the length of the lens. I usually use it to make judgments about the highlights. If I look at something and I think I am okay and I will take that picture and the highlights are totally burned out then I get suspicious and recheck things. It is only accurate up to a point and it is affected by how long you let it develop, and the temperature. It is like a fourth light meter. You've got your Spectra and your Weston and your Spotmeter and then you have that.

Finally, a few words should be said about the viewing glass or contrast filter. It is basically a filter of a certain density designed to better judge the contrast as it will be rendered on film. For black-and-white film a Kodak Wrat-

ten filter #90 (olive) is used and for color film it is a Neutral Density of 0.9. Unfortunately, at a low key, a viewing glass is not very useful.

John Alonzo, ASC

I use a contrast viewing glass just as a reference point, not always, sometimes when I have a slight problem like shooting a man against a window, it sort of helps me to evaluate.

All the light meters and other devices are just tools to help in shaping the aesthetic concept. The art of filmmaking should never become subservient to technology. An understanding of the scientific processes employed, though, will make the cameraman less dependent on the measurements. The old adage that you have to know the rules to break the rules, is truly illustrated in exponometry and in cinematography as a whole, so the issue of rigid ratios between the key and the fill light should have its place mainly when shooting tests. In the end, it is often intuition that wins out over all the measurements and Polaroids and contrast viewing glasses.

Caleb Deschanel, ASC

As far as the direction of light and the amount of fill light, that part of it is really by eye and is more intuitive. You make a decision about how you want to see something and it can be partially a conscious decision, and it is partially how you feel about it. Sometimes you just feel that you should do something a certain way. You have to answer to that. Good directors will respond to those intuitions and will accept them as [an] equally practical means for making a judgment as being intellectual about it.

Giving yourself a reason for something is oftentimes after the fact. Lots of times people demand a reason for you doing something a certain way. But if you have to spend a lot of time coming up with reasons, when you are dealing with an inspiration, or intuition, it makes no sense. You should be able to say, well, I don't think that's right. I mean that is my feeling.

Just as a cinematographer must be aware of whether his eye is tired when he is judging the brightness range, it is also important to be aware of the fact that the human eye adapts quickly to slight color shifts in light unless there is a reference point in the field of view for example, one area of true white light.

Jordan Cronenweth, ASC

Color is relative. If you want to have a warm feeling to a scene, you need a non-warm refer- ence, otherwise the eye will adjust and pretty soon they are seeing overall warm as a more neutral color light. But if you keep a reference in the frame, like another practical that is not as warm as the one you are using, or reflection of something in a mirror, that gives you a reference. As long as you keep that alive in there, the audience will never start assimilating the warm light as normal light. In a day interior scene with the feeling of the daylight in the windows, put the practicals on in the room. People will have nice warm light from the practicals and yet when they come by the window they will be in daylight (accentuated by a colder light). As far as unfiltered windows (on locations) are concerned, I personally don't like that much difference in the color temperature. I am particularly sensitive to blue, I don't like it.

COLOR GELATINS

Generally we can say that cinematographers today are much more daring in their departure from the exact color temperature of the light required for a given film than were their colleagues two decades ago. On the whole, the changes are rather toward psychologically warmer, more orange light for everyday situations. For this purpose lights are covered with gels, such as the traditional #54, the CT Orange series by Lee, or the Rosco MT series.

Allen Daviau, ASC

I rarely like the normal 3200° K for anything. I like to use the pale gold 54 gel in different strengths as a warming element. Unless I am representing something right near a white light where it would be normal. For a feeling of a lamp shade or what have you, I would throw a 54 gel on all my source lights. It does not read golden. But sometimes you will see the back light bluer than if the same light was coming from the front. And if I throw in a 54 gel, it will make it neutral. Light loss on the 54 is negligible, very slight. Unless you double or triple it.

Another way to warm up the lights is by putting them on dimmers to lower the color temperature (in degrees Kelvin). For this purpose as well as for the adjustment of brightness, practical lamps are often used with a rheostat on the line.

On location, and even on studio sets, fluorescent tubes are sometimes left unfiltered for a more realistic feeling. But when filtering is needed and tubes with correct color temperature are not available, conversion gels and color compensating and color correctng filters can be used.

Several approaches in filtering can be used.

The aim is to obtain a uniform color temperature of all the lights so that the laboratory can correct it during the timing of the print. If natural daylight prevails and the tubes are also fluorescent daylight or cool white, the windows can be covered with a green gel called Tough Plusgreen/Windowgreen (Rosco). If we wish to use tungsten 3200°K lights simultaneously, we need to cover them with Tough Plusgreen 50 (Rosco). Should day-type lamps, like FAY lights be used as well, the proper gel in this situation would be Tough Plusgreen/Windowgreen (Rosco).

When the lighting situation indicates that it is more convenient to filter the fluorescent daylight tubes rather than the windows and tungsten lamps, Tough Minusgreen (Rosco) gels are employed, sometimes in the form of sleeves for the individual fluorescent tubes. The Minusgreen covered tubes create a disquietingly purple illumination and often a Polaroid photograph is needed to put us at ease that this "purple" illumination will indeed match the daylight. Lee filters also provide a range of gels for fluorescent correction.

A scene entirely lit by fluorescent light can also be corrected with filters used on the camera lens. Several companies offer two filters, FLB and FLD for the correction of the average fluorescent tubes of the warm and daylight types respectively.

For more exact types of fluorescent tubes, a wider range of filters may be needed. The American Cinematographer Manual and Kodak publications provide various filter recommendations for such purposes.

One can avoid using filters altogether where there are fluorescent tubes that closely match daylight, such as Optima 50 or Vita-Lite (Duro Test) or Chroma 50 (General Electric). To match tungsten illumination use Optima 32 (Duro Test) and Deluxe Warm White (General Electric).

Finally, a few words should be said about correcting fluorescent illumination that does not match the film emulsion during the timing in the lab. Let's remember that timing deals with the whole frame and can be totally effective only when all the light sources we wish to correct are the same color characteristic. There is also some danger in full fluorescent correction.

Allen Daviau, ASC

It is no problem for the lab to make the fluorescent correction. The one thing I will caution you about is allowing the lab to make the full fluorescent correction. There is something that occurs in removing all the green from the print that raises the inherent contrast. And then you'll get an extremely hard black. Harder than I like. As a result, when I am shooting in fluorescent I tend to use a low contrast filter, like Tiffen LC 3. And people would say, Isn't that strange, you are shooting under fluorescent light, it is so flat, why would you want to use a low contrast filter? But I found out the hard way that without this correction you'll wind up with extremely contrasty blacks.

IMAGE MANIPULATION BY FILTERS, NETS, AND OTHER OPTICAL MEDIA

The cinematographer has an impressive range of filters and nets at his disposal, to manipulate an image in the camera. Some, like graduated filters, are employed to selectively change the density of the image, or, like low contrast and fog filters, to change the contrast of the image. Others, like diffusers are specifically used to soften the definition of the image.

The first thing to remember is that any filter, particularly a glass one, will have an effect on the performance of the lens.

Ralph Woolsey, ASC

When the camera has inside filter capability I would use it every time possible, chiefly for convenience, plus the advantage of not having to look through a heavy filter when operating. It is easier to make quick changes or to divide filter combinations. The main problem in having an inside filter is that it must be far enough from the film so that an imperfection or accidental piece of dirt will not produce a sharp shadow. And since the image is shifted about one third the thickness of the filter, the usual rule of thumb is not to use inside filters when shooting interiors. Certainly avoid them if you are working wider than T/2 unless you can critically eye-focus. And of course the focus is much more critical with a wide-angle than a long-focus lens.

The most commonly used filters in the group discussed here are neutral densities. They allow the cinematographer to use wider lens apertures (f/stops) by cutting down the amount of light, mostly on bright exterior locations.

Caleb Deschanel, ASC

If I stop down to f/22 it is usually on a real long lens. With long lenses I always like to shoot as far down as I can for depth of field. For anything wider than 200mm I would use neutral densities. Generally, the NDs I use are Pancro Mirrors. They are a little more accurate. They are special filters that are mirrors basically, a certain percentage mirrors. When

you go to N.9 in ordinary filters, you will get a certain amount of yellow, which you will not get with Pancro.

A neutral density filter that does not cover the whole frame comes as a graduated or an attenuator. The graduate filter (grad) has a soft bleed line that separates the ND part of the filter from the clear part. Custom designed filters may have this dividing line at different levels and angles to fit a particular horizon line or other frame division. On occasion a net in front of the lens may serve a similar function.

Ralph Woolsey, ASC

To control areas of great brightness in a large interior you could use, in a static shot, a graduated filter on the lens; or put a net with a nice clear edge on a stand, right next to the matte box where it would be out of focus. This net would darken the problem area, such as a hot window or wall. You can shoot through it and then pan off it to the darker part of the set. Another method is to pull the net sideways while panning, or in the opposite direction of any camera movement. If smoothly done it can be blended with close foreground action and never noticed, so it works well. Cinematographers have often used these tricks on exteriors where bright areas were too large or inaccessible to control in any other way.

The attenuator is designed to give a gradual darkening of the frame. It may be two stops darker on one end (ND.6) and then gradually lose its density until the other end becomes clear glass.

Vilmos Zsigmond, ASC

Sometimes I use an attenuator to make the sky look more dramatic, but it is difficult to use it when the camera moves a lot and I do *not like to limit my director. I don't want to tell my director, You cannot move the camera now. I do not like static filming, which works best for graduates and attenuators. I like the camera to be free to move all the time. It's very difficult to have it both ways, to have camera movement and still use graduates or attenuators.*

For creating a darker and more saturated sky, blue graduates are also available. For a sunset effect an orange graduate can be used. Filter manufacturers such as Lee can make grads to order in various colors. At times the blue sky can be darkened by using a polarizing filter if the sun is to one side. It polarizes the sky more than the foreground scene, so there is no problem with the bleed line of a graduate. But panning is also problematic because the change of angle in relation to the sun will also change the rate of polarization. At high altitudes the sky is usually sufficiently dark by itself.

Ralph Woolsey, ASC

Because the sky at high altitudes appears darker, the use of a Pola filter can make it really black if desired. This filter is very useful, not only as an ND but also for its added angular capabilities. The angle can be changed during a shot in order to obtain certain effects. Reflections in a glass surface can be eliminated with a Polarizer, and then on cue the Pola can be rotated to fade in a reflection or ghost effect.

Modern lenses render the image with high definition that is often too harsh for the given subject matter. Several filters were designed to diffuse the image, lower the contrast, and desaturate the color in various degrees. In this group are diffusion filters, single and double fog filters, low contrast screens, frost filters, Harrison's Black Dot Texture Screens, nets,

and several filters for specific effects such as star filters. Most of these filters come in a range of five densities. Finally we can use clear optical glass smeared with substances such as petroleum jelly or glycerin.

The usage of all the filters discussed here requires tests to arrive at the desired effect under the conditions of the given film stock, lighting, photographed subject, and expected processing in the laboratory. It is important to keep in mind that this discussion on diffusing filters pertains mainly to 35mm and larger formats. The 16mm image is generally softer and on the whole does not need more diffusion unless special visual design demands it.

Any filter positioned in front of the lens may cause car headlights and other bright sources to appear on film as double images. To prevent this phenomenon, some cameras (Panavision) can be equipped with matte boxes that provide filter holders positioned at an adjustable angle so that the filter plane is not parallel to the lens surface. This allows the troublesome reflections to be directed away from the lens.

Cinematographers often differ in their preferences for certain filters. Here are several opinions.

Vilmos Zsigmond, ASC

Double fog gives a little glow from the highlights, which seems to me to be similar to the way the eye sees. I do not think that people see in clinical, sharp detail; I think that the human eye is more kind, softer. You do not see the pores in the people's faces as a sharp Cooke lens does. You usually do not come that close to the person. So I think that the diffusion on the lens makes it more realistic.

When choosing a filter, don't be misled by the names fog and double fog. The names of those filters are totally wrong. They should have never been named that way because ac-

cording to the name you would think that double fog has a double effect. Double fog gives you a sharp image, all it really does is to give you a glow around the light sources. Regular fog is foggier and not as sharp. Regular fog has more of a diffusion effect than a double fog.

Low contrast filters really deal with contrast. They do not glow on the highlights. I have very little use for these filters. For some reason I have not learned to use them. I hardly ever use the traditional diffusers. I do not like to take my pictures out of focus. And what those diffusions are actually doing is throwing things out of focus. Again, I have not used them that much.

Caleb Deschanel, ASC

I don't like fog filters. I used LCs from time to time and there are these Frost Filters that they have. They are another kind of diffusion, they basically soften the edge of highlights. They are made by Wilson in England. They don't affect the low end [the black] as much as low contrasts do. They sort of soften the highlights. My tendency is to not use much at all. I prefer keeping things fairly clean.

Haskell Wexler, ASC

I use low contrast filters when there is heavy contrast on an exterior. Instead of flashing I would just throw in a #2 or #3 or #4 low contrast filter. I use diffusion filters on people when required. I would use Mitchell diffusion A, B, and so on.

I find nets useful because you do not have to worry about the kicks on the glass. They flare differently than the fog filters. Say, on a lamp the fog would flare out when the net would crisscross.

It is important to know the differences between the filters made by different manufac-

turers. I know for example that Harrison fog filters are stronger than Tiffen® fog filters.

Harrison and Harrison also make a couple of useful filters not mentioned by these cinematographers: the scenic fog filter and the black dot texture screen.

The Scenic Fog could be described as a fog graduated filter. You can situate it to obtain a light fog effect in the foreground and a denser fog in the upper part of the frame. This would resemble a natural situation.

The Black Dot Texture Screen represents a new kind of diffusion filter which gives you diffusion without the milkiness and the halos around the light sources.

To soften the outer areas of the frame while keeping the center image clear, Tiffen makes the Center-Spot filter. The same company offers a series of star filters that create star effects on any light glint in the scene, and for a more colorful and stronger effect the Vari-Burst filter.

One of the oldest diffusion devices is a net. Traditionally, cinematographers assemble a personal set of nets in various densities and shades, ranging from millinery veils to an assortment of ladies' pantyhose.

Philip Lathrop, ASC

When I use black nets on the lens for female close-ups, I use them in combination with Mitchell diffusion filters. Double Fog is better than the Low Contrast filters, because you do not get out of focus as easily. LC looks to me always out of focus. Single Fog is more for a fog effect.

James Crabe, ASC

White gauze is very effective, it probably does a little bit of what the Lightflex does. Just by virtue of it being white. And some white gauzes were actually backlit for the incredible complex silent movies where the great glamour shots of Gloria Swanson needed this kind of flare. It is pretty difficult now with the zoom lenses that are used as often as they are. In old days the matte box could be extended as far as it can go, to be just off the shot and keep a lot of that spurious light from hitting the lens.

The problem of spurious back light is the reason why black nets are preferred to white ones for the normal, not flared, net effect. Other color nets are also used.

Michael D. Margulies, ASC

I have some pink nets and some black nets. Apart from their diffusing quality, a pink net has some psychological effect on an actress. It puts her at ease because she sees this net and feels that I have a net just for her, that I am taking some little special caring.

Ladies' pantyhose, a great source of nets, are available in a variety of shades and densities to choose from.

Vilmos Zsigmond, ASC

Pantyhose is a very beautiful thing actually. It is like using a scrim. It creates a very beautiful effect. It gives you sharpness and it gives you softness at the same time. The only disadvantage to pantyhose is that it has a funny effect on light sources, like a cross-star effect that many times you do not like to use.

It is important to remember with all these filters that the image seen through the camera is more diffused than the image that will appear on the film. More accurate evaluation is possible when looking through a combination of the viewing glass and diffusion or fog filters.

James Crabe, ASC

The ground glass, even though it is pretty accurate most of the time, does often play tricks on you. If you look through the camera that is heavily diffused, it usually looks more heavily diffused through the camera than it does when you see the final result, so you have to be pretty confident about what you are doing, because often people will look through the camera and say, You must be kidding, I cannot even see him, whereas in actual fact the diffusion is less severe.

One should also remember that the effect of the same fog filter will differ depending on the focal length of the lens and on the f/stop at which the lens is set.

James Plannette

At 25mm a fog filter does not have as much effect as it has at 250mm. At 25mm you may use a one-fourth double fog where at 250mm you will use one-eighth double fog and it will look the same. Therefore if you cannot change filters during zoom (like a sliding graduate filter) it will have much more effect at 250mm. With sliding diffusion you could theoretically slide it during the zoom-in from one-fourth to one-eighth. You really have to keep in mind the effects that filters have at different focal lengths.

At the same time, if lenses of a similar focal length are used for a close-up and then for a wider shot, the close-up should be given more diffusion than the wide shot. These are very general rules, it is essential to shoot tests for the particular circumstances.

The diffusion effect will also change with the f/stop. Stopping down decreases the effect of a diffusion filter, particularly in the range from f/8 onward. Fog filter results are similarly affected. The wider the lens opening, the more "blossoming" effect the fog filter will produce. Exposure also needs to be considered. Underexposed parts of a scene will be less affected by diffusion than overexposed areas.

Fog, double fog, and low contrast filters do not require more exposure. On the contrary, lowered contrast, especially in already less contrasty subjects, may appear as overexposed images and therefore some minor exposure reduction is sometimes needed. When using low contrast screens exposure reductions of one-half to one and one-half stops may sometimes be required to prevent a flare effect. A Black Dot Texture Screen requires approximately 1 stop more light to compensate for its density. A professional diffusion filter, which usually consists of a glass with a finely ground pattern laminated onto an optical glass, does not require any exposure correction. On the other hand a homemade diffusion device like a clear glass smeared or sprayed with petroleum or glycerine, or nets like pantyhose, should be tested for an exposure compensation. The easiest exposure test consists of holding such a "filter" in front of an exposure meter. But only shooting tests on film will allow a proper evaluation of all the characteristics of such a device.

One of the most important reasons for the rather wide use of fog filters and nets is their ability to desaturate color. Cinematographers of today are usually not interested in obtaining highly saturated "postcard" colors.

Jordan Cronenweth, ASC

There are really three places to control color: In front of the camera, in the camera, and in the lab. Some colors need more desaturation than others, but that is a selective thing and that has to be done by wardrobe, set dressing, paints used, colors that you allow the sky to

be. I think that blue, almost unlike any other color on film, calls attention to itself immediately when you see it on the screen, and oftentimes to the point of distraction. I find red to be second to blue in calling attention to itself.

Whereas Cronenweth finds particular colors distracting, Robert Wise finds excessive saturation annoying.

Robert Wise

To me more often than not color is too rich, too full of color, too unreal. The very nature of photography is not quite realistic. I have found that if you wanted to get something really low, really down, really degraded, you had to dress it and paint it and treat it and knock it down. To the eye it seemed to be too much, but it was right to the camera. I very much favor, if possible, to desaturate it, to knock down some of the extremes. But it depends on the film that you are doing, of course.

Finally we should mention the times when the use of *any* diffusion is not recommended.

Michael D. Margulies, ASC

When shooting footage with subsequent optical printing in mind, besides having a full negative you might want to have a crisp, clean negative without a diffusion on the lens, for optical effects.

WORKING WITH SMOKE

Working with fog filters is relatively easy when compared with real smoke or fog situations. Smoke works in depth. It affects light sources as well as the surfaces on which light falls.

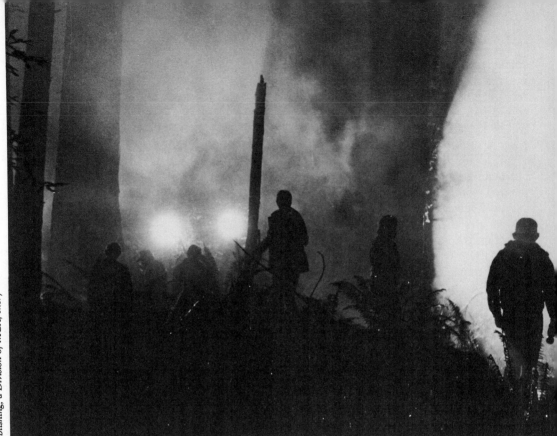

Backlighting makes the smoke visible in this scene from *E.T. the ExtraTerrestrial.*

Allen Daviau, ASC

The secret in learning to work with smoke is that you must get to do some tests. Reading with a spot meter you try to find some average reading. You are lighting air. Your exposure index is based upon the reflectivity of the smoke in the air. This is what makes it very difficult even with a spot meter to read. And to be truthful, the most valuable is your eye, judging the density of the smoke by eye. And evaluating when the smoke is ready. You say, Smoke it up! and the smoke starts swirling around and building up density. You are waiting for it to stop moving and finally you are ready to go. You roll the camera and it may be still moving, but finally you say, okay,

and the director says, Action! just when the smoke stops moving. In my tests for E.T. I bracketed the exposure in half stops. I was higher up in my printing scale than I thought I was going to be. We printed at #40, 44, 30. This way if the smoke turned out to be less dense and therefore less reflective, there would be still enough exposure to print in the middle of the scale.

LIGHTFLEX®

Lightflex represents a sophisticated system of image enhancement in the camera. It is attached to the camera in front of the lens in place of the matte box. The Lightflex reflects soft light into the lens and onto the film as the scene is photographed. This light increases the level of shadow detail, thus reducing the contrast. This considerably expands the contrast range of the film, which is determined by the intensity of the reflected light.

Either white or colored light can be used in the Lightflex System. Colored light is modulated by the filter pack in the path of the Lightflex Quartz light source. The basic filter trays contain gel formulas to color correct for exterior sunlight, interior daylight, studio tungsten light, and exterior night. There are also filter packs for candlelight and sepia effects. More specialized filters are custom-made to create such effects as a rainbow in the sky, a sunset, a moon, or lightning. A motorized transport mechanism allows for the movement of the filter gels to create color changes during the shot. Since the colors overlaid by Lightflex will only affect the shadows, the key-lit areas will remain in their original colors.

The amount of color overlay can be regulated and evaluated in the viewfinder before shooting. Sets and costumes can be coloristically modulated.

By adding light to the shadowy parts of the frame, Lightflex reduces the need for fill light, making the production faster and more economical, and the working conditions for the actors more comfortable. The absence of fill light also means fewer shadows in the picture.

The picture enhancing potential of a cinematographer is greatly expanded by this system.

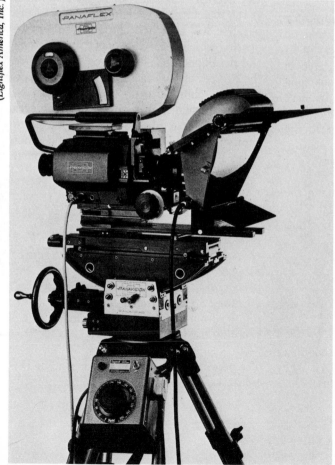

The Lightflex® System is a unique method for extending the practical latitude of the film emulsion.

IMAGE MANIPULATION IN THE LABORATORY

The film laboratory represents the next place where the image can be manipulated. For example, an exposed film can be reexposed to a controlled light in the process known as flashing. Or, it can be manipulated during development by varying the length of developing time. An extended development—pushing or forcing—will result in a denser negative. Finally, the print made from the negative or reversal, whether it is a projection print or an intermediate, is timed to have densities and color balances that match the aesthetic concept of the cinematographer.

POSTFLASHING

Postflashing can be described as reexposing the film to a weak light, which will make no practical difference to the already heavily exposed highlights, but will be noticeable in shadows as an overall exposure, changing deep blacks into shades of gray and therefore reducing the overall contrast of the image. This procedure can be done either to the camera original, whether a negative or a reversal, or it can be done to an interpositive or print. Flashing an interpositive or print affects the highlights. Instead of making the shadows less dark, it makes the highlights less bright. It will still lower the overall contrast, but it will have a different look.

Richard Kline, ASC

When I did Camelot, I think that I was one of the first people to do flashing. The labs were not doing it, so I did it myself on the set. I would preexpose the film before shooting, on a white card. You would "wide open" the lens and expose it way out of focus. This would increase the speed of the film and create muted, rich colors.

Flashing can be done beforehand (preflashing) but this is more a thing of the past. Today cinematographers prefer postflashing in the highly controlled lab environment.

Vilmos Zsigmond, ASC

Flashing is a terrific technique to use on period pictures. It creates the right look and it also gives you a lot of exposure in the shadows, so you do not have to worry about not having enough fill light.

The degrees of flashing can be predetermined as the increment by which the density of the negative will be raised above the minimum density, which is the density of the unexposed and developed film stock. In general practice the degrees of flashing are designated in percentages. Unfortunately, there seems to be some confusion as to what these percentages represent. These values differ from one lab to another, so 30 percent in one lab does not mean 30 percent in the next one. Therefore it is essential to conduct tests at a given lab.

Jordan Cronenweth, ASC

You send them a piece of the negative long enough to do the percentages on, from zero to fifty percent, or whatever you want to see, and you control the material. You control what you want to see affected by it, by what you put in front of the camera when you are shooting the test.

The percentage of flashing will depend on the contrast of the scene and on the f/stop used.

Philip Lathrop, ASC

I would use flashing for high contrast exteriors, for example, a street with one side in shadow. Among other considerations, the contrast of the scene, and so on, your flashing will differ according to how much you will stop down your lens. The more you stop down, the more you have to flash. You may be flashing ten to fifteen percent on the interiors at f/4, and on the exteriors at f/11 you will have to flash twenty-five percent to match these two scenes. You could control it by using the same f/stop and cutting down light with ND filters, but outside I like to see more depth of field, to have everything sharp.

PROCESSING

The next stage at which an exposed image is affected by the lab is development. It requires stringent quality control to assure consistency from day to day. On the request of a cameraman his film can be "forced developed" (pushed) to make up for an underexposure. It means that the film will require an extended development time to produce more density in the image. Today, with fast emulsions, pushing is used less frequently for gaining additional film speed. One-stop pushing, on Eastman negatives, should have hardly any effect on the look of the film, but extensive pushing will raise the grain and deteriorate the black.

Allen Daviau, ASC

I don't believe that pushing inherently gives a higher contrast. In fact, in many circumstances I feel that pushing film deteriorates the black. I try to avoid pushing film except in a true emergency. Particularly since we have high speed stock. Pushing is an option, but in general I am rather a purist, I don't like to push the film, I do like a healthy negative.

TIMING AND PRINTING

The widest range of image manipulation is offered at the printing stage. The printing machine exposes the film stock to a light that can be precisely controlled both in its intensity and its color quality.

The light hitting the film is composed of three primary or three complementary colors, depending on the printer. Therefore one lab may call its lights RGB (red, green, blue), whereas another will work with CMY (cyan, magenta, yellow). Regulating the amount of individual colors used in printing is called timing (or grading in England), hence the timer (or grader).

The printer machine has fifty or more light intensities, called lights, to choose from. Eight lights equals approximately one lens stop. The ideal printing lights for a correctly exposed scene differ from lab to lab and from cinematographer to cinematographer.

With Eastman negatives the printing light for the yellow or blue designation is always lower than the other printing lights, giving for example a set of lights for a given scene as 30–30–23 instead of 30–30–30. Usually the range of printing lights from 25 to 40 represents a well-exposed negative.

An underexposed, thinner negative will require lower number lights, although it is called "printing up". On the other hand, a well-exposed, dense negative requires higher lights and is called "printing down". Printing up means printing lighter; printing down means printing darker. We can state here the relationship between exposing the negative and timing the print as follows: Expose the negative well and print it down for rich color and rich black.

John Alonzo, ASC

If you want rich blacks, you expose to your key light and you fill your actor as full as you want, and then print him down. As you are printing him down, the background will get rich and velvet black. But if you do not want rich black, then you add light to it so that you have a soft gray or a soft black, but not a jet black.

You underexpose the negative and print up for less contrast and more grain. Too much underexposure causes the blacks to get milky and lowers the contrast. Too much overexposure also lowers the contrast. It is important to remember that when we are talking about under- and overexposure we understand it in terms of the whole frame. It is quite normal that parts of a scene are under- or overexposed, yet the scene prints in the middle of the scale. These extremes are often purposefully designed by the cinematographer for the creation of a certain mood.

Vilmos Zsigmond, ASC

In many paintings people's faces are not always painted in full light. You remember it and you say, well, I will underexpose, but it is not really underexposing, it is underlighting selectively. Many cameramen develop a technique of underexposing everything, they do that for the look of the picture. But the problem is that darkening everything to the same degree from the beginning of the picture to the end would become boring. It is also very dangerous. The slightest mistake that you make, for example, if the f/stop is not working correctly on the lens: you are already on the very edge, on the threshold when underexposing; and now a half stop more underexposure caused by a lens malfunction can be disastrous. I do not like to work that way. I like to stay safe in the middle. My dailies always print in the middle of the scale. Around #30. Whatever I wish to appear dark, I will light dark. But still, it is perfectly exposed. Everything will be printed at the same light level.

To obtain the desired look of the print, a cinematographer must establish good communication with the timer (the technician in charge of timing) as early as possible, preferably during the testing in the preproduction period. For financial reasons, elaborate timing is usually done only on the edited film, when *answer prints* are being made.

During the shooting, the lab provides "one-light dailies." In reality these dailies are usually printed at about four lights, which ideally the cinematographer had a chance to test with the lab. These separate lights are usually for Day Exterior, Day Interior, Night Exterior, and Night Interior. Apart from financial savings, one-light dailies allow the cinematographer to judge his exposures against constant values.

Many cinematographers feel very strongly about the importance of communication with the timer and some have expressed it well in these interviews.

John Alonzo, ASC

I discuss timing in advance with Technicolor for instance; this is the lab that I am dealing with now. The first tests may be printed in two different ways, because in this picture I want a light warm look to it. So the lab representative showed me two sets of prints, two sets of printing lights. And I said, okay, we will stick with those lights, let's try these lights for everything. Then, I went back and did some more testing with actors, exposing in different ranges and they printed them on these preselected lights. Now what that means to me is that when I saw them and there were some errors in them, I could understand where they came from, if it was my exposure, or whatever it might have been. We try to preselect the lights for the look of the picture. For interior, exterior, day and night. Then we might get into a situation when we shoot late in the day when the sun is very, very yellow and I will warn the laboratory to back off on the yellow, we have too much yellow in this. Or if it is early in the morning and the light is too blue and it is supposed to look like sunset or late afternoon, I would say, add yellow to it.

Usually cinematographers will leave the exact amount of correction to the judgment of a timer. Some, like Richard Kline, give precise instruction as to the degree of color change.

Richard Kline, ASC

I work very closely with the lab. I shoot the test and I establish a light [number] that I like. Actually three different lights for red, green and blue. Also one light for incandescent and one light for daylight. Then, as we film, I might want to use the scale. As the day changes I may want to take the yellow out. We start early in the morning so it is a bluer light. Throughout the day I shift color values by changing the numbers in the report. It is never just Day Exterior or Night Exterior. It is Day Exterior and exact light that it prints for every take, for every color. Some labs use Y, C, M [Yellow, Cyan, Magenta], others use R, G, B [Red, Green, Blue].

With incandescent lighting I may want to give it a different color value. I don't want it to be just normal. So I may put some gels on the lamps and in addition change even more through timing. Because the more gels you put on lights, the more you will cut their light output. And then it is also time consuming to

put the gels on, and I can do it quicker by just changing the color. I also alter the densities, because I might want to borrow a stop. Maybe I am lacking a stop [in exposure]. Or another reason might be that I want more contrast or less contrast. Slight underexposure will lower the contrast. Another situation would be when I am using a soft light, but I do not want it to be quite as soft as I lit it. So I would add contrast in the printing. I would overexpose and print it high on the scale. As much as a stop or two stops. The higher you print it on the scale, the more contrasty it will be. When I go to the lab I insist on several things: That one man services me, that he sees the dailies personally, and that the dailies are printed on the same printer—the same machine. But you have to live with a certain degree of tolerance.

Over the years cinematographers may change their methods of working with a lab. It will depend on the approach to picture manipulation with which the cinematographer feels comfortable at any given time.

Vilmos Zsigmond, ASC

I try to create the mood with lighting, filters, and so on, but if I cannot do it, I will sometimes ask the lab to print some scenes colder or warmer, say for the sunset tones. I will ask them to do this for the dailies.

I used to establish separate printing lights for the day and for the night scenes. Now I want them to be printed using the exact same light. I use less lighting at night and still print on the same light (#30), so night looks darker than day. Having one printing light, the lab makes fewer mistakes.

I change my ASA rating on the light meter when working on a night scene. You have to learn to underlight night and to light the day normally. For example, if a daylight scene needs 50 FC with f/4, then for night I will need only 25 FC for f/4.

I like my night interiors warmer and sometimes if I don't want to use gels, I may establish with the lab that my nights will be printed warmer. On Heaven's Gate we had a scene in a canvas tent, so we had the tent painted to have it warmer.

To work with the lab effectively we have to eliminate as many variables as possible by introducing standards and reference points. One such reference point is the gray scale, and many cinematographers provide their timer with a gray scale for each lighting situation.

Allen Daviau, ASC

I always shoot a gray scale in each situation. If I am all day in an interior, though, I may shoot the gray scale just once. It acts as a control for me to see how the lab is maintaining its consistency in printing color. Even though my printing light is locked some dailies' supervisors appreciate seeing the gray scale. It lets them know that everything is working correctly at the lab, that nobody made a mistake on the printing light setting. I find that the gray scale is just one more guarantee of consistency. If I shoot the gray scale in a normal color temperature light source in each lighting situation, even though every light in this scene may have gelatin on it, the fact that I have shot that gray scale in white light gives a point of reference for the timer. I give him a simple instruction: Time color to gray scale. By this I mean that he shouldn't base the density reading on the gray scale totally, although I will try to keep this density as close to my key light situation as possible, but to evaluate the use of the three colors in the printing light in such a way as to give me a true gray scale. And then I will not talk to him about the color at all. I will say, Evaluate the color by this gray scale and then don't be alarmed if there is a warm source or a cool source or anything else in the room.

Where the gray scale helps to maintain the color standards, the densities of the dailies are established by predetermining the printing lights.

Allen Daviau, ASC

In the feature film situation you want to lock your printing lights as early as possible. And this is usually determined by a combination of tests that you do before the production starts and how you evaluate the first few days of dailies from the lab. The advantage of locking in the printing lights on a feature film is that you then have a standard. You have eliminated one more variable.

Once you establish a lighting style, you also want to make that lighting style relate to the print. Therefore you want to lock your daily printing lights in, for the given situations in the film as early as you possibly can.

Normally you would have a day exterior light, maybe a night exterior light, and an interior light that usually functions for both day and night. Once this is established, you have eliminated the variable of the film being looked at by a timer at night. It comes straight off the negative processor and goes to a negative assembly. They look in the book and find the printing light. When the slate and the camera report states, This is day exterior, for example, then it will be assembled on the roll with all the other exterior scenes and then printed at your Day Exterior printing light. The same thing with interiors and so on. If, in the course of the picture, you run into a very special circumstance such as fluorescent, mercury vapor, whatever, then you will give a special reference to the lab, and you will say, I want this evaluated by the timer. Or sometimes you can literally call a change in the printing light right on the camera report, simply by saying, I had to underexpose the negative half a stop, please print this scene up four points.

Basically when you are working from locked lights, it allows you to shade your scenes in the negative. I like to work with a heavier negative, a negative that prints somewhere in the midthirties, which I find to be a very good place to print. Theoretically the normal printing light is 27 across. But I find that I am more in the middle thirties. First of all I like the look of the heavier negative. I feel that the blacks are more solid, that I get a snappier looking piece of film, and at the same time it gives me the latitude to print up. And if I have to print a scene lighter when I am going for an answer print, I have more "meat" in the negative to be able to print up without my blacks milking out.

Once I establish that printing light that gives me the snap that I am looking for, then I have a freedom in lighting to shade my negative. If something is going to go dark in the scene, I can let it fall dark. And the next morning, my dailies, printed on a fixed light, will reflect what I have done in reducing the amount of light in a certain area of the screen. When I know that the basic exposure of my key light is resulting in a negative that prints at this light, and that the highlights are properly rendered, then I can do anything I want with the shadows just by manipulating the light or the lack of light in the scene to give me the shading that I want in the negative. It makes timing the film much simpler, and also it is less likely that anybody is going to come and change the look of the picture later because I put that look into the negative.

When you work to a standard that you've established, and when you preconceive this shading in the negative while shooting the film, your whole operation of printing the answer print and the release print is much more straightforward. You do this to get the technology out of your head, and then you can really concentrate on the creative aspects of lighting and the dramatic aspects of telling the story with light.

With all the standards and points of reference established, timing still remains a human function and should not become just a mechanical operation. Constant communication with the timer allows the cinematographer to obtain in the dailies the fine nuances that may otherwise be lost due to the imperfections of the timing process.

Allen Daviau, ASC

Your dailies are being timed on a Hazeltine analyzer, which is basically a color television film chain. The timer places the negative into this machine and the electronic aspect of it changes—reverses—the polarity. The negative image is changed into a positive image on a color TV screen. It is not as simple as it sounds in that usually this image is not perfect. The timer must evaluate within the limitations of the picture which the Hazeltine is giving him in trying to translate the look of this image on this crude television screen, to what will be the next morning on positive film, on the screen. So the less you ask the timer to do at the dailies stage, the better off you are.

Let's take for example a studio situation where I am having the sun come through the window. Maybe I put a gelatin on what is supposed to be my sun to create a late afternoon sunset effect. I don't want the timer saying, "Gee, why is this light orange?" and turning the knobs to give me normal color. So with the combination of the simple communications [that] this is late afternoon interior warm effect and [the use of] the gray scale as a standard, he will know what he is trying to put into the print and [how] to interpret that negative for you. And I find that the more you work with the laboratory and with one night-dailies timer, the less you have to say and the more familiar a timer becomes with your style. Oftentimes you will talk to him the next day and he will say, "Well, how was it last night?" You'll say, "Well, it's fine. Maybe a touch too red or a touch too light." That is the information he will file into his mind, regarding your taste. Anybody who deals with color on the Hazeltine puts together a mental filing system of the preferences of the cinematographer that he or she works with on a daily basis. And that information will come up the next time they evaluate a film of yours for printing.

There is one variable that tends to come up more in commercials than in feature film productions. This is the emulsion, which may vary slightly from one batch to another. This requires more tests and more communication with the lab.

Allen Daviau, ASC

On a feature film you try to shoot with the emulsion batch you tested and you stay with this batch number throughout the picture. If you have to change the emulsion number, you must run another test to see how it varies, if at all, from the one you had been using. But in commercials, many times you are forced into a situation when you are using different emulsions. Different companies have deals with different laboratories. Working in commercials you are facing such varied circumstances every day that you have no chance to work at one fixed printing light. So you have a system of communicating with the lab on a day-to-day basis to let them know what you expect to see from what you photograph. I

found that the simpler you keep this communication the better off you are. In many cases, as you work for some years with a certain lab and with a certain dailies supervisor or night dailies timer, these communications can oftentimes be one or two words. If you are using gels in the scene, make sure to state that you are going for a warm or a cool effect in some areas of the scene, and again I stress the use of the gray scale as being one of the best pieces of communication and evaluation of standards for the timer.

Generally, when timing commercials the communication with the timer needs to be more exact than in features, because in commercials people who view the dailies are less experienced in evaluating the potentials of the print.

Allen Daviau, ASC

In the feature situation, once you have the trust of the director, the producer and so on, you could say, "Oh well, this print is a little light and maybe it is a little bluer than I would like, but let's not worry about it, we will fix that in the answer print." And no one will worry about it because they trust your taste, they know your reputation for what you will do later, that you will follow through in the lab. So you won't even bother to make a reprint at this stage. I don't believe in reprinting the negative unless it is absolutely necessary because the fewer times the camera negative is handled the better condition it is going to be in when you go to make the prints from it at the end. But in the case of commercials you have people who may not be as sophisticated in their understanding of film technology. There may be the advertising agency people, the client company people, totally unfamiliar with filmmaking, or relatively so, and all they know is what they see on the screen. And they are convinced that this is exactly what their commercial is going to look like. So suddenly your dailies hit the screen six points lighter and greener and these people are going to have coronaries on the spot. The whole show is for the dailies. They are spending a tremendous amount of money, their agency had convinced their client that they have the finest people on earth to do this commercial, and when they come in they want to get the impression of what it is going to look like on the air. Even though we all would know that this is simply a bad print and that it can be corrected, these people may not. And even if you tell them, they may not believe it. So there is the necessity of being able to predict where the print will fall. This all has to do with your philosophy of exposing the film properly in accordance with the type of lighting effect that you are trying to get and also in terms of speaking to the lab.

Cinematographers who take great care to obtain the best results in their dailies must be equally involved with the conditions in which these dailies will be viewed by all the people concerned.

Allen Daviau, ASC

Something that will hold true both with commercials and with features are the circumstances in which people view the dailies. The conditions of the screening room. In some cases, I find screening rooms to be appallingly substandard, even in major studios. The light on the screen is supposed to give us the reflectance of 16-foot lamberts on a blank screen with the projector running. In many cases I found both in studio situations and in regular rental screening rooms, and certainly in the theaters, that the light is either appallingly low or in one case, in New York, so bright that they must have had 25-foot lam-

berts in this screening room. It just washed out everything.

You quickly learn that if the projection is not good you really have to become a tyrant, you must insist that the projection standards on which your dailies are viewed are proper. Sometimes on location you are using one of these little Italian portable projectors. You have to make sure that one person is responsible for the projection to be on standard brightness and in focus, or you will get blamed for the mistakes in the projection. People will look at the image and in many cases they don't understand that the image is perfectly in focus and bright enough but the projector is at fault. You will take the rap for shoddy projection. Therefore you have to go and personally check it and approve it before you allow other people to see the film projected in this situation.

Finally, when the dailies are edited into a fine-cut work print, a cinematographer who cares about his work will insist on participating in the timing of the answer print.

Allen Daviau, ASC

When you sit down with the timer to do the answer print and you screen the work print, you are looking at your dailies cut together into a film. Now you go through a process of what I call picking the keys. It means pointing out to the timer the key scenes. You may be saying, "Now, this we really love just the way it is, don't change a thing. Make it look just like this master. Now, that close-up is perfect. Maybe this close-up should be a point darker. Make this close-up match that one." So he will say into his tape recorder, "Key off the first close-up of man, darken woman shot to look the same." You find that he is making his notes for the time when he sits down at the Hazeltine. He will also have a record of where your printing lights were from your dailies.

Sometimes you will change your mind entirely about how you want the scene to look, when you see it in context. Often there is originally a scene which you considered as transition. For example, if a time transition to carry you from midday to late afternoon is cut out in the course of editing the film, you will have to reevaluate how you print the two scenes that no longer have the transition between them. Now you have to reinterpret that negative, give it a little different look, different meaning perhaps. I also find that when I am screening with the timer, I love to screen the picture with the soundtrack, even if it is just at an early crude stage, so that the timer understands the story and gets into the feeling.

And as early as possible, ideally before you locked the timing, it would be good if you both could hear the music while looking at the image. Many times your response to the music will require a warmer or darker print than you would have thought when evaluating an image alone. The more elements the timer is exposed to—dialogue, music, and so on—the better he can do his job. This is true for all the positions in filmmaking. I think that the crew should be allowed to come to dailies and feel a sense of participation in the film.

I feel the same about the timer. He should have that same ability to respond to telling the story. We are all working in our different areas of telling a story. And the less everyone feels as merely a technician, the better it is for the film. So that first screening of the work print with the timer is probably the most important part of timing the picture. Later when the lab is ready for you with a first answer print, you sit there and you start fine tuning and really getting down to little tiny things. And people might think that we are crazy in how much importance we would put on one point of lightness or darkness, or one point of warm or cold, but many times it makes a vast difference in how the scene will play. Whether the scene is supposed to be funny or tragic or whatever.

At this point of working on the film your response is so highly sensitive that you are one big nerve watching the film on the screen, and those little things are extremely important to you. When you approve the answer print you have to say, This is the standard. This is the way I intend the film to look. And then it is the laboratory's job to deliver to the motion picture theaters as many prints as close to that answer print as possible.

People will say: But who is ever going to see it like that? Who cares? Nobody is going to notice it. Well, we hope that people won't sit there and notice things like the printing points but rather what they feel should be similar to the impact of the music, the quality of the interpretation of a line of dialogue, why somebody's eyes look a certain way in a certain kind of light. All of these little tiny things that might seem insignificant are what adds up to make a film an emotionally powerful experience. And if you do not follow through at that stage in the laboratory, you are abdicating a huge portion of your responsibility. Maybe the lab will do a beautiful job on their own. But I think that you are not being serious about your work if you don't take part in it.

VIDEO TRANSFER

Today, the cinematographer's image control does not end in the lab. Considering that most theatrical films are at some stage seen on television, many cinematographers are wisely participating in the film-to-tape transfer of their work.

Allen Daviau, ASC

As motion pictures developed ancillary markets other than network television, or local television, we saw two things arise. One was the pay television systems that were created during the 70s; HBO, Cinemax, The Movie Channel, or the Z channel in Los Angeles. As they became popular, it became apparent that the engineering standards of these organizations were much higher than those of the networks.

The second thing that arose was the video rental market. People can now go out and either buy or rent a movie and can do this even before it is aired on network television.

The transfer of feature films onto video for home screening, whether over a pay channel or through a home video system needs a higher quality of transfer than the standard method used by the networks. The pay channels and rental companies were promising the movie theater experience in one's own home.

Allen Daviau, ASC

Even the nonprofessional would ask professionals in television and motion pictures: "Why is it that the commercials look so much better than most television programs?"

The production values of television commercials, are of top motion picture standards, and are often technically superior in the way the image is moved from film to tape. This type of transfer is far more sophisticated than that used for network programming, which was simply handed to the networks on the standard projection contrast print and projected onto a TV camera and corrected "on the fly."

Originally the companies making top quality commercials used low contrast print stock that was manufactured in Europe. This low contrast stock made a somewhat better transfer to video, but it was the introduction of the Rank Cintel Flying Spot Scanner that made the greatest difference in quality of the video image.

It increased the quality from a 16mm or 35mm image by doing a transfer from the original negative rather than from the print. This procedure reverses the polarity of the negative image and gives a full tonal range positive image in the video transfer. It also allows for scene to scene color correction, much in the same manner that one would do in a film lab making an answer print. It is a process analogous to the Hazeltine, but it offers a greater range of corrections than the Hazeltine was ever designed to do.

The Hazeltine analyzer is simply an intermediate device between the negative and the print stock, whereas the Rank Cintel process results in a final product in itself. In other words, from a film image into an electronic image.

By being able to go scene to scene, making individual color corrections if you want, the capability of the newer Rank Cintel is such that you can practically correct every frame individually. If, inside a shot, you want to do correction, if a shot has a wide range of exposures, such as when panning from a very light area to a dark area that might be acceptable for a motion picture screen, but is too great a range for a video image, you can now make a correction inside the shot on a Rank Cintel, literally dissolving the image to itself, from the lighter value to the darker one, and it is imperceptible even to the most sophisticated viewer if it is done correctly.

When you are working from a really good originating medium, such as an original negative, or dupe negative, or interpositive, you can do an amazing range of things to alter color density and to some extent, contrast. You certainly can flatten the picture out, in a manner analogous to flashing, with your black level control. With your white level control, your highlights, you can control contrast to a great degree, but not as much as the blacks. Your overall tone and mood of the picture is really in the control of the transferring engineer.

We want to see the people involved most intimately with the picture making the transfer decisions with the engineer. The good engineering personnel want someone directly involved in the film there when they do the transfer. All too often there is, in too many companies, an attitude that they don't even want the cinematographer or director to know when the transfer is being done, because, "Well, you just come in and slow things down." Because the cinematographer will take the time to make something right, yes, it is going to cost a little more to get it right, but this is going out and in its own way is becoming a bigger part of posterity than the release print. Release prints are usually junked after their initial run, and these tapes and video discs will be out there for many years. People will be watching these things and judging the film by them. So, again, I feel that it is extremely important for the cinematographer to become involved in this aspect of postproduction.

The Flying Spot Scanner is very unlike the old telecine film chain, which was basically a television camera with three tubes, an optical system and a film projector. These tubes, like all camera tubes, have decay factors that are uneven and lag factors which cause comet tails or streaking colors when the film image pans a bright object across a dark frame. If you cut from a very bright scene to a very dark scene, you observe this decay still happening on the television screen. Unlike the film chain

system the Flying Spot Scanner works in reverse. The scanning of the film is done through the film itself, in other words, it literally projects a raster with the appropriate number of scanning lines (525 in the U.S., 625 in Europe). It scans the film frame line by line. On the opposite side of the film are a series of color photocel receptors (red, green, blue) that react to the changes in color and density that results from the white light raster projected through the film. You have no color registration problems. Once your tube is installed in the correct position, there is no focus problem, nothing connected to an optical system to distort the film. The other advantage that you have, which is very important in transferring films today, is the fact that you can reposition, you can choose a portion of the frame rather than the entire frame to transfer. This is particularly important with cinemascope format or 1:1.66. You can pan and scan the anamorphic frame, or you can even take a normal film frame and blow it up slightly. You can do little moves inside the frame, or zooms. These are things that you do not want to see overused, but sometimes it can make an impact in a different way on the television screen. These are the things that you want to keep in the control of the people that made the film, and not as the decision of an engineer who could arbitrarily make a choice about panning and scanning and blowing up.

I find the experience of sitting down with a video transfer engineer and running a film in a theater quite comparable to sitting in the lab theater with the timer and running the work print with him, and pointing out what in the work print is good and what is not, what we hope to achieve in the answer print. I find it a similar stage, taking the final answer print of the film and showing it to a video transfer engineer, talking about what we want to preserve in the video transfer and perhaps even some things that we can improve along the way. There are some subtleties that we can accomplish in a video transfer that cannot be done on film, simply because we can control the color, and intensity of highlights separately from the shadows. We can, in fact, make a high-end change that does not hurt the shadow areas, and vice versa. The original photography of the scene is, of course, still the determining factor in what happens. You cannot put something in an image that is not there to start with. You can only take certain things and enhance them. In this regard it is extremely exciting to be able to work with scenes on a scene-to-scene basis. You can often give a smoother dramatic flow to the images simply by the work that you do on the video transfer.

Video transfers can be made with any generation of the film. Each has inherent advantages and disadvantages.

Allen Daviau, ASC

Your procedure working with the low contrast print stock is to go ahead and make your answer print, as you would normally do, on regular contrast stock until you have the look that you want. Then you make the corresponding print with the same corrections on the low contrast stock. You do not project that print, but put it on the Rank Cintel and work with it there. It is certainly less contrasty than the old print stock, but not quite as flat as the interpositive. I am not yet convinced that anything equals the quality of working with the negative, or the interpositive. These two allow for much more control in the transfer, particularly in dark scenes with an interpositive. Ideally, you want to use both because different scenes transfer better with different materials.

Since you have access to the interpositive,

the negative and the original magnetic sound when they are fresh and clean, you should do that transfer as an immediate part of the postproduction process. The film should not be considered finished until those responsible for the film have supervised that. You owe it to your own work and to the film that you have made to see it through the final stage, the stage in which many people will see the film for the first time.

When you have the opportunity to work with the interpositive or the negative, you are able to have as extreme contrast ratios as in your original photography and preserve the ratios when the image comes home. The only difficulty one still has with television is to have a scene with a dark object, or a person in front of a large very bright area, like an extremely burned-out window or sky. Reference white and reference black are still important to have if you are shooting for television.

Another problem is that the majority of the audience still watches on cheaply made receivers that, unfortunately, if there is not a reference white and reference black somewhere in the picture, will tend to produce a mass of gray regardless of the dramatic intent of the scene. You have to be extremely careful of this in night scenes. It is one area where, in cinema, we can photograph a very low key night scene with no light references in it whatsoever and make the audience strain to perceive something in the dark, and be able to achieve a mood and a feeling that way. Unfortunately, when that piece of film is put on video, no matter how carefully it is transferred, the poor television receiver will tend to make a gray murk out of it. But the next few years will bring about such drastic improvements in television receivers, that eventually we will not have to worry about this.

I think it is a very important thing in any area, whether you originate on film or originate on video, to ask yourself, What is the ultimate use? Where is this image going to wind up? Where do I need this image to look the best? Is it on home television, is it on a closed-circuit affair, is it on the big screen of the Cinerama Dome? We have to know where the most important use is going to be, and design according to the engineering requirements of that.

It used to be that the networks strongly suggested that photography for programs for television be done with a very flat lighting ratio because contrast buildup was a problem in the way they transferred films for television.

Now, when you have the opportunity to work with the interpositive or the negative, you are able to have extreme contrast ratios in your original photography, and preserve it exactly this way when the image comes home. It really just gives us an additional tool to encourage the use of gutsy contrast ratios.

Steven Spielberg has a theory that I think is quite correct. He says that the most extreme photography in terms of contrast ratio will carry through in the final process, be it in the motion picture theater or on the home receiver, even if those conditions are bad. So when we look for dramatic images, the ones that tend to get hurt the most and that hurt the cinematographer very much, are those that are built on subtlety and smoothness of tone. Those wonderful creamy delicacies have a chance to be hurt the most by a bad print, a dim projector, a terribly tuned receiver. The images that tend to have inherent contrast power survive better.

We have followed image manipulation all the way from the camera to the video transfer. At every stage the cinematographer has to make significant technical and aesthetic choices which directly affect his visual concept. There is an impressive technology to be employed and rules which can be broken creatively and intelligently. What should become clear is the fact that film lighting is not isolated from the rest of the photographic process, but that it is constantly related to image manipulations at the various stages of film photography. We should keep it in mind when examining the lighting techniques in the following chapters.

CHAPTER **Four**

Strategy of Lighting

THE VISUAL style the director seeks for a film will influence the decisions the cinematographer makes about lighting the scenes. There are several general choices he must make about his lighting technique. Will it be hard or soft? Will it be high- or low-key? Will it be lit to a great extent with practicals or from sources outside the frame? Each of these basic decisions will greatly affect the look of the film.

HARD VERSUS SOFT

Before we go deeper into the subject of composing with lights we have to look at the character of light itself. Light can be hard, soft or gradations in between. Hard light casts strong shadows and the softest light is shadowless. Hard light is generated from a small source whereas soft light comes from a large one.

The hardest source of light known in nature is the noonday sun; an overcast sky is the softest source known. It is as if a diffusion material has been stretched from horizon to horizon. The illumination comes from all directions and cancels out the shadows.

Over the years lighting designers, cinematographers, and gaffers have designed a vast array of lighting instruments to produce both hard and soft lights.

The hardest light in general use is the arc. Its light, created between two carbon electrodes, is smaller and brighter than the filament of an incandescent bulb. A Fresnel lens is used with an arc to bring the light into a narrow beam. Incandescent lights with Fresnel lenses also fall in the range of hard lights. Open-ended lights can be hard or soft depending on the size of the reflector and on the type and positioning of the bulb. The softest are boxlike soft lights and a variety of lighting instruments made in the studio that consist of rows of bulbs behind a diffusion screen. Even softer sources can be created by placing very large diffusion screens in front of conventional lights or by bouncing light off large reflective screens onto the subject.

Soft light produces much lower light levels for the same wattage used than hard light and it falls off with distance much faster. In the days of slow emulsions, its use was limited mainly to a general fill function. With the advent of fast color film stocks, however, soft light sources became adequate as the main modelling light. Many leading cameramen developed a style of lighting that utilizes soft light as the chief light source in a majority of scenes. Other equally distinguished cinematographers continue to favor the predominantly directional focusable key lights; these should be chosen carefully for a particular area and function. There is, of course, a middle ground, which might be to use predominantly soft light but accentuate modelling with some harder sources.

Soft light technique is basically area lighting, which creates a more natural look. Since less equipment is involved it actually helps to keep the production moving at a better pace, especially when less professional actors and directors are involved. It also allows the actors more freedom of movement on the set. These attributes become rather important with today's budget considerations. There is a drawback to using soft light, however. It is difficult to control because, originating as it does from a large source, it spreads in all directions. Therefore huge black screens (flags, teasers) are needed to cut off the light from certain parts of the set.

Soft light falls off rather sharply also; therefore it must be positioned relatively close to the subject. That becomes problematical in a wide angle shot when a large area of the set is in the frame.

Jordan Cronenweth, ASC

Soft lighting is much more difficult to control than hard lighting. It is not what you light that counts but what you don't light. Anybody can go back there and turn on a beautiful soft light; take a light and bounce it off a white card and get 10 footcandles or 15 footcandles and say, Ready. But to control it you have to do many things. You can take it off the actor and just hit the back wall and silhouette him, or you can take it off the back wall. You can make a shadow. You can put a bottomer on it, or a topper, or a sider.

Soft lighting gained its popularity because it gives the scene a more natural, less "filmic" look than hard lighting. At the same time it has a danger of lacking character. In the final analysis, it is just another "brush" to paint with, but not the only one.

Caleb Deschanel, ASC

I think that soft lighting is very limiting. There are certain scenes or certain locations that call for that, or certain kinds of moods or atmosphere. I think that soft lighting mainly came as a result of the fact that film reacts a little bit differently than our eye does to light. Soft light was a means of achieving on film what we have a tendency to see with our own eyes. You very rarely see lighting in real life with real strong back light.

A cinematographer would be unwise to judge a style of lighting on its own merit. Sometimes the qualities of soft light that seem less interesting are just the qualities needed to serve the story.

Caleb Deschanel, ASC

The argument between hard and soft light is kind of weak because in a sense you really make your judgment based upon whatever the story is. There is a tendency to think that the philosophy is soft or hard lighting, but in reality the philosophy is what film I am doing. Basically you should have at your disposal any range of lighting styles.

One has to have practical experience in both styles of lighting to be able to mix and match them effectively.

Haskell Wexler, ASC

Everybody should still work in hard light as well. Not to do it and to say that it has to be all soft light is like throwing away part of the artist's palette. I think that the more variety you can have, the better it will look. To be able to light well in hard light makes the soft lighting a piece of cake, because a soft light is very forgiving. Soft light, uncontrolled, is still acceptable photographically. It is really hard for soft light to look bad, but it is not hard for hard light to look bad.

Wexler has hit on an important point here. He continues:

One reason why soft lighting is so popular is due to the fact that there is more improvisation today which is tolerated by the soft light. It is possible to utilize in soft lighting what we have learned from hard lighting and a lot of good cameramen actually do that.

In immediate and practical terms, the character of light will be initially designated by the time of day. Day interiors are affected by sunlit windows. Many cinematographers call sunlight coming through the windows "sourcy" light, meaning that it is well defined in its origin. Practicals, or lights visible in the scene, are also sourcy.

Vilmos Zsigmond, ASC

Lighting depends on the picture. I really believe that daylight scenes should be lit softly except for harsh sunlight coming through the window, which is sourcy. But most daylight scenes are very soft and should be handled like a bounced light, no shadows and all that. But night interiors and night exteriors are, in real life, very sourcy. Sometimes you have hard light with practicals. Candlelight is a sourcy light. You really try to follow reality as much as possible. I do not like to light with hard sources anymore unless that is the way it is in real life. Almost everything nowadays is done through some diffusion material, unless you elect to be sourcy.

If you go too soft in the lighting, it just becomes boring. The difficult thing is really to light softly but to create a contrast at the same time. This is a difficult thing to do. Soft lighting can be more or less directional depending on the mood of a scene and the kind of set.

Directional light can be made soft through diffusing and bouncing. Soft light can only become partially directional with the use of flags, grids and teasers. Creating varying degrees of softness and directionality becomes one of the important methods used to create mood through lighting.

Richard Kline, ASC

In directional lighting we will take a unit and we can slip in a soft material like a spun glass a diffusion material which softens the light. You can use frosts and you can also bounce the directional light, which I do quite often.

Take a very strong light and bounce it off the card and then box it in with gobos, rather than [using] the generality of the overall soft light. It all depends on a scene. When I do a film I try to get a variety of looks because if the whole picture is soft-lit it becomes boring, and I have seen that quite often. Yes, it is pretty; each frame is gorgeous; but after a while it is meaningless because it is repetitious. It is a question of the overall picture so you have the variety of looks, and not just for the sake of variety. Most of the time in a story there is generally a night and a day, which require different looks. There are different times of a day and there are different rooms, which could dictate a different look. Sometimes you achieve it strictly through a bounce light. A bathroom or a kitchen, which are usually soft during the day, are ideal places. This might be a place to use the overall soft light, I think, but then again you come into a living room and it is usually down a bit, moodier, even if it is very soft. There are usually darker areas; you can make a set look soft and still go directional.

Experienced cinematographers see soft and hard light as two extremes in the whole range of light characteristics, each useful for certain applications.

James Crabe, ASC

To try to differentiate lighting generally by saying that there is hard lighting and there is soft lighting, one has to remember that there are a million variations between hard lighting and soft lighting, too. I certainly think that today the tendency is to use more soft sources that are more akin to what we experience in life, except in a tungsten situation at night where light bulbs and small sources are casting hard shadows. Much of what we see is bounced light and with the faster film it can be done.

I think the pendulum always swings [first] one way and [then] the other when you think that at the very beginning of motion pictures, the first studios were covered with muslin that would allow only soft light to come through. But, of course, there are many possibilities and effects available to soft lighting. Anyone who dismisses it as being easier to do or just a cheap shot is not really thinking about it. It is difficult with soft lighting to keep the sources out of the shot, usually because you often want them around a little bit. You can always put a Junior up, out of the set, or a Baby, or something, but to have a large radiating source like a bounce card from an interesting angle, particularly on real locations, quite often takes a lot of effort and thought.

Although cinematography began with soft lighting, for a good fifty years hard lighting predominated. The slow emulsions required lights with a "kick" to them. The resulting style was characterized by sharp shadows and well-defined areas of light. This created a rather dramatic, stylized quality. Since the sixties the trend toward more realistic treatment of the story has led the way to soft lighting. But the pendulum continues to swing.

LOW KEY, HIGH KEY

One of the most decisive factors creating the visual mood through lighting is the question of contrast and light distribution known as the Low Key and High Key styles. These

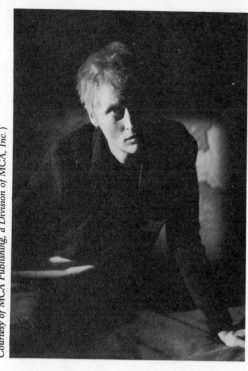

Low key effect is created by the use of one hard light source and predominant shadows. The lighter part of the face is played against a dark background. *Sophie's Choice*, Nestor Almendros (ASC), cinematographer.

The candle scene is in low key but with an upbeat mood. Lighting comes at an angle approximating the candle light. Street light patterns outside the windows provide more depth and separation of the planes. *Sophie's Choice*, Nestor Almendros (ASC), cinematographer.

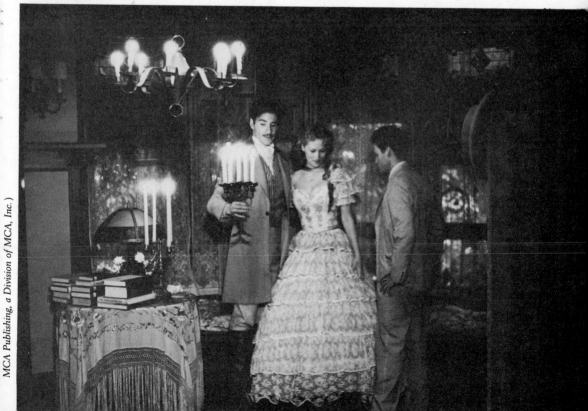

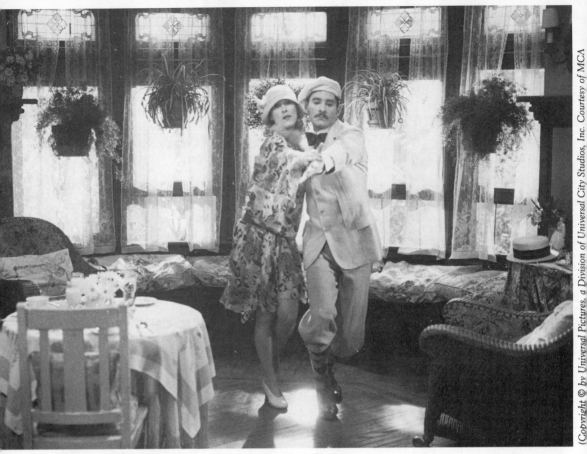

The same room as in the candle scene is lit to a high key effect with strong daylight outside the windows and rather flat lighting of the actors. *Sophie's Choice*, Nestor Almendros (ASC), cinematographer.

styles should not be confused with hard and soft lighting, though there are many parallels and similarities.

In a Low Key scene the majority of the picture is underlit, but some parts are correctly exposed or even overexposed. If, for example, there is a shot of a prisoner in a dark cell, perhaps a small window in the upper corner will be quite bright and one quarter of his face will be correctly exposed, but the remainder of the frame will be a few stops underexposed and no fill light will be used. The result is an overall impression of Low Key because the eye compares the dark areas with the few that are well lit.

Underexposing all the areas would lead to a murky picture without sufficient contrast and visual impact. We have to remember that it is by comparison of brightnesses and shadows that our eyes comprehend the lighting values in the frame. As many cinematographers state: "What you do *not* light is often more important than what you *do* light." In black-and-white pictures the brightness range is all there is. In color, the hues and saturation will also contribute to the overall gradation.

High Key represents the opposite concept. Here most of the frame is well lit with a lot of soft fill light. Sets are rather light in color. If the heavy shadows of Low Key are intended

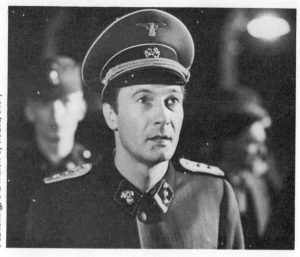

The SS officer is crosslit and well filled in to give him a more self-assured and domineering character. *Sophie's Choice*, Nestor Almendros (ASC), cinematographer.

Lighting a night scene from the camera side rather than from three-quarters back is not typical, but is very effective here. The actress looks drab against the dark background, which is in keeping with the mood of the scene. *Sophie's Choice*, Nestor Almendros (ASC), cinematographer.

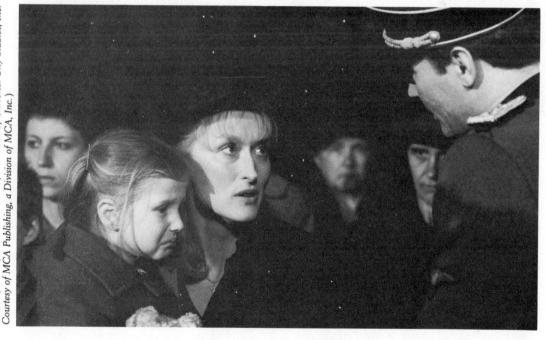

to introduce an element of suspense, the shadowless High Key leaves nothing to the audience's imagination.

To understand High and Low Key styles better we should take a closer look at charac-

ter and the functions performed by the key, fill and back lights.

In the hard, directional lighting style, the traditional concept of key light, fill light and back light was clearly defined. Today, a soft

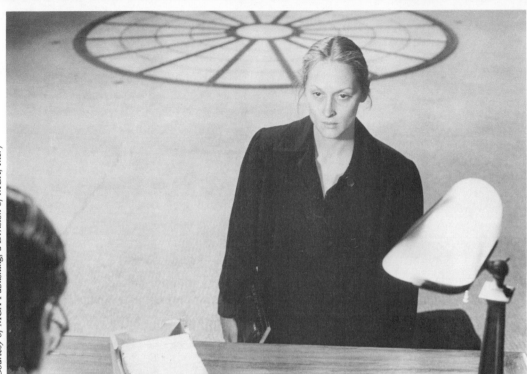

In this scene, flat lighting, together with a high camera angle, helps to create the mood of dejection and alienation. The reverse shot shows the unfriendly library clerk looking down at Sophie (Meryl Streep). His lighting includes a kicker which gives him a more self-assured look. The light reflections in his eyeglasses add to the ominous effect. *Sophie's Choice*, Nestor Almendros (ASC), cinematographer.

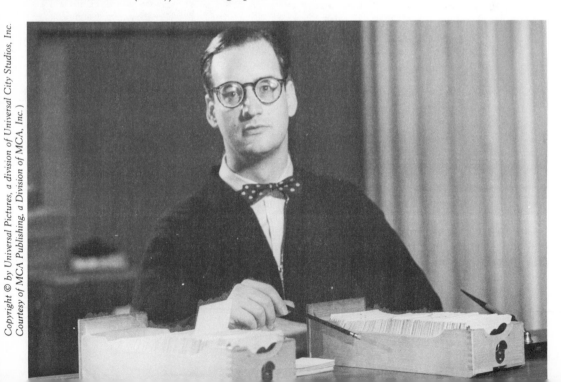

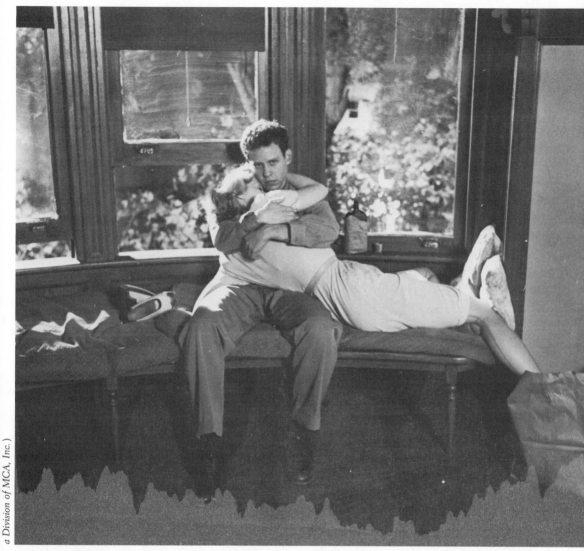

Strong backlight is logically motivated by the street lamp. The ambient room light justifies the soft front light. *Sophie's Choice*, Nestor Almendros (ASC), cinematographer.

light, enveloping objects and bouncing off surfaces creates a seemingly less clear distinction, and yet with a little bit of common sense we can always analyze the sources. The main source of light, which gives character to the scene, is the key light, even if it is extremely soft. Although with softer keys the fill light is not always needed, it remains an important light when the key light comes as crosslighting, for example, from the side (half light) or even from three-quarters back.

Richmond Aguilar

Fill light is a very important light. It is taken for granted, but it sets the mood and it can save your life in exposure. It starts picking up details in the background, things that you would not see otherwise.

In terms of placement, fill light can be described as being rather close to the lens axis, for example, slightly above the lens or opposite the key light, or both.

Back light traditionally fulfilled the function of separating people from the background. This function was necessary in black-and-white photography. It became less important with color, where the elements in the frame are separated from each other by their hue. Some more radical cinematographers reject back light altogether as artificial but with the advent of softer key light the majority of cinematographers find back lights useful.

Depending on the angle these accentuating, textural lights have many names. Back light usually means a light directly behind the subject, in line with the lens. A back light that does not indicate the source but just lights the hair is appropriately called the hair light. Also from the back comes the rim light or rimmer, which gives just a thin rim of light to the subject. The next light farther to the side is the kicker, which gives a certain sheen to the cheek as seen from the camera position. Farther yet to the side is a liner, which could be defined as a kicker, but is forward enough so that it does not produce any sheen. Glow light comes more from the side and basically creates a little glow on the shadowy side of the face but does not produce any shadows of its own: it has no "kick" to it. For the sake of clarity I have tried to systematize all these terms, but in practice they are used less precisely and sometimes interchangeably. The liner may mean the rimmer, or the kicker. Various cinematographers and gaffers develop their own nomenclature over the years.

This variety of light directions represents part of the "palette" of the cinematographer, to be used judiciously when and where it is needed. Incidentally, back lighting need not

The actress' profile is delineated by a rim light. Her key light comes from the right. *Sophie's Choice*, Nestor Almendros (ASC), cinematographer.

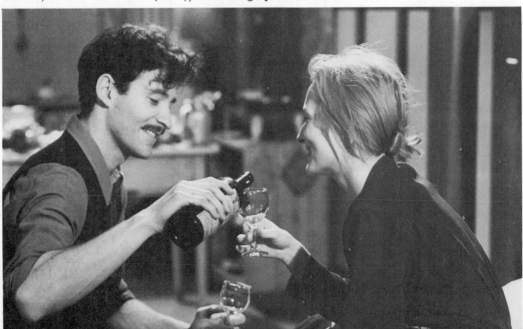

be a hard, directional light. Many people use soft light to create the effects of separation and light rim on a subject.

Richmond Aguilar

I use almost exclusively soft light for back light. It gives a little bit more area of highlight and the light is less harsh, so you see the outline but you are not conscious of the light being there. On a location interior you are limited by the height of the ceiling. Under these circumstances your back lights are low. If you are shooting a party with a lot of people milling around, it is quite disturbing when people block the back light. But if you use a soft light up there, or more than one, then when someone is blocked from one light he still gets some from another back light. It is a very soft, easy change; you do not have that harsh on and off shadows.

A harder light that gives a real punch may be referred to as a zinger.

Richard Hart

A lot of cinematographers like that "zing." It usually gives a rim-hot back light on hair to

line out the profile, like a kicker. When someone says "I want a real kicker in there," they don't necessarily mean kicker in the terms that we used to use them. Kicker was the three-fourth back light. Now lots of times it is a term used for just a real hard punch from some direction. It may be a total half light that someone steps into at a point. "Give me a real punch right there," "real kicker," "zinger"; they all mean the same thing.

We will conclude this review of back lights and kickers with a few words of caution.

Jordan Cronenweth, ASC

In lighting, time is a big factor. A trend in lighting is to get more and more simple, the judicious use of back lights and rim lights and kick lights. It stems from the fact that they all take time, so you put them where you absolutely have to have separation. You see unnecessary kickers every night on every channel on television. Lots of guys put them in out of habit, I guess, because of the "key light, back light, fill light" principle. Sometimes it is nice to have a face that is just almost melting into the background; it depends on what you are doing.

SOURCES OF LIGHT

Once the character of light is decided for a given scene, the cinematographer's task is to decide the practical and hypothetical sources of light and the direction of lighting. These choices will be influenced by the script and the director's concept of covering the scene. The more camera setups you can get from the director in advance, the less danger of "painting yourself into a corner" with lighting.

Therefore most cinematographers insist on seeing the run-through of the whole scene before lighting it.

Vilmos Zsigmond, ASC

The sequence of lighting a scene depends upon how a director works with actors. Unfortunately, many times actors have a late call, so usually you will talk to the director the night before or that morning. You ask him what he will do in that scene. He will rehearse with the stand-ins, walk it through, and he will establish a few things. For example, let's say somebody walks in through the door and sits down in a certain place. I prerig the lighting for this move. When the actors arrive, even if I am not finished, I will ask the director to have a rehearsal to finalize the action, because many times it will change. The actor will come in with a different idea, and they will change the whole thing. Maybe he won't come through the door anymore; maybe he will come from the other side of the room and that means that you would end up doing your job twice. I don't want to do that, so I like to get a rehearsal as soon as possible. When everything is locked in, the stand-ins will walk it for me; then I light the stand-ins. When this is done, usually you can shoot the scene. Most of the set can be prerigged to a certain degree.

Cinematographer Allen Daviau suggests lighting the windows on the set even before the rehearsal begins. In this way the light sources are suggested to the director and may, in turn, influence his staging of the scene.

Haskell Wexler, ASC

When lighting a set, prerigging is a time-saving practice, and it allows you to see the lighting problems in advance. The sooner you will get something lit, the sooner you can see whether you have made a mistake or not. This way it will not happen when everyone is waiting and when for reasons of time economy you would have to live with your wrong decisions.

Although prerigging may save time in a long run, on fast schedules it may be considered a luxury that cannot be afforded. Gaffer Richmond ("Aggie") Aguilar who frequently works with cinematographer Laszlo Kovacs, discusses ways to work around more restrictive budgets.

Richmond Aguilar

To a certain extent, it is dictated by how much time you have and what you are allowed to work with. When I started working with Laszlo Kovacs, I would be roughing-in when he was working with the director blocking the scene. I would be lighting the set from the background, or maybe outside, working toward the foreground, to the principals in front of the camera. By that time he will know where they will be on their marks and whether he will want to key the scene from the window or not. So, essentially, we would be working in the same time without too much coordination. I got very familiar with what he likes so it would work out very well without talking back and forth. In those early pictures, there was not a lot of time to release the set to the crew. We were lighting when they were rehearsing. Now in a major production you will have a rehearsal and a scene will be blocked out by a director, and we will be excused from the set. But on a very pressured schedule, we may have to work simultaneously, with the director rehearsing. It depends a lot upon a director and the people around him if they can work in this situation. Some want absolute quiet and privacy. That is a luxury which you cannot afford in a television schedule.

I start lighting from the background because we do not really know what the actors will do in front. When the director is working on that, I will go and do the windows outside and we will talk and establish, for example, that perhaps the sun comes through the window back there, so we have something to work from. The other school is to light the foreground action and to cut it off from where you don't want it, and then work your background. The basic question is: Where the hell will you start lighting the scene? Every scene has a key to it, something that will work for you. You see the light through a window or from a chandelier; those are obvious things. But, there are other scenes that are less obvious; a stained glass window perhaps, or maybe a plain room with one door open and a shaft of light coming down the hallway; something that would be appropriate for the dramatics. You find this one key, and if you like it you work from there. Many times it is awfully hard to get that one thing.

Deciding on light sources involves the aesthetic philosophy of the cinematographer. The two basic orientations are sometimes referred to as "Naturalism" and "Pictorialism." The naturalistic school of lighting would follow the natural, logically established sources of light in the scene. The pictorialists on the other hand would use light angles that violate this logic if they achieve a more pleasing picture as a result. Of course, there is no cut-and-dried division between these two approaches. It is more a matter of give-and-take between the logic of the source and the compositional requirement of the frame. Generally, most cinematographers believe in justifying the source of light.

Richard Kline, ASC

I establish a source. The position of light can change in various setups but the general character of the source will still look the same on the screen. You just need to enhance the source. Now, whether it needs more light or stronger light, it will still be the same in character.

John Alonzo, ASC

Jimmy Wong Howe once told me: Start with the source as the premise, but if the source as the premise does not work and does not look right, then change the source, just make up a source. And that is the best way because in the end result, you do not know how they are going to cut the picture. No director will start with the shot of a window and say, "Here is the light coming from this direction," and then cut to the actor. You may never see the window in the entire scene.

It is the overall character of the light direction that matters. The exact angle of light will never be scrutinized by the audience as long as it is not disorienting.

Vilmos Zsigmond, ASC

It is good to follow practicals but I am not dogmatic. When you see that a person needs another key, you can either start putting light sources on the other side and change everything around, which becomes ridiculous eventually because you will change the look of the room, or you can cheat. Now, how do you cheat? You can always cheat with light sources and the audience will never catch you. Who says that there cannot be a light source outside the frame? If I never shoot in that direction, I never reveal the cheat. You can get away with many things. If I was forced to cheat during the day, I would turn on some lights and use mixed light. But I like to justify the lighting. It is very important that people are lit realistically from existing light sources. And if you cheat, you cheat with light sources that you do not see but you feel that they could be there.

Sometimes the light direction is established by what "feels right" even if the logic of source is violated.

James Plannette

If you are photographing a scene and there is a light source in the picture, even 50 feet away, the direction of light should come from this source, even if in the previous shot another source was visible and another direction

of light established. If it came from the same direction, but a new source of light was visible, it would be distracting. The audience may not be able to verbalize what bothers them, but something would be bothering them.

LONG SHOT AND CLOSE-UP

Once the light directions are established, the time comes to execute the lighting strategy for the master shot and the coverage of the scene in closer shots. The extent to which the lighting will have to change from a long shot to a close-up really depends on many aspects of a scene. With predominantly overhead soft lighting for a master shot, the eye sockets can look cavernous. Close-ups will most likely require some "cleaning of the eyes," which means filling them in with lower angle light to get rid of the shadows. In hard, directional lighting, the changes will often depend upon the individual features of the person in close-up and on the composition of the frame, which tends to be affected more by hard directional light. Many cinematographers feel that if they spend more time and care on lighting the long shot, then there will be fewer delays and problems when they move into close-up coverage.

Vilmos Zsigmond, ASC

I usually spend a lot of time lighting a master and I usually do the rest of the shooting with very few changes. I prefer to spend twenty-five percent more time to light a master than an average cameraman would do, but then I use much less time on the close-ups. Directors do not like to wait too long after the master for the close-ups because they lose the

level of the performance. Many times a director will set up two cameras and get a master and a close-up at the same time. Of course, I don't like to use this technique too much because you end up doing the close-up with a long lens, in a lighting set for a master shot. This is sometimes limiting, especially when working on location. In case where I cannot light the master right, I will correct it in the close-up. I always try to bring the light through windows or from light sources, so it looks right and it can be used for the master and the close-up as well.

Coming closer to a close-up may require a change in the lighting ratio to better match these two shots.

Caleb Deschanel, ASC

You have to make certain adjustments for close-ups. You can generally use a higher lighting ratio in a close-up then you do in a long shot. Some of it depends on how hot the background is and many other things, but if you are in a setting, generally you get farther back and details that you would pick up in a close-up get lost and just become totally black or extremely dark, so that you don't see any details. It is not an absolute rule because each scene is different. If you have a very hot background, then that rule changes, but if it is a dark background, then when you are getting closer, when the image becomes large in frame, you start seeing details in shadows even at the same lighting ratio as when the object was farther away. There is also more grain there to create the detail.

The background may need adjusting as well when coming to a close-up. For example, in a long shot the shadow on a wall is halfway up the wall. In a close-up, actors may be only against white, so you have to lower the shadow line.

Specific lighting procedures always depend on the subject.

Haskell Wexler, ASC

You have to know what the scene is. Let's suppose that it is a motel room. Two people are seated at the end of their beds watching the TV set. You rig a light that would simulate the light from the TV set. Now the director probably wants to turn the light between the two beds on or off, so you rig that light into a switcher. Generally speaking, we do not let the actors turn the lights on or off

in a scene. They put their hands on the switch and we switch them off. You might have a small "coffin box" or a small square soft light on top of a set, so that there is an ambient exposure light, so to speak.

Sometimes you just light the room. You take the existing sources in the room and you enhance them visibly. You light the room for a naturalistic film and then, when they come to a close-up, you hit the eyes a little bit but not so much that it destroys the lighting character of the room. You do change the lighting when coming to a close-up but nobody should know it. Unless, again, you are trying to make a dramatic point. Sometimes you can make a dramatic point that is not necessarily realistic. I can imagine a film where someone is starting to cry and it is a very high dramatic moment in a film that is not realistic in its concept. You can rig a light to a dimmer to slowly brighten the person's eyes. It is perfectly legitimate in this film. In a realistic film, when you go to a close-up, you have to keep the change in the same character as the other shots. The light that was hitting on the right side of the face in the master should not hit on the left side in a close-up.

IN THE STUDIO AND ON LOCATION

The actual painting with light, creating the three-dimensional composition to be ultimately recorded on the two-dimensional film, has to be approached differently in the studio and on location. The challenge of a dark stage holds an immense appeal for some cinematographers.

Conrad Hall, ASC

Starting on a dark stage is the most wonderful, joyful evolvement ever and it is just a

metaphor of what all life should be like. It is as if you are coming into a problem that you have to face and there it is, like a life to live. What are you going to do? You have choices to make. It is not like there is one way to do it, and you have to figure out how to make those choices. I have gone about it starting with a concept. A concept gives you enough information to start talking to somebody else that you are working with, because at this point you are going into a teamwork operation. So, the concept has to be spoken, articulated, and everyone on the crew has to be imbued with that concept. Now we are all working with one concept instead of everybody working with his own idea. And, I am working with the director's concept, and then [come] a lot of discussions, because sometimes you know just how to do it and sometimes you don't.

In the past, the total control in the studio setting was often blamed for an unrealistic treatment of the story material.

James Plannette

When you are shooting a night street scene on a back lot everything looks too perfect. You get on a back lot of some studio, and you have arcs and towers, and you have everything you want and so you end up shooting at f/4 instead of at f/2.8, and so the headlights do not look the same and the neon signs in the windows don't look so bright as they look when you shoot real exterior, and everybody has a perfect key light, because you have lights on top of the buildings and you've got the towers and all of a sudden it is the studio. So even if you are shooting on a back lot, pretend that you are not. That is the problem in the studio with scaffolds and lights on them, that everybody has a backlight: that says, Studio.

Some filmmakers find the limitations of location shooting more reassuring.

James Crabe, ASC

When working in sets you are creating everything yourself from the ground up. It is all artificial. When you are going to a natural location, walking through the door, you are aware of where you can put the camera, and where you cannot. You are affected psychologically by the lighting of the place when you see it in the natural situation. You may try to emulate that. It is a lot different from coming to a studio where the grips can tell you, any wall can come out, everything is wild, you can shoot anything you want to shoot. Some directors like the control, being able to design everything, and a lot of directors are terrified of that aspect and prefer to let the natural aspects of the location dictate the staging.

There is no question that the studio allows for much more precise and sophisticated lighting.

Conrad Hall, ASC

In the studio you have total control. I love the distance that you can have from your lights because I hate to see somebody walking close to a wall with a larger-than-life shadow of himself. That means that the light source is very close. But in the studio, when you can have your light source thirty or forty feet away, an actor can walk any place in the room and he does not burn up when he walks to a window.

Of course some location interiors are so vast that they combine the best of both worlds: space and authenticity. Irrespective of the type of interior where the scene takes place, the cinematographer has to decide on the look of it.

All the lighting strategies should serve only one thing: The story. It is the mark of a good cinematographer that he is not creating beautiful pictures for their own sake but that his vision helps to tell the story in the most effective way. And we can only hope that the stories that come our way will be worth telling in the first place.

CHAPTER Five

Lighting a Scene

IN THE previous chapter, we dealt with the character and quality of light and with the strategy of establishing lighting directions. Let's look now at the actual creation and control of light on the set. The unique problems of location lighting will be dealt with in Chapter Six.

As we mentioned in the previous chapter, when compared with location, the studio provides a cinematographer with much more freedom. He can put the lights where he wants them and he can leave them there for the required period. On location, a small change of a camera angle may result in dismantling many lights which would become visible in the shot and starting from scratch. This relighting wastes valuable time. On a sound stage, larger lighting units can be used from greater distances. Farther away from the source, the intensity of light changes less with distance and therefore will be more even. There is also more room on the stage for setting up Century stands with flags, nets, scrims, and other devices to modulate the lights.

One could say that sound stages have made a spectacular comeback. During the sixties, filmmakers equipped with lighter cameras and lights and faster emulsions almost abandoned stages in favor of real locations. The prevailing philosophy of those years claimed that locations provided realism that was hard, if not impossible, to obtain on the stage. There was much truth to it but the practical drawbacks became quite serious as well. The camera "liberated" from the stage became imprisoned by the confines of small interiors. The sound recorded on location was often unusable. The legal trouble of negotiating with private property owners with high financial expectations made it very expensive from the production point of view. The realization came that in many ways the sound stage offered freedom that locations were lacking. Perhaps today a happy medium is achieved. Choosing to shoot on a sound stage or on location is based on both creative and logistical considerations. It is interesting to note that even though film emulsions are much faster than they were fifteen years ago, and filming is possible with very little light, sound stages are far from becoming obsolete.

DAY INTERIOR

For day interiors windows are the most logical light sources. Cinematographers feel more and more uneasy about the key light coming from high above and creating what is considered a "film look" as opposed to the reality of light coming from the window or the practical light sources inside. Here the time of day will obviously influence the character of the lighting. If the major light source is the window (perhaps with tracing paper on the glass) then an arc or a tener (10K) "punching" through it can be hoisted up or down to simulate the position of the sun.

When it is very early in the morning or very late in the afternoon, light coming into the room will be at a very low angle, almost parallel. Any additional lights will follow this pattern. For a sunset or a sunrise effect, an orange gel on an arc will warm up the light.

Generally, when a scene in the script is des-

In this example the window was established as the source of light. Only the man sitting behind the desk is in the direct lightbeam from the window. The remaining areas are keyed only approximately from the window side, to preserve the general logic of the light source. The soft light on the right side provides the general fill.

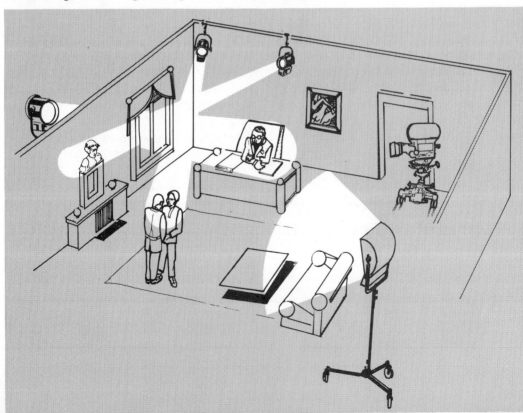

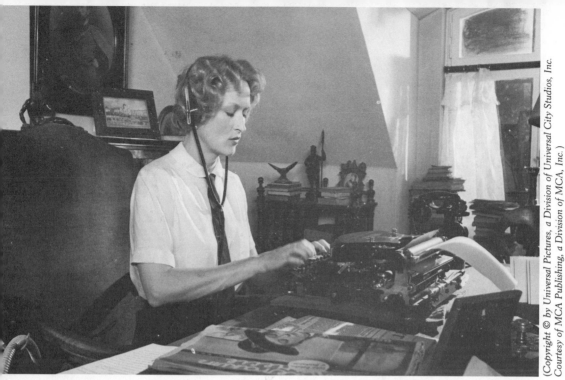

Hard key light coming from the window as a crosslight is balanced by fill light coming from the 750-watt soft light with diffusion. *Sophie's Choice*, Nestor Almendros (ASC), cinematographer.

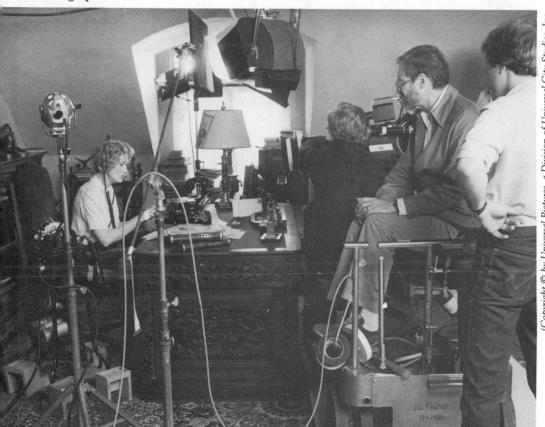

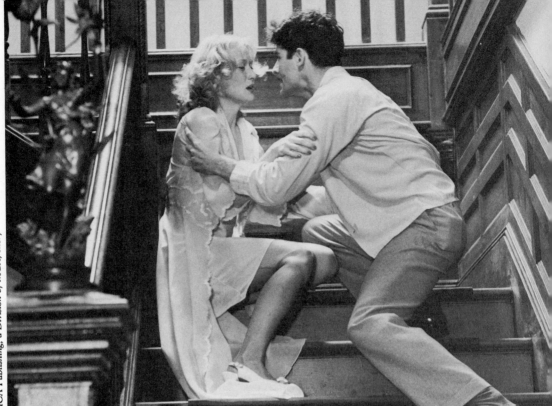

A daylight scene with strong backlight, indicating bright sunlight. *Sophie's Choice*, Nestor Almendros (ASC), cinematographer.

ignated as Day Interior, a specific hour of the day is not frequently established. The cinematographer creates a general daylight.

Vilmos Zsigmond, ASC

I cheat a lot in daylight interiors because I never think of the sun as being as high overhead as it is in California in the summer. I assume the location is in Sweden or in Ireland where the sun travels low around the sky even in the summer months. I cheat on the time of day because it is rarely important that you play a scene at a specific time. If a scene calls for day, it could be 10 A.M.; why does it have to be noon? I determine it when I read the script. When you are making a detective story, though, and the time may be very important, then I would follow a scheme of

exact hours and play with the shadows. But very seldom would you have a story like that. So for me, day is 10 A.M. or 3 P.M., but it is never 12 noon.

The effect of shafts of light coming through venetian blinds, so often used in the detective films of the 40s, is as popular among today's cinematographers as it was forty years ago. Either an arc or a 10K lamp is used without a lens to create a sharper shadow. The shadow cast by rain-spattered windows can also be heightened by removing the lens from the lamp. When a Fresnel lens is removed from an arc, it should be replaced with a Pyrex glass to protect the actors and the crew from the burning rays of ultraviolet radiation. The lens should never be removed from an HMI

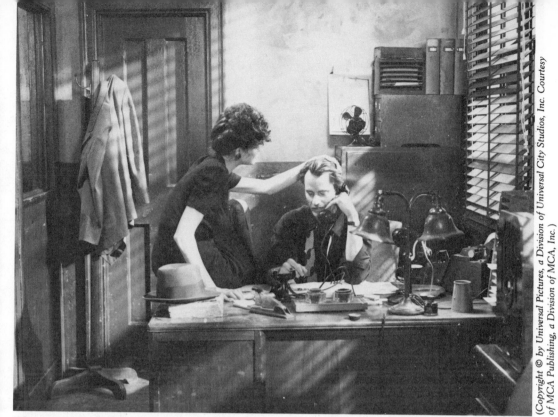

The venetian blind effect was enhanced by using a 10K light with the lens removed to obtain a sharper shadow pattern. *Frances*, Laszlo Kovacs (ASC), cinematographer.

To create the shadow pattern, a venetian blind was hung in the middle of the room, and a 2K light with the lens removed (an open eye junior) was used to light it. A soft light was added to partially fill in the shadows. *Frances*, Laszlo Kovacs (ASC), cinematographer.

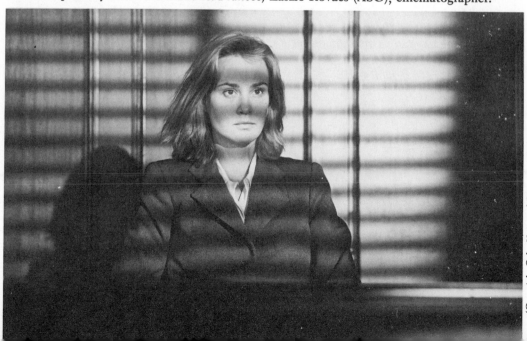

light. Day interior logically requires a rather soft light, except for harsh sunlight coming through the window. The upper parts of the walls tend to be darker, depending on the angle of the sun.

When the windows are visible in the shot, what is seen through them becomes an important concern of the cinematographer. Here, the set designer's cooperation should make our lives a little bit easier. The exterior on the studio set will usually consist of a backdrop and some scenery elements such as greenery and architectural details. A Translite backing is often employed nowadays. It is a backdrop made of huge photographic enlargements glued on a thin material and lit from behind by an equally large bank of photofloods. The black-and-white enlargements are painted over to the required hue and saturation. A rule of thumb for the cinematographer is to light it darker than what looks right. A net in front will soften it and add more depth. There are also nets used on windows to modulate the background.

Allen Daviau, ASC

The intensity of the window has to be realistic enough that you miss that there is nothing out there. At the same time it cannot be so hot and such a big part of the frame that it pulls the eye away from the compositional point that you try to draw it to.

I don't think that there will ever be an absolute solution to working on stage with windows during the day interiors. I hate backings with a passion. If somebody gives me a backing, I usually try to burn it out so that it is almost not there. Background paintings seem to have been developed for black-and-white films. And for some reasons the black and white can accept it being graphically present.

To create a hot window, but with a little detail behind it, you can put a bobbinet [white gauze] stretched on the frame in the window, and you backlight this net. Then you put greenery out there and frontlight the greenery. If you angle the bobbinet across the window, the amount of light that you put on that net determines how transparent it is. If I have a ficus or other bush standing out there and I put a lot of light on it to make the greenery come through, but still it looks too artificial, I can backlight the bobbinet and have the greenery virtually disappear. Or have just some movement of the bush there, just the shadow.

I don't feel that you can do any kind of a large-scale day exterior on a stage and have people believe it. It is just something that an eye knows that it isn't really out there. Tracing paper in the window and a light behind it is a wonderful way of sourcing; it is as true a window source as you can have if you can get away with it. And you can even see a piece of the window as long as it is not too big a part of the frame. It is a lovely source.

NIGHT INTERIOR

For night scenes, hard, directional lighting is more justified. This does not mean that night character cannot be created with soft lighting. It is done all the time. It really depends on the type of practical sources visible in the frame and above all, on the visual concept of the film. For example, black-and-white photography requires directional light in order to separate the objects in the frame. Therefore, more units are used to light the scene. The sets are basically lit separately from the action. The illusion of night is created by the angle and the distribution of light. The angle of the light tends to be less frontal for a night effect. The percentage of well-lit areas in the frame is smaller. One strategy is to underlight foreground objects or even characters in relation to what is behind them.

Richmond Aguilar

Every item in the room has an optimum angle to be lit from. Say you have a lamp in the corner of a living room; you may light the chair with the light coming from one side of the lamp and you will light the couch from another side and you will light the flowers on the coffee table maybe from above. So you will end up using several units to imitate that one source. Then when people are moving around it complicates it even further. Of course, you have to take many liberties with justifying your sources.

Any time you have a source of light in the frame it adds definition to the picture; it gives you a reason for your source. Say that we have a few people around the table. If there is one lamp in the middle of the table, then you have to light each person from the center. So essentially, if you have five people sitting, you need five lights, unless you double up on one. But if you put it to the side, you can light them all with one light as a source and then just fill in from the front. And if one person gets up and walks away he does not have to walk through the light; he is still lit from one side. It looks real. This way then, on a lower budget film, you can make it easier for yourself by keeping your source to one side of the frame.

The lighting at the dinner table simulates an overhead chandelier. "Babies" are used with diffusion. A practical lamp in the background helps to create the feeling of depth on the set and adds to the night mood of the scene. *Frances*, Laszlo Kovacs (ASC), cinematographer.

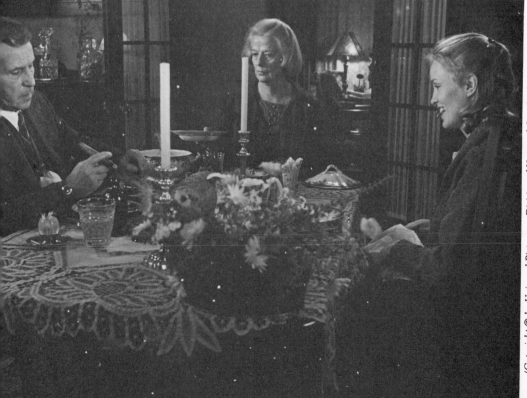

CONTROLLING HARD LIGHT

In real life we are used to having only one shadow. On the set each hard light casts a shadow. Multiple shadows on film are distracting. Cinematographers take great care to minimize multiple shadows.

COPING WITH SHADOWS AND MODULATING HARD LIGHT

Michael D. Margulies, ASC

I like to work without shadows even from a hard light, because when you see a shadow and it is from a cinema light, you know that you are looking at a film. And, if you can see a film without shadows I think that it brings you more to the realm of reality, which is what the film is trying to do in the first place.

Richmond Aguilar

One shadow seems to be legitimate and logical. But when you get two, it takes the attention away from the actor. Sven Nykvist will accept one shadow if he absolutely has to, but definitely not two. He is the whole school in himself when it comes to simplicity. Beautiful simplicity is not necessarily easy. We in Hollywood would tend to overlight. He knows that there is place for real glamour, and he will take time to create the lighting for a visual effect. But if the rest of it is not important for the dramatics, he will do it simply. Expressions like "simpler is better," or "simplicity is a key to beauty," bear out.

The creation of softer or harder shadows to take the light away from certain areas constitute methods of controlling light and creating

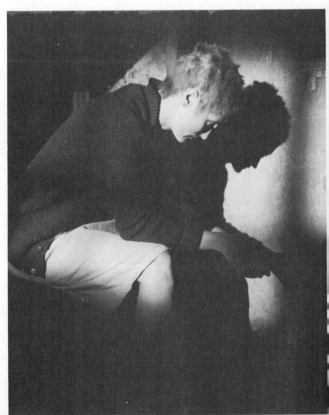

One hard light source creates one shadow, used here successfully, for a dramatic effect. *Sophie's Choice*, Nestor Almendros (ASC), cinematographer.

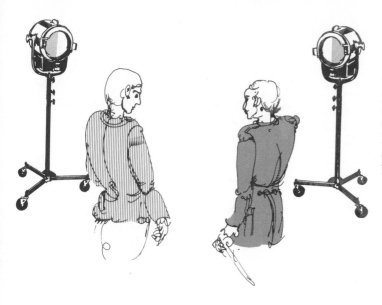

A two-light setup to cover a two-person scene. The half-scrims are used to even out the illumination. Here the key light for one person serves as the backlight for the other.

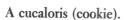

A cucaloris (cookie).

(Mole-Richardson Co., Hollywood, Calif., U.S.A.)

A cutter is used to project a shadow over the area where a microphone shadow would be visible on the wall.

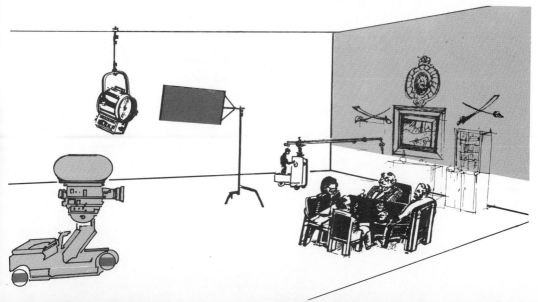

mood in the scene. A large arsenal of light-restricting devices has been developed over the years specifically for hard lights; they are often too small to be used with soft light. From ever-present scrims and barndoors on the lamps, to cutters, fingers, sticks and cucoloris, they all help to keep the light from being in one tonality. They come in a variety of sizes and shapes to hold back the light from carefully selected and often very small areas. Some are designed for very specific uses. The cutter, for example, is often used to hide the shadow of the microphone.

James Crabe, ASC

The microphone is very often close to where you want to put the light. The actor faces both his key and his microphone, so in the old days, it was handled by sharper lights and harder cutters. Movie audiences over the years got accustomed to seeing walls that always had shadows on the top and were always bright on the bottom. It also made the shot look more attractive. Even so, it was used to hide the microphone shadows. Soft light can sometimes be more deceiving because a hard light shadow is really easy to see, but soft light shadow can be very difficult to discern. Everyone has to keep a close watch. You've often got to use lights that are on stands on the floor to get them under the microphone itself in order to cut that out. It is therefore very important for the soundman and his boom man to watch the rehearsals, because nowadays the directors are much tougher on crews. In the old days it might be a dolly, a track that makes a simple little movement. But today, with zoom lenses and all of the other techniques used, the miking of a scene can be really complicated.

Evenly lit flat areas often need to be broken up with shadows. Devices used to restrict light range from solid flags to translucent netting.

Philip Lathrop, ASC

When you have to light frontally because location limitations do not allow other angles, then you need many nets and cutters to break up the light and take it off the foreground. I have had as many as twenty cutters on occasion.

Another way to limit the frontal light coverage, is by putting up cardboards with slits, holes, and so forth, in front of the light source. This method is often used in the so-called, new lighting style which, at the time of this writing, is often used in television commercials and is characterized by hard-edged frontal lighting.

Hard, directional light is also modulated by nets in various shapes and sizes.

Harry Wolf, ASC

When I have a man sitting at a desk and a wall is very close behind him, it is very difficult to take the light off the wall. So what I do is, I take a double net and I take my lighter and I burn a hole in the middle of it and I put it in front of the key light. Now I've got the key on him but everything else is down. I use it very often.

This method can also be used to diminish the roundness of a face. A hole in the net will allow more light in the center of the face. By moving the net nearer then farther from the light, we will obtain a softer or harder shadow. Nets of different shapes are used for different problems.

Ralph Woolsey, ASC

White is probably the most troublesome thing to deal with where tonal control is concerned. You have to do something in a close-up shot where a face is competing with a brilliant white shirt, which is sure to be an eye-catcher; it will almost burn a hole in the film. For hard-light lighting the "chin scrim" was once used. It was shaped like a crescent moon and was often hand-held to shade a white blouse or tuxedo shirt. Today on medical shows the doctors and nurses wear green outfits and there are green drapes in the operating rooms. That practice did not start because of films, but happened because it lessened eyestrain. But it certainly helped in filming, as many of us who struggled with glaring white sheets and uniforms can attest. Today, where props and wardrobe are controlled, gray-tinted materials are used, or light-colored fabrics, all of which finally reproduce as white. Otherwise a lot of time may be necessary in "aging down" white pillars, window frames, tin roofs and the like when they are obtrusively bright areas. Often temporary paint can be sprayed on small props, and dulling spray can do wonders with brilliant kicks. The subject is very extensive; a book could be written.

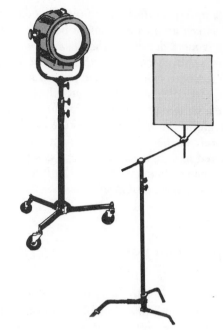

When a scrim is positioned at an angle it becomes optically denser and cuts down the light more effectively.

One of the most common uses of nets and metal scrims is to create an even light intensity when the actor is moving toward the light. For example, the half scrim covers the lower part of the light so that it equalizes the illumination when the actor moves closer to the light. This also can be achieved with a net positioned on a C-stand in front of the lamp. You can also use nets as "floaters". This means a net moved into a certain position during the shot. For example, when an actor is crossing a hot light you can "float" a net in front of it.

The light-cutting power of any net is affected by its distance from the light source.

Ralph Woolsey, ASC

When you use a single net or wire scrim very close to a directional light, it will darken the affected area about half a stop. But if you take

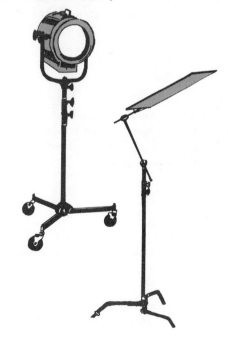

the same net ten feet away from the light, it will darken an area even more because now there is more density as the openings of the net are relatively closer together. To use a net at its intended value you have to keep it close and perpendicular to the source beam. To make a scrim more dense you can foreshorten its angle to the light, thus making the holes relatively smaller. And by turning a solid flag centered in a light beam you can use it as a poor man's dimmer, provided this change does not make a visible shadow.

When lighting with hard light one usually lights and modulates the sets separately from the scene taking part in the foreground.

Richmond Aguilar

Normally you light your sets pretty much separately from your action in the hard light, and you are using any number of units. You can use one 10K to light the set, put a cucaloris on it, or put a shadow across the wall and you break it enough to create some kind of mood.

CONTROLLING SOFT LIGHT

So far, we have discussed the lighting of a scene with hard, directional light and its manipulations by cutters and scrims. When a small, hard source is replaced with a large, soft one, the light-controlling devices grow in size. Generally there are three categories of soft light: commercially built box-type luminaires, any lamp with diffusion in front of it, or light from any source bounced off a reflective surface. The categories are frequently combined. A hard-soft light quality, for example, can be created by projecting a hard lamp through silk, or a soft-soft quality can be achieved by bouncing light off a white card

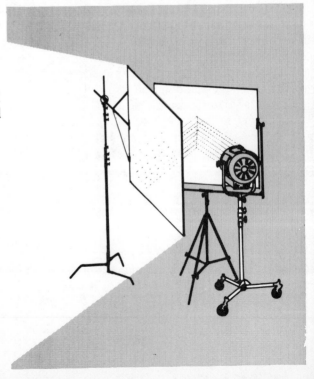

A hard light source can be made doubly soft when it is first bounced off a white board and then directed through a diffusion screen.

and then passing it through tracing paper. Quartz halogen units are good for this purpose because they are small and produce strong light.

COMMERCIAL SOFT LIGHT

The box-type soft lights are generally more controllable than the other methods. Some cinematographers, such as Laszlo Kovacs, use them regularly.

Richmond Aguilar

We like the so-called Four Bangers, for instance. They are about 18 inches square with four 1000-watt bulbs. Eighteen inches does not seem too big when you talk about soft light nowadays, but it is soft enough and yet small enough to have punch, to reach a little bit, and it is controllable. We like to have a little more definition. We use very little diffusion on it but we put the grid on, usually. The globes are situated in a well about one foot from the reflective surface so it is a powerful,

4000-watt Super Softlite with an "egg crate," which helps to control the pattern of the light.

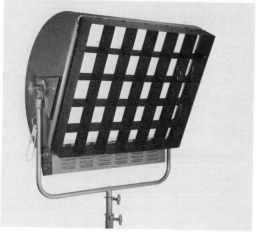

small soft light with a bit of a punch. If you get any bigger than that, your light does not seem to reach that far and, of course, it is not that directional. So it is a kind of a compromise.

The grid on a soft light that Aguilar mentions here is a truly useful accessory. Often called egg crate, it has enough depth to give certain direction to the light and to limit the spread.

Richmond Aguilar

The egg crate grids are very useful when you are working in small spaces and you want to use soft lights but there is no room to put flags up in front to control it. So you can put these grids on to direct the soft light in about a 45 degree angle and do most of your control. You save three flags maybe and you control the exposure. For example, you can have three people on a couch lit from one side and rather than using nets you can give them an equal exposure with the use of the grid. The source is big enough to be soft, yet it is not so big that it wraps around, or soft to a point of losing some details in the features. It is soft enough to eliminate hard shadows, yet hard enough to be directional. You can put it over the camera, in a hallway, for example, where you are limited in space and you can tip that grid to a position where it will cut a certain amount of light in the foreground. You will get a very even footcandle reading on a person walking toward the camera. Sometimes, when the ceiling is not high enough, you may have to tip it up when the person is coming forward because otherwise he or she would walk directly into it.

DIFFUSED LIGHT

The second type of soft light is created with diffusion screens. There is a variety of materi-

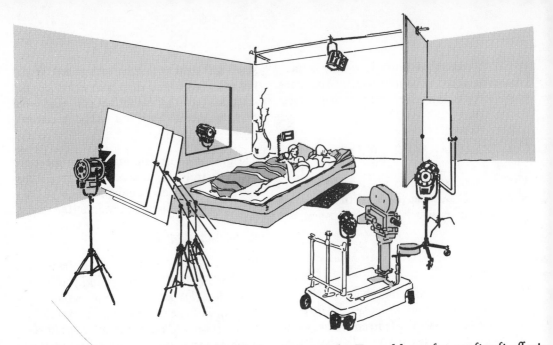

Bedroom scene lighting using a triple diffusion in front of a Fresnel lamp for a soft-soft effect.

als, from tracing paper, silk, and bleached muslin, to a vast choice of sophisticated diffusers offered by such companies as Rosco and Lee. Tracing paper is a great favorite of many leading cinematographers. Often it is mounted together with a sheet of clear plastic to prevent any rustling sound. Tracing paper comes in different densities and it is essential that it does not change the color temperature of the light, although some slight shift toward warmer tone can often be expected. (I use "warmer" here as a psychological expression, not as regards in Kelvin rating, which would represent a drop in color temperature.) If the only available tracing paper is too much on the brownish side, a blue gel may be necessary to bring it back to the correct rating. Rosco materials like Grid Cloth, Rolux, Soft and Tough Frost, Tough White Diffusion, Tough Silk, and Tough Spun provide a good choice of densities and characteristics. "Tough" indicates that the material will not char or yellow readily when used on hot lights. Lee Filters offer a similar selection of diffusion materials. All these products are used to increase the size of a light source.

Richmond Aguilar

A frame of a diffusing material, when it is lit from behind, becomes a source of light itself. But the character of this source will depend on the size of diffusion screen, the type of lamp and its distance from this frame. If the lamp has a wide spread, the diffused light will have a wider pattern itself and will perhaps cover more area than we need it to cover. In other words, the angle at which the light attacks the surface of the diffusion is related to how much it spreads the light on the subject. If it is a wide angle, the light may be flared out beyond the subject. The softness of the light depends on the size of the source. So, the closer the diffusion is to the source, the smaller the pattern of light and the harder the light. Therefore, we can control the softness of diffusion by regulating the distance between the sources and the diffusion screen.

When we need large soft light but with a longer throw and more control, an arc may be the right lamp to use behind the diffusion screen.

Ralph Woolsey, ASC

The carbon arc has a highly specular quality. Therefore if you project it through a diffusion material like half-density Frost, you will get a softened but directional light which will give you more control. By comparison, a 10K is not a very specular source; you cannot make a sharp shadow with it, no matter what, even with the lens removed, because the 10K filament is very large, whereas the arc is almost a point source. If you have a frame of diffusion sufficiently dense, like Tough Frost or Soft Frost, placed far enough from the light so it fills the whole frame, then you produce a new light source the size of your diffusion screen. When using arcs, a piece of half-density spun glass on the lamp will reduce its directional quality when using soft diffusion material out front. There is even a difference in the quality of soft light that you get from a diffused Baby 10K, as compared with either the regular or Big-Eye 10Ks. My favorite soft light effect requires considerable studio space and a huge piece of Soft Frost, way back from the set and fairly low. Through this a standard 10K is directed to produce wonderful soft, low shadows, as though the light were filtered through a large window or windows. This lighting can fill a large area, if it is placed far enough away, with a minimum of falloff. Actors can move freely about, and you can direct additional spots through the same diffusion panel at differing angles to supplement or carry out an effect. By raising this type of diffused source, everything from the above effect to overhead skylighting can be achieved. And adding color to the lamp will sell a sunset or other feeling as needed.

In The Iceman Cometh we used many soft light sources, but to project it farther we utilized Baby 10Ks, which are very bright but small, and we hung Soft Frost in front of them. We also had a couple of arcs outside the set, shooting through large panels of Frost some distance away. When someone came through the front door he would step in front of this light, which would make him extremely bright. By using shutters on these arcs, remotely controlled near the camera, we could easily change the brightness during a shot. This was more accurate than having someone moving nets or flags in front of the arcs.

Another aspect to consider is the distance of the soft light to the subject.

Richmond Aguilar

The quality of the light will be harder the further away you move it, because the source will get smaller. The biggest light we know is the sun—bigger than the Earth—but its light produces such a hard shadow because it is so far away that it is a pinpoint source. The softness of the light depends on the size of the source. An 8K soft light which is about four by four feet in size, will give you shadows if it is too far away. Another factor governing the hardness of your shadow is the distance between your subject and the wall. The closer it is to the wall, the harder the shadow. So to summarize it, the softness of light is dictated by the size of the source, the distance to the subject, and when we are talking about shadows, the distance between the subject and the surface on which the shadow is falling.

BOUNCED LIGHT

The third type of soft light is the bounced light. When the reflecting surface is large and matte in texture, it will provide an extremely

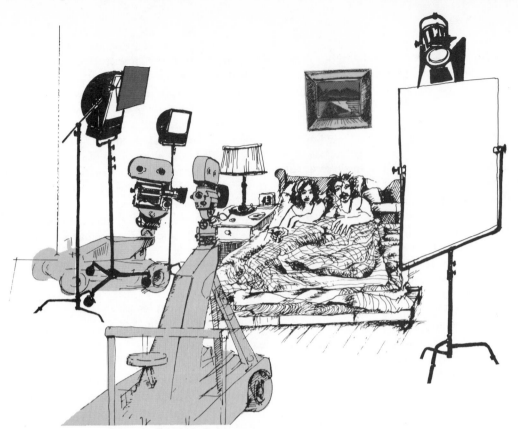

Soft key light in this scene is motivated by the practical lamp so that it comes from the side. The general fill is provided by bouncing the light off a foam-core board.

The approximate lighting pattern of this scene is shown in the previous illustration. This is a good example of creating a night mood using only soft and reflected light.

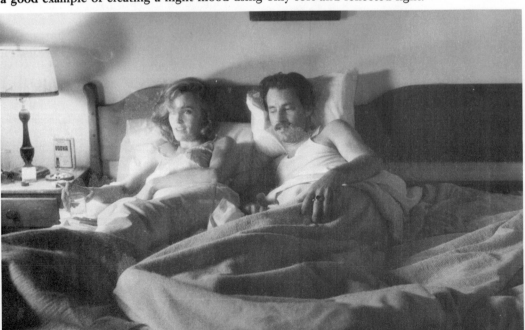

soft light, but its throw will be rather limited. Any white wall or ceiling can be utilized for bouncing light, but there is a range of materials carried by the grip department for this purpose. Styrofoam "bead boards" are considered to have the most matte surface and therefore reflect the softest light. They are extremely lightweight and can be easily broken into different shapes, but they cannot be bent. Next in softness are show cards, also known as art cards. They have a very good white on one side and black on the other. Slightly less white and with a bit more sheen are foam-core boards which come in larger sizes (4' x 8') than show cards. They can be bent into a corner. They are very good when a little more direction for the light is needed. The most directional, yet soft, are large white plastic Griffolyn sheets, often stretched on 12' x 12' frames. This material, originally

used for covering haystacks on farms or goods on trucks, was adopted by the film industry as an excellent reflector for bouncing light into a larger general area from a slightly greater distance than the other reflecting materials would allow.

For certain specific applications a diffusing material such as bleached muslin can also be used for bouncing. I once observed Jordan Cronenweth and his gaffer James Plannette lighting a car commercial. Several sheets of bleached muslin were sewn together and stretched above the stage on which the cars were displayed. Several Master Lights, positioned on the floor, were pointed upward and their light bounced off the muslin. Thus, areas of this white canopy were reflected in the cars, which were truly "painted with light."

The car is "painted with light" bounced off a bleached muslin stretched above the stage. PAR lamps work very well with this technique.

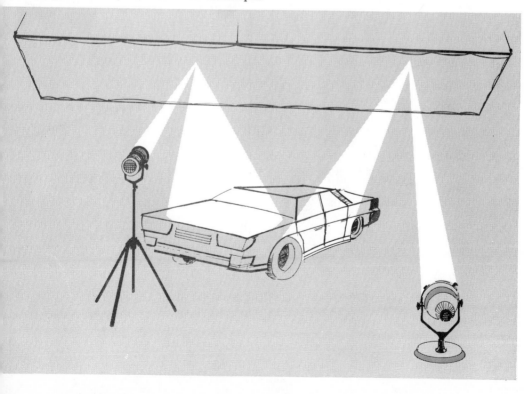

MODULATED BOUNCED AND DIFFUSED LIGHT

The soft quality of bounced light is similar to diffused light and so are the problems of controlling it. For a lighthearted comedy, when the light illuminates the whole set, the task is easy. But when a more dramatic situation occurs and the intention is to light it soft, yet with several areas kept at low key, it requires skill and time to do it right with bounced and diffused light. You need to work with big flags and teasers, which are large frames with black cloth stretched on them, and you need space to be able to position reflecting boards at a proper distance and angle. Angle is very important to provide modelling for the faces and to avoid unwanted light spills on the walls.

There is a practical point to remember when controlling such light sources. All flags and scrims used to modulate the distribution

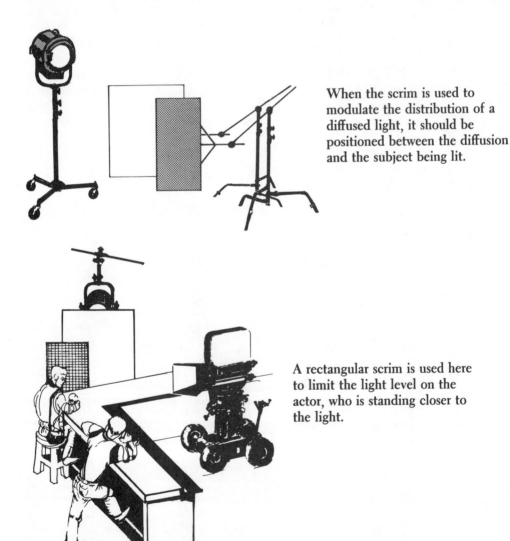

When the scrim is used to modulate the distribution of a diffused light, it should be positioned between the diffusion and the subject being lit.

A rectangular scrim is used here to limit the light level on the actor, who is standing closer to the light.

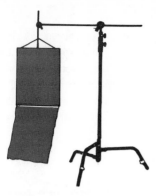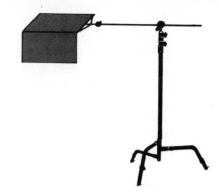

Custom-made cloth flaps will extend the existing flag. When not needed, they are folded back and secured with Velcro attachments.

of light should be positioned *in front of the diffusion screen* and not between the lamp and the screen. After all, in a situation like this, the diffusion material becomes the effective light source to be controlled. Another principle to remember is that the softer the light, the larger the flags needed to control it, and the farther away from the source the flags will have to be. Behind a large diffusion screen, one can combine several hard lights as a supersource. The light quality will be better if these lamps are farther away from the diffusion material but the intensity of the transmitted light will then decrease.

TREATMENT OF WALLS

One of the practical differences between hard and soft lighting is the treatment of walls. With directional light covering the exactly defined areas, the walls have to be treated separately with lights specifically positioned for this purpose. In a soft lighting technique our efforts go in the direction of limiting the amount of soft light reaching the walls. We do it with very large flags, and with teasers hanging over the set or positioned on stands on the floor. That does not mean that the walls will be entirely lit by the light designed for the action. Some cameramen will still try to light them separately.

When you wish to put a break on a wall, for example, above an actor's head, you have to use the flag closer to the subject especially when using a soft light. A flag used closer to the soft light source will cut the general output but not the exact area.

Controlling the walls is also required when lighting from the top. For such overhead, soft lighting, coffin lights, are used. The black velvet skirts can be rolled up and down to control the light falling on the walls or on a particular area.

Another method for overhead illumination consists of covering the entire set with silk or bleached muslin and lighting from above.

Richmond Aguilar

We use silk or bleached muslin to drape over the set as the overhead diffusion. Above this 'ceiling' we use 5 and 10Ks so that we can direct the light through it and still have a little bit of control. It softens the light out, but leaves enough punch to reach the opposite side of the set. Such light crosses over the people who are standing directly underneath.

To control such lighting, one puts a border of cardboard strips around the ceiling to shade the walls.

Dark panelling, typical for courtroom and boardroom sets or locations, is notorious for "sucking up" light. There are two ways to bring up their appearance: side lighting for texture or reflecting into them large white surfaces such as Griffolyn.

COMBINING HARD AND SOFT LIGHTING

Ideally, a variety of softness and direction in lighting is needed.

Haskell Wexler, ASC

The degree of soft lighting is something to consider. You can light it with hard lights but put either a Croniecone on each unit or a Spun Glass. Spun glass is not supersoft but it is not hard either. There are degrees of soft light. For combining soft light with the punch-through hard light, you have zingers. Any directional light can be a zinger. In Coming Home, I had a soft-lit set with strong daylight coming in. The highlights were two, three or four stops overexposed, which is the way daylight is. I think that it is more interesting this way. A soft light is basically boring. If you see a film that is all soft-lit, it puts you to sleep. In order to keep it from being utterly bland you take some other units, still soft with some direction to it, so that instead of having a face evenly lit from the top with one cheek getting exactly as much as the other cheek, there will be a modelling light like a key light. It would not be hard but more as if a practical lamp was lit nearby. This also helps to clean up the eyes.

Sometimes this overall soft light comes from a side. For example, Sven Nykvist (ASC),

likes to establish the general level of exposure with a large soft source from one side. For this purpose, Nykvist likes to bounce light off the foam-core boards positioned as high as the stands will permit. For a day interior situation, the window often will become the large soft source from one side. In such a case, it will probably have the function of a key light. If there is a ceiling over a set, Nykvist will often bounce a nice fill light off it.

Richmond Aguilar has worked as Nykvist's gaffer on several films. He pays great attention to fill light in general. He feels that it is more critical than is usually considered, especially for the background. On the subject of fill light coming from above he has this observation:

Richmond Aguilar

When you use an overhead fill, you do not have a shadow running across the back wall when somebody walks through, because you are not filling from the camera position. You are filling from the overhead. It gives you just what you need in the set and it gives a nice rim on things.

Aguilar explains the intricacies of the proper use of fill light.

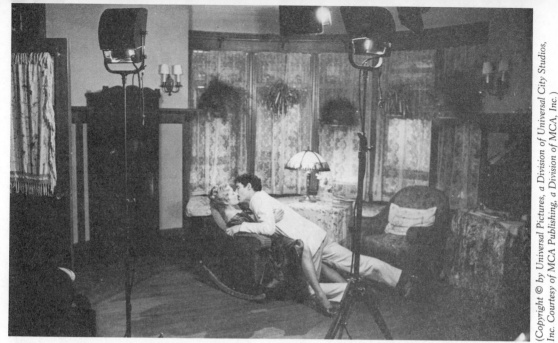

This production photo illustrates the use of small 750-watt soft lights to provide the fill for this evening scene. *Sophie's Choice*, Nestor Almendros (ASC), cinematographer.

If you are close to the person at a table and you fill him just right and it falls off to the background, the background starts getting muddy. So, you put your main fill light further back or you have a second fill light so it does not fall off that fast. It is more critical than people think. Hollywood theory is to fill from the direction of the lens, but even Nykvist and other people will fill from the side opposite to the key, as long as it does not give a second nose shadow. You can move a fill light during the shot. If the fill light is big enough, you are not going to have a shadow. The movement of light might show a little bit on your foreground furniture, for example, but you can cut it off with a flag. If you are moving fill light, it is because you usually have somebody pretty close to the camera and if there is that much movement that close, you can get away with an awful lot. We have always one light stand with wheels on it for the fill light. Generally, stands with wheels

are just a nuisance on location, but I always have one for the fill light.

There is one more place where you can have your fill light source. A white card can be put on the floor to reflect the overhead lighting into the face. Sometimes the floor can be painted white for such a purpose.

On sets with low ceilings, the light bounced off the ceiling may become too bright for an actor standing directly under the strongest reflection. In such a case, a black net can be suspended horizontally above his head to cut down the intensity.

On occasion the fill light can be greatly reduced if the shadows are visually enhanced with the use of Lightflex® (described in Chapter Three). It is especially useful when large background areas would otherwise require several arcs. Nykvist used Lightflex to bring out the detail in the facade of the Louvre when it was in the background of a scene in *Swann in Love*.

USING PRACTICAL LAMPS

Night scene lighting is most often built around the lights visible in the scene, known as practicals. This is the area where cinematographers and art directors cooperate very closely. Especially when using softer sources to light the scene, one depends on the practicals to add the highlight effects to create a wider range of brightnesses. Sometimes a practical lamp is positioned outside the frame but in such configuration that it will be reflected in some glass surfaces, like a picture frame, to add more visual interest to the scene. Practical lamps will justify our lighting angles.

James Crabe, ASC

Usually, if there is a choice of a couple of lamps in the room, you can pretty much cheat almost anything. But I guess that the more light you add, the less effective the light is. A room usually looks more romantic and cozy if there is one light going and every time you add another one, it tends to diminish that

charm. I think that it is really important, particularly when working in the sets.

Often the practicals are put on dimmers to control their brightness. This way they can be used more effectively as actual lighting sources. The practicals in the frame can be reduced in intensity and the practicals out of frame can be boosted to provide sufficient light for proper exposure without upsetting the balance in the frame. This is not always possible.

Jordan Cronenweth, ASC

If you have a situation, for example, at night when there is one light in the center of the room and that is the only light source that you want to have there, obviously if you kept the light source down in intensity so that the photograph would be normal looking, you would have not enough light to carry people a few feet away from light. In that case, you would let the practical be bright. If it is a few

Here, the practical light is augmented by a soft overhead source and fill light from the right and left sides. Careful examination of the shadows and highlights enables one to interpret the lighting plot. *Sophie's Choice*, Nestor Almendros (ASC), cinematographer.

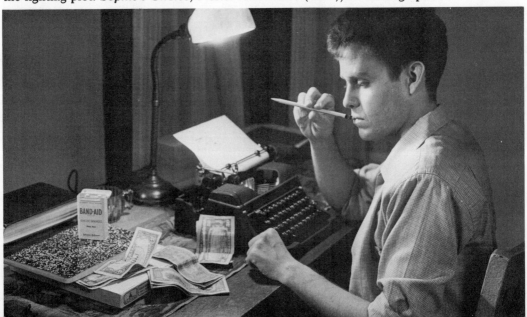

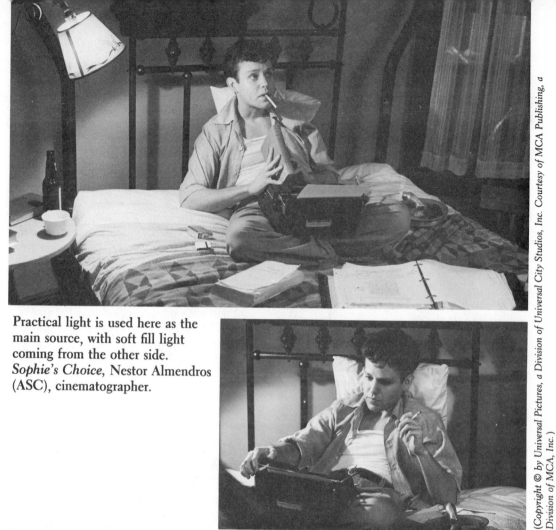

Practical light is used here as the
main source, with soft fill light
coming from the other side.
Sophie's Choice, Nestor Almendros
(ASC), cinematographer.

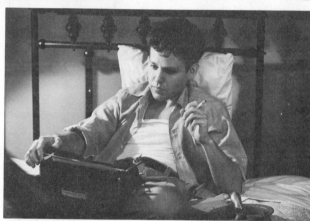

The same set in daylight. The shadow pattern on the bed and wall indicates a window and
motivates the direction of the key light. *Sophie's Choice*, Nestor Almendros (ASC),
cinematographer.

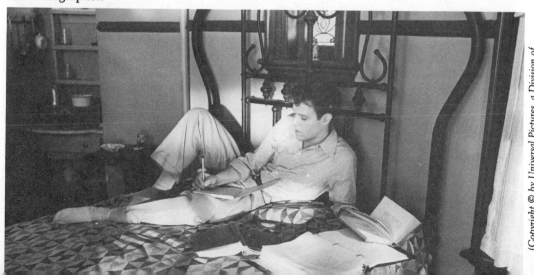

stops overexposed it makes very little difference in the overall look of the scene. It also depends on the area in the composition that it occupies. Assuming that you have a long shot initially, the globe will occupy a very small area of the room. You would set it up so that you will have dark things in the foreground, perhaps, depending on the kind of effect that you want to go for, the foreground objects will be silhouetted, the center room objects will be cross-lit from the globe and the back objects behind the light source will be more or less flat-lit depending on how far away they are. I would not worry about the flare from the globe. Generally speaking, if there is a flare you can see it. A halo would be acceptable. It would be a visual element to the scene. Now let's make it even more interesting. Let's have them get into a fight around this lamp that is maybe sitting on the floor and they knock it over and the bulb goes out. You have to be able to see something, so even if there is no other light source in the scene, you have to take dramatic license.

Practicals are very difficult to judge. They always photograph at least a hundred percent brighter than they appear. In night interiors, when the practicals are all in proper balance, it looks very dim and muddy to the eye.

When you are using a lamp as a light source as well as compositional element, the part of the lamp that is facing toward the camera can sometimes be darkened with nets in a lampshade, so that the part that the camera sees is two stops below the back part which may be lighting someone behind the lamp. Or, you can hang little light bulbs on the back of the lampshade.

MANIPULATING PRACTICALS

This tiny peanut bulb can also be placed behind a wine decanter or glass teapot to make the liquid sparkle. Bright sources, like bare bulbs, are usually darkened with a brown hairspray. Hairspray is an invaluable accessory for the cinematographer.

Michael D. Margulies, ASC

When a practical is too hot, a brown hairspray can possibly take it down. A can of Streaks 'n' Tips® is always a couple of feet away from the camera. Also, a beige masking tape can be used on chandeliers or other practical lights. It allows the light to come through but it softens it. It is a masking tape in 1 inch or 2 inch depending on the size of a lamp. For example, on flame-shaped bulbs, you will stick on a piece of tape the size of a nickel, just to cover the filament, the hot spot. Light goes through and around it and you cannot see the tape. A Scotch tape would be like a half single net. Masking tape is like a full single net.

Richmond Aguilar

Streaks 'n' Tips hairspray washes out very well and dries very quickly. You can use it on hot globes. We use it primarily to darken the camera side of a light; for example, a bare bulb hanging over a poker table. You keep spraying it till it looks good through the camera.

SPECIAL PRACTICALS

Some portable practical lights—lanterns, candles, and flashlights—require special attention. As with all practicals, the main problem is to make the visible source not too bright for the latitude of the film emulsion and at the same time to produce enough light to illuminate the subject close to this source. Let's start with the lantern.

James Plannette

Fix a Mini Mole socket with an Inky bulb on the back of the lantern, away from the camera, and hopefully hide the cable; for example, up the sleeve and always on a Variac. When you put a globe inside the lantern and do all the necessary things, like frosting the glass, and you have it on a Variac or dimmer and fluctuate the light, it still looks like what it really is. So it is better to have the normal wick inside the lantern and the bulb behind the lantern.

When, for staging and lighting reasons we decide to use a bulb inside the lantern instead of a wick, we will put an 85 gel sleeve around the bulb or paint the bulb orange-yellow.

Gaffers devise very ingenious ways of making lanterns look real. Hal Trusell who worked with cinematographer Nestor Almendros (ASC) describes the preparation of such lanterns ("Lighting *Goin' South*," *American Cinematographer*, March 1979). They scraped vertical lines on the painted bulb. The bulb was inside the transparent chimney sprayed heavily with dulling spray on the camera side. To add realism they would create the effect of a smoking wick by dropping smoldering bits of incense into the lantern's chimney. These lanterns were operated on AC run through a household dimmer. The portable lanterns, equipped with a tiny Philips #12336 bulb in place of the lantern's wick, were run on small 12-volt batteries made by Yamaha and hidden in the lantern's bottom.

Generally, the lanterns themselves will not be adequate to light the scene and some, usually smaller units, will be employed. These lamps will be gelled to match the lanterns and often will be moved during the shot.

Harry Wolf, ASC

I am working now on a period set, so all my night interiors are in a lantern light. So we have lanterns with peanut bulbs hidden behind, and I put 54 gels on all the lamps. Characters in the picture, when they walk with a candle, are followed by light. I have done it many ways. For example, I have done it with a fellow with a light on a shoulder walking alongside the actor. These are things that you learn as you go along. You cannot learn these things in school.

Often there is an elaborate setup of lights on dimmers that are modulated depending on the movements of the actor carrying the lantern. Moving shots, of course, require proper staging so that the lantern is carried on one side to hide a "gimmick" bulb. The camping industry can also provide us with practical lanterns.

Jordan Cronenweth, ASC

The Coleman lantern is a nice light source but it will burn out the film tolerance. You can age the front side of the lamp, or a net can be inserted in the shade.

Some scripts require candles on the set. There are a variety of ways to handle this problem.

Jordan Cronenweth, ASC

There is also a special candle that is hollow and has space-age insulation and gimmick globe. There is a slot in the back of this candle. But the best is a real thing so shoot tests with a real candle. Maybe a thicker wick will give more light. For ambient light in the room, bounce amber light off a card or ceiling above the actor's head.

There are also practical candles fitted with a tiny globe which stays behind the wick and is hidden by the flame. In this case, the wick is especially thick.

There are several modern solutions to the practical flashlight problem. Sport shops sell powerful flashlights for divers that work on higher voltage than the bulb is designed for. This provides more light output and cuts down the life of the bulb to 1½ hours. Then there are flashlights available with krypton gas bulbs. Usually a propman will provide the practical flashlight.

Jordan Cronenweth, ASC

Using a flashlight is a matter of staging. Color temperature does not matter with flashlights.

Actors can do a lot to help the cameraman. You can hide white cards in places where the flashlight will be directed.

Let's now look at a lamp which is essentially a soft light, but under certain circumstances can become a practical. It is known as a Japanese Lantern. It is basically a large, round, white paper lampshade with a light bulb inside. It gives a very nice soft light and it can be easily positioned on the end of a pole wherever it is needed. Should it reflect in some glass surface in the frame, it will pass for a practical light on the set.

Caleb Deschanel, ASC

In Being There I used Japanese lanterns basically as a replacement for lampshades because

An interior location lit by the Japanese lanterns and practical lamps on the tables. This basic lighting scheme may be complemented with some more directional lights for particular camera angles.

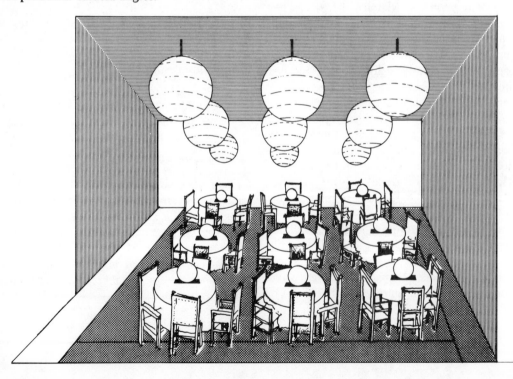

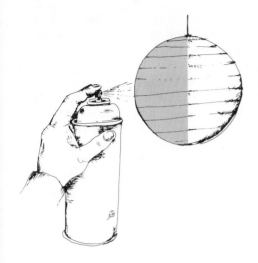

Japanese lantern sprayed on the side to control its light output and direction.

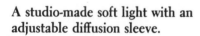

A studio-made soft light with an adjustable diffusion sleeve.

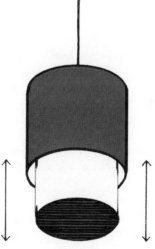

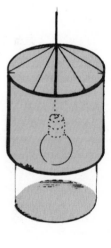

they were a lot easier to put in place. You can hang it from the ceiling more easily than you could a lamp. They were never in frame. You could take a cheap Japanese lantern and you could spray paint a quarter of it black or half or three-quarters of it black, and you could control the shape of the source a bit more than you could if you were using fixed lights. What happens is, that lots of times you will get into a situation where you have a Baby with diffusion in front of it and then you have all these flags and everything else. And this is something that you can literally put at the end of a C-stand and hang down, and by putting a wire on it, you can control its direction. And, if you've got reflections from it, you wouldn't be getting reflections of something that would be bothersome, you get the reflection of some round object that could be a lampshade. Sometimes you will get into a situation where you have no control over what you're getting in way of reflections. When you cannot control it I always prefer something that has a certain logic.

Sometimes practical lamps help in creating false perspective on the set.

Caleb Deschanel, ASC

In Being There we were supposedly in the Washington Post newsroom. It was a much smaller room and my gaffer, Gary Holt, built some lights that were just triangles which continued after the perspective of the overhead fluorescents. When you looked at it, it looked like the fluorescents went on forever, but in reality they just ended. There were just lights that came down at an angle. We simply adjusted this angle to be the same as the perspective in the ceiling. So you have the light that is vertical but it is a "V" shape, so that when you see it on film and it is lined up perfectly, it appears as if the lights go off into the distance. I am sure it has been done hundreds of times before but it was new for me.

(Fluorescent tubes are the most visible practicals in many buildings, but because of the color temperature problem, they were discussed in Chapter Three.)

MIRRORS

Glass walls and mirrors are perpetual headaches for lighting people. We all know that the angle of incidence equals the angle of reflection so the lamps that are positioned from the camera side will reflect more easily. The camera itself may be a problem as well. The cooperation of the production designer is absolutely essential in overcoming these obstacles.

Jordan Cronenweth, ASC

Mirrors are time-consuming and make the production more expensive. Use low camera angles. Work with the set designer. Light from lower positions. Otherwise, there may come a 'trap time' when a wide shot will make positioning lights very difficult.

John Alonzo, ASC

On Scarface, the production designer put all the mirrors on gimbals, so I could tip them one way or the other and throw the reflections in a different direction.

There are sets where it is almost impossible to prevent the camera and lights from reflecting on glass walls. In such situations a two-way mirror is the practical answer.

Caleb Deschanel, ASC

In Being There we did an interesting scene; we built a set for when Peter Sellers is being made up for the television show. It was all mirrors and it was impossible to be inside the room without actually seeing yourself. So we actually made one end of it from a two-way glass and shot through that. No matter where you looked, you would not see the camera because the camera was actually filming through the mirror.

PROCESS SHOTS

One of the important facilities offered by the sound stage is back and front projection. Generally known as process or process shot or process screen, it allows for the combination of previously filmed background footage projected on a screen with the live action in front of it. Lighting for process correctly is a matter of keeping the light off the screen and balancing the foreground and the background in brightness.

Ralph Woolsey, ASC

When using back projection you must keep all front light off the screen, so you would avoid soft lighting. With high-speed films it is possible when desired to keep the screen a little farther from the foreground because of increased depth of field. More space between the subject and the screen makes it easier to shadow the screen.

James Plannette

Balance of lighting is most important. When on an exterior, people in the foreground are brighter than the background, the scene looks like a bad process. That is what happens in a process scene: they overlight the foreground and people are actually edged from the background and it looks phony. But you can make it look like a bad process shot by just lighting the foreground too much.

In shooting a helicopter, they used a back projection screen behind the helicopter and then used another projection screen behind the camera, so it was reflected in the bubble of the helicopter, which really gave a feeling of reality. You can do the same with an automobile where it will be reflected in the windshield. On a low budget film, you can do it with a mirror so the rear screen projection is
then reflected in the mirror which bounces back into the windshield. It is not an idea way but it works also.

A process system known as front projection uses a high-reflectance screen material, such as Scotchlight made by the 3M Company. This screen consists of millions of flint glass bead lenses, enabling it to reflect over 200 times more light than is reflected by someone's white shirt. Furthermore, virtually all the light is reflected directly back to the source. A very thin, optically perfect glass is placed at a 45° angle to combine the optical axes of the camera and the projector. When the camera and projector are perfectly aligned and equipped with compatible lenses, the image from the projector is reflected by the optical glass onto the screen. The screen returns almost all the light back through the glass into the camera. Because of the high-gain reflection, the projection can be of low intensity and will therefore not show on the actor. Because the camera and projector are aligned on the same optical axis, the actor's body will cover his own shadow.

Compared to back projection, lighting front projection is much easier. Because the high-reflectance screen reflects lights back into their own source in a very narrow angle, there is no need to worry much about side lights washing out your projected background. Even a conventional 45° key light presents no problem because any of its light that happens to hit the screen will not be reflected into the projector/camera. If anywhere, it will be sent back to the key light.

There are many good uses for high-reflectance screens. For example, you can make a moon out of it for the backdrop and project a small light source into it from the camera direction, or you can have a costume made of

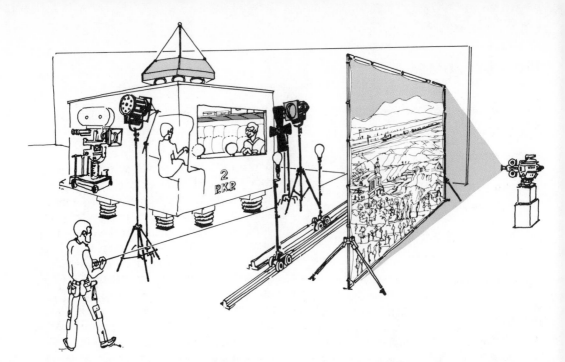

These two drawings illustrate a sophisticated lighting design for a train compartment scene shot against a back projected night exterior. The train interior is softly lit by an overhead light diffused through a bleached muslin ceiling and by a fill light mounted over the window and bounced off a white card positioned next to the camera. Outside effects are created by rotating blades which produce moving shadows and by lights that are moved during the shot (similar to Jordan Cronenweth's solution to this problem in *Best Friends*).

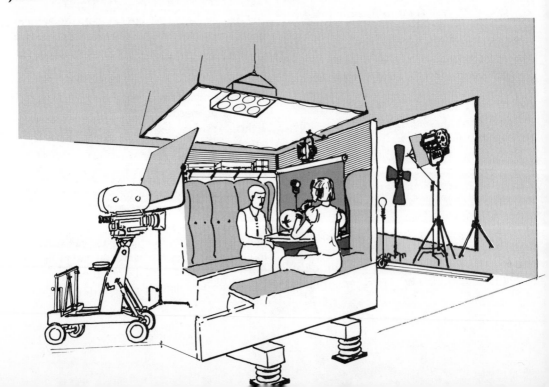

this material and project some effects onto it or parts of the costume painted with this substance.

Jordan Cronenweth described to me such an application used in *Altered States*. To cre-

ate a particular effect on Emily's body, bubbling water was underlit with color gels and filmed. This was then projected slightly out of focus onto a bodysuit Emily wore that had veins painted on it with Scotchlight.

LIGHTING FACES

The human face is the most studied subject that ever appeared before the lens or on the painter's canvas. Still photographers and painters before them worked out several ways of minimizing certain features of the human

face and augmenting others. The general direction and angle of the key light will establish the mood in which the face is lit. Over the years we have seen countless angelic maidens haloed by light from above as well as

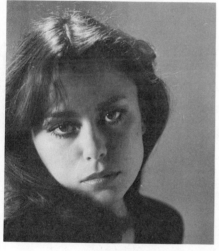

A close-up lit by a soft light key which is also bounced off the foam-core board to provide the fill. Backlight comes from a hard Fresnel source.

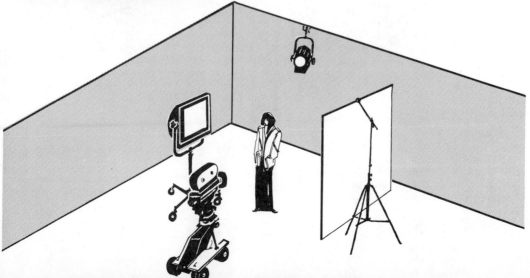

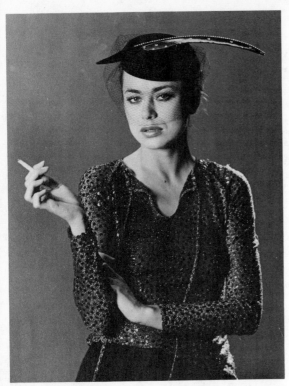

The same lighting design with additional kicker and eyelight.

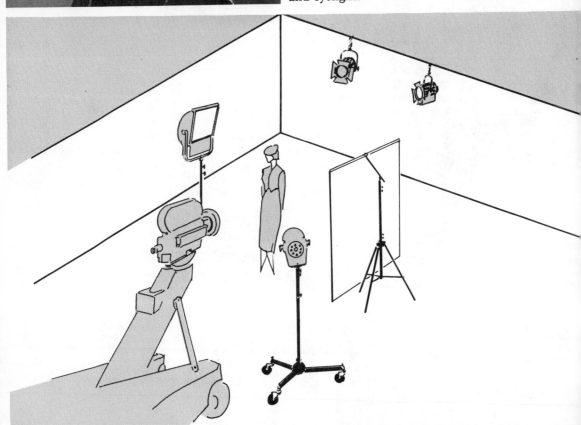

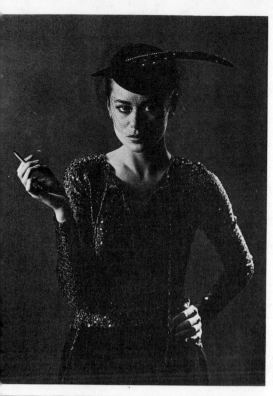

The same lighting design, but the white
foam-core board is replaced by a black gobo.

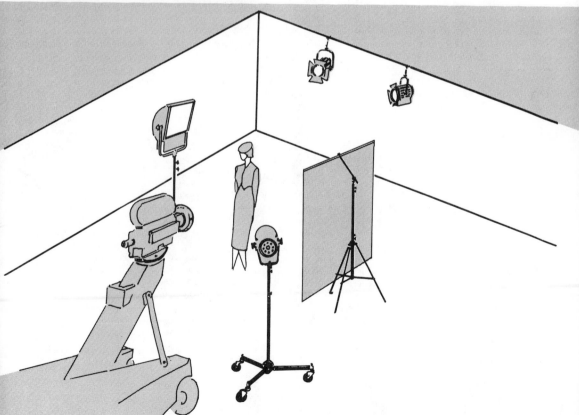

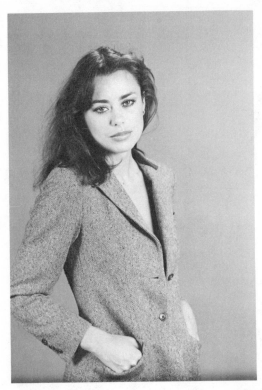

This close-up is lit by two soft lights further diffused through Tough Frost plastic material. Backlight remains hard as in the previous setups.

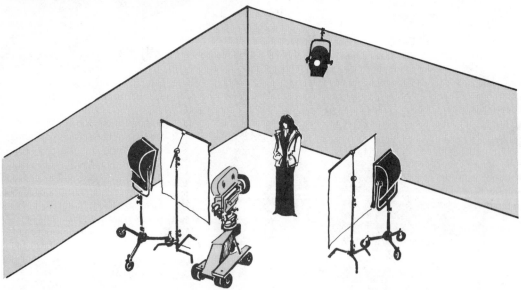

Jezebels who are always lit from a low angle. As the saying goes, good people are lit from heaven and the bad people are lit from hell. These cliches are not as obvious in today's more natural and often softer lighting, yet the angles of light and the composition of light in the frame remain as the most powerful tools for the creation of mood and for the shaping of the actor's face.

Many techniques employed in the past are still useful to the cinematographer who has a more difficult problem to solve than the still photographer. His subject moves.

Conrad Hall, ASC

We are dealing with moving pictures and people are in various positions and in many different kinds of light. They cannot be in the same type of light unless you soft light them. Then there is no problem. But if you have a person by a window in bright light and then you take him to a corner in dim light, and you make him turn on the light, then you have those three different equations to deal with. You might have a hard half-light on him and then you might have a no-light look when you see his face in a soft dimness and then he comes in and turns on the light and he is very brightly lit.

The best way to learn how to light the human face, whether it is stationary or moving, is through experimentation. The still camera, Super 8 film or video are all affordable tools for such studies. Even careful observation of people in everyday light can be helpful.

Conrad Hall, ASC

I work with the person. If a person is meant to be unattractive, then you are lighting for unattractiveness. I study the actors' faces very carefully. I watch them like a hawk all the time when they are drinking coffee, talking to anybody else, moving around. I try to imbue myself with the qualities that I find and the things that happen by accident in nature that appeal to me and apply to the type of lighting used for the story.

Actors are often sensitive about particular features. Any of these "flaws" can be diminished or accentuated to serve the story.

John Alonzo, ASC

If a person has a double chin and is conscious about it and doesn't want to show it, you raise the key up higher and put a dark shadow under the chin. If they have a bump on one side of the nose, you try to keep the key on the other side. If they have a large nose, you try to shoot them straight on. There are a lot of different little tricks, but the actor has to be cooperative to do that. They have to be aware of that.

One rule of thumb is to position the light side of the face against the darker background to define the shape of the face and to create separation and depth. Wall color and brightness can cause the face to blend into the wall. Rarely is this a desired effect. Should you wish to deemphasize a bald head or large ears, the above may be useful. When lighting an actor with these features, be careful with the back light, or avoid it altogether. You can also use nets to keep them in shadow. Sometimes a round face needs extra attention.

Richmond Aguilar

When you deal with a round face and you do not want to accentuate it, usually you will go high with your light which brings up the top of the face and the light falls off at the cheekbones giving you a longer shape of the face.

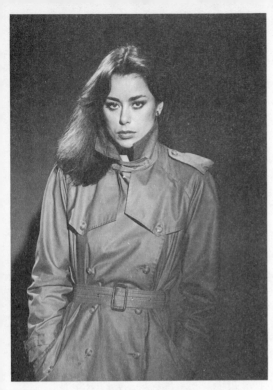

The key light, eyelight, kicker and backlight are all Fresnel lights in this setup.

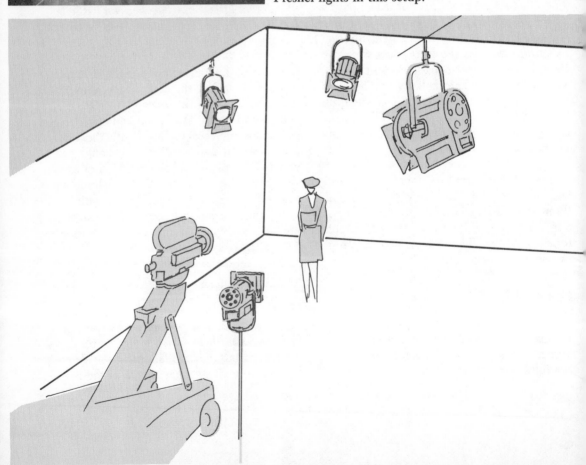

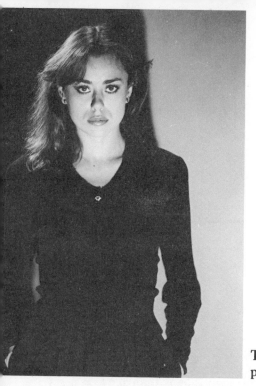

The floor angle key and high angle kicker are positioned on the same axis.

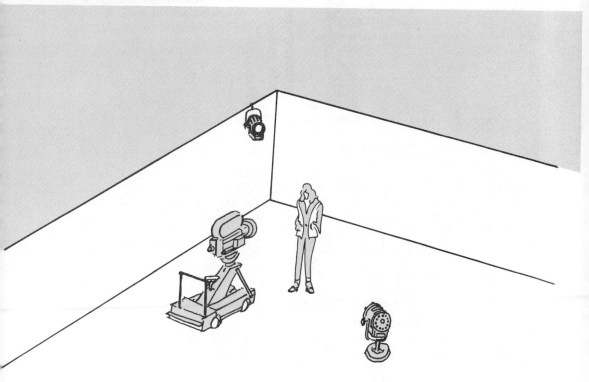

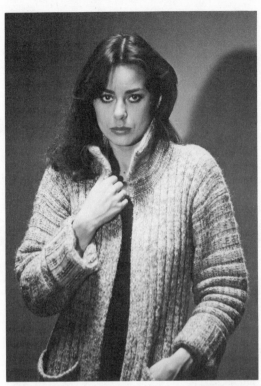

A soft light is hung from above as a key.
Additional eyelight is used on the stand to
accentuate the eyes.

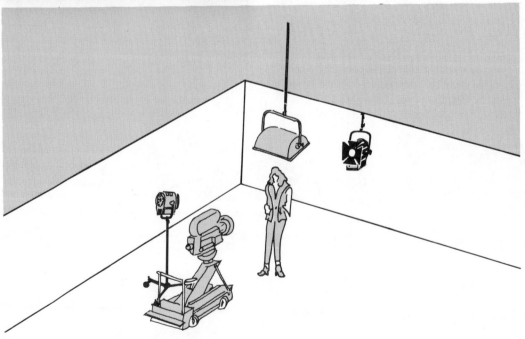

FILM LIGHTING

You would not come up from the front with a soft light, because that makes the face even flatter and rounder with the light clear back to the ears.

One soon learns that deep-set eyes and large noses are usually the main problems to deal with and these are the features most commented on by the cinematographers interviewed.

Ralph Woolsey, ASC

Sometimes you get problems like deep-set eyes, or heavy eyebrows. Some performers cannot stand light very well, particularly outdoors, and they squint, and need help in opening their eyes. You may have to set up an overhead butterfly or other scrim, or take the sun off and replace it with another source. Reflectors are impossible for some to face, especially if such persons are not used to them.

Once on a western, we had a leading actor who wore one of those hats with a straight brim, pulled down right over his eyes. To fill the eyes in the outdoor scenes I started to use a small hand-held reflector, down under the camera lens. And he said, "No, no, you cannot use that. I can't stand it." I was a little surprised because he was an experienced actor, but I replied, "OK, but you'll look like a raccoon if I don't." We then agreed not to use it, and look at the dailies for proof. Of course nobody could see his eyes on the screen, and he agreed to the reflector right away. We could not always get the best angle for using that reflector directly from the sun, so once in a while we directed a mirror into it. The reflector was small and soft, and I would ease it on gradually for comfort.

Try to prevent a kicker light from hitting the nose. If the light is just hitting the tip of a nose that has some irregularity, the result might be annoying in a close-up. By having a person turn slightly, you sometimes get a nice line along the length of the nose, and if straight it looks okay. But to avoid that one little angle that might look bad during the action, you work to get the light around to a better position. Fortunately, women often have enough hair to keep us out of trouble with nose kicks. But since performers do move in movies, we can't lock them in one gorgeous angle anyway; however we do relight for close-ups and try to restrict movement in these. In films of the twenties and thirties, actors were often fixed in beautifully lit positions, and cinematographers even used burned-out gauzes which would diffuse the image around a person, which would greatly restrict movement. The wide screen and freedom to move around have required more flexibility in lighting, and some compromise.

Richmond Aguilar

Generally you are concerned about the eyes, how to get the light into the eyes most effectively. For deeply set eyes, you have to light fairly low and to the front. You cannot go around to the side with your light and very high, because the eyes will be shadowed. The bridge of the nose is also a feature to be careful about because you might be able to get the light into the eyes from a certain position, only to see that it gives a bad nose shadow. Then you have to compromise with that. Generally, you try to avoid the kicker hitting the tip of the nose at all costs. It is this hot spot in the middle of the face and we are not used to it. A long diagonal nose shadow is also not too flattering. Soft light softens the prominence of that shadow. We do an awful lot of lighting with a soft light. Even at night we have been doing more soft light work than so-called hard night scenes. We would use soft light on the principal actors and hard light maybe on the walls to control the set. Soft lighting the action, eliminates the obtrusive shadows when actors move, so that you do not have shadows busily playing around in the picture.

Michael D. Margulies, ASC

A nose shadow does not stay the same because the actor or actress is not long enough in that position to put that shadow in a specific place. Several times I have asked an actor or actress to look only in a certain direction so that the shadow would stay at a certain angle. Many times I have gotten cooperation and then many times I have not. They do not want to be tied down. The new school of contemporary actors does not want to be restricted. In the early days of Hollywood, before the development of the soft light as we know it, in the dramatic, directional style of lighting, the actors were much more restricted in their movements and head positions.

When a kicker catches the tip of the nose it is always brought to my attention by the gaffer or the grip. Usually it does not bother me, in fact it is a little sparkle, a little highlight, that looks nice. Now, this is basically on men. I do take more care of the ladies and I try to avoid that. Another thing to watch out for when lighting women from a side with a hard light, is the shadow from long eyelashes. To me it is an ugly line on the bridge of her nose and that bothers me. Then I will go with my key up and fuller. It is hard to sidelight a lady with long eyelashes without getting that line.

The only anatomy of the face that is a problem for the cinematographer is the eye socket. When the eyes are deep set, then very often you have to come up with an eyelight. The top light or a ceiling bounced light will give you dark "wells." Some actors with experience know that they have that type of an eye and they will be aware of an eyelight or a lack

of one. For an eyelight, I just use an Inky with barndoors closed and taped on the edge and with some diffusion.

When dealing with older, more difficult to light female faces, it is wise to make tests in advance.

Philip Lathrop, ASC

You generally do it when you make a hair test or a wardrobe test. You do a makeup test at the same time. The makeup test is really for a cameraman.

One way to light a close-up of a woman with many wrinkles, is to take a 10K far away, frontal and up, and cover it with diffusion on the light and then a few feet away put another diffusion in front of it. It gives a good modeling and soft shadows. By using a 10K, I get the light which goes right around the face.

There are times when the mood of the scene does not allow for a full frontal lighting. In such circumstances, Lathrop suggests minimizing wrinkles by lighting the face at a half-key level and adding a kicker at full key value. He also uses lots of shadows on faces like that, such as putting a net across a part of the face.

James Crabe, ASC

To help the problem of aging actresses, you do it the old way: you put the key light over the lens, maybe you soften it a little bit, but not too much because you still want maybe the underside of the chin to go dark. Sometimes using soft light is not the most glamorous way of lighting women. At least on Mae West, in Sextet, we tried to use a rather hard frontal key and some Mitchell-type diffusion on the lens. I shot some test shots with Mae. When she saw them, she said, I need more

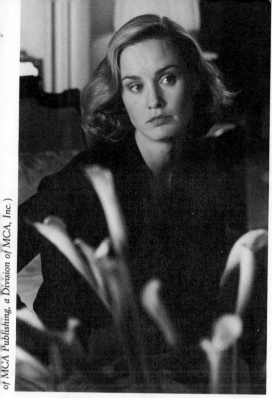

For this night interior lighting, a soft 4K light was used to create a soft, yet quite directional lighting. Jessica Lange in *Frances*, Laszlo Kovacs (ASC), cinematographer.

light on my eyes and my teeth. When you think about eyes and teeth you realize that you can lose them if you have key lights too high. We all know that a real high key light makes dark sockets but in older people, sometimes their teeth are withdrawn back behind the lip. If you do not get the light low, you do not see the teeth. It is hard to beat that rule: To keep the light low, keep it over the lens, maybe slightly in the direction the person is looking—the old Hollywood kind of lighting, with some nice fill coming from the camera side.

Another kind of Hollywood edict about close-ups of women is that you never shoot them looking down; you never shoot with a low camera; not to say that I haven't. You have people sitting around a table; you want a dynamic shot so maybe you have a low camera and you are looking up slightly. Very often these ladies who are camerawise get very nervous when they see a camera down

below and they will say, "Oh, put the camera up." Now maybe a cameraman will say, "No, this is very good, we are going to relight this," or the director will say, "Believe me, Betty, it looks great"; but generally speaking they get very nervous when the camera is down, because whenever they look down, their jowls come out and the fold-up double chins and all that stuff. Whereas in the traditional movie two-shot, a man and a woman standing together, the woman is always looking up, the man is always looking down and he has a little more rugged key light. This is Hollywood lighting. So already the face is pulled to a good position. The key light is very close to the lens and above it usually with some nice fill coming through. That is how they often like to see themselves, and often maybe remember themselves. It must be very tough on some of these ladies to see themselves on the reruns on television and then look in the mirror.

Von Sternberg claimed to have invented everything including Marlene Dietrich and Marlene Dietrich lighting. He used a very exotic effect achieved by putting a very sharp, unfiltered light up high in front to bring out the cheekbones and the nose shadow, sometimes called the butterfly shadow.

In the old close-ups you see the shadow of each individual eyelash. It was really sharp, and of course being sharp the light could be cut off the hair and off the clothing and just have that wonderful glowing madonna light coming at you. It is just a matter of putting the light in precisely the right position; but the higher a key goes, the more accurately the head has to be placed to keep that effect on.

Traditionally it seems that the most interesting placement of key lights for defining the planes of the face is rather like architectural lighting on the building. Usually you see a building in three-quarters with the one side diminishing sharply. The key light, or the sun, will hit from outside and will leave the shadow side toward the camera. Of course, this is a type of light that painters use a lot in their effects and it delineates the planes of the face. However, with some women you cannot go that far. You suddenly realize that even though it is aesthetically correct and renders the subject in the way you like to see them, there is a scar that shows now, or something that was not visible before, so you cheat it around to the front. Of course a lot of old movies would pretty much disregard the lighting continuity and people never even knew it. The key light would be one way for the master shot or the two-shot and then you cut in and the key is now on the other side. I am not quite sure if you can get away with that today. If the key light is a small Fresnel light, it is going to cast a different kind of highlight on the face rather than a big one. If there is any moisture on the face and you are using a very large reflector, it can cast kind of a phantom reflection over much of the face. Instead of getting a snappy, more concise shadow, such a reflector can produce a skeletal effect.

There is a peculiar problem when lighting some leading actresses that has more to do with psychology than with lighting.

Jordan Cronenweth, ASC

There have been leading ladies down through the years that have been told by directors and/or cameramen that they look better from this side than the other and when they get power, they end up insisting that they should be photographed from that side. I would hate to work with someone like that. That would be a terrible pain in the neck for a cameraman and a horrible problem for a director, always having to stage for that, to make people walk around in a funny way in order to end up with her on the right and him on the left.

Of course, some leading men are just as difficult to work with.

Beware also of actors who put on their own makeup. They're not as consistent as the professionals. The makeup artist is the cinematographer's ally. It is important to coordinate the makeup of the actors appearing in the same scene to avoid lighting problems.

LIGHTING FOR SKIN TONES

The true test of a cinematographer's lighting skills comes when he or she has to deal with actors vastly differing in their skin tones. When a multiracial cast appears in one scene, the brightness range considerations are tremendous. On top of that, different skin textures require different amounts of light.

John Alonzo, ASC

You have to consider different variations in color among black people. You have some black people who have a lot of blue that comes out of their skin, so you have to use a warm light, and eyelight to change it. There are some black people who have very, very reddish-brownish skin. You may use a piece of half-blue on the lights just to bring them back to balance, but when a black person and a white person are standing next to each other, it is not a matter of adding more light to a black person, it is taking light off the white person.

Conrad Hall, ASC

As a cinematographer you have to deal photographically with people of different skin colors in one scene. If the black skin is absorbing the light, you have to put some lotion on the skin to create reflective quality. As soon as you have moisture, you have the reflective quality. Then, when you have some light bounced off the white card behind you, a black person's skin will reflect the quality of that light. You will get exposure without adding any more light. It is a question of makeup. I do not do anything different for black people than I do for white people except when somebody's skin is dry and has no reflective quality.

Michael D. Margulies, ASC

I light black people with an orange light, using for example ½ MTs or full MTs [gels]. I would not use kicker lights in this case. Outside, an incandescent tungsten light without correction would give the warm light that complements the dark skin. I would not want the shine. In a mixed group it may balance out when the black person is lit and the white one is underlit. It is the same with a white dress next to a black dress.

James Plannette

One of the great fallacies about lighting black people is that you have to light them on a kick-angle in order to see them. What happens is that you light a black surface, whether it is a face, or a wall, or a piano. Anything like that with either a kicker or a backlight will, as a surface, go blue. If you light somebody with black hair, his hair turns blue. So then if you put an amber gel on the light, it becomes normal again. The only thing that black people need is more light. It is as simple as that. It doesn't have to come from any particular direction. It just has to be more. There are all sorts of skin tones. When you photograph children, they don't require nearly as much light as adults. Children tend to be very fair, so using your meter on a child or a black person is ridiculous because it does not matter what the meter says. So, you light somebody who's got sort of an average white skin tone and you balance the other by eye. The problem is when, for example, one of us here is black and the other is not and now we are photographing the scene and we got the balance just right. All of a sudden, for some reason, we switch chairs. Big problem! Say that I am a white person. My light is covered with a silk and your light is open. And then we switch; this silk comes off and another one on the opposite lamp comes on. Silk generally would do it.

Such light change may also be created with dimmers if the color shift caused by dimming is acceptable.

CLOSE-UP ACCESSORIES

When lighting faces we have to deal with hairstyles, with wardrobe and particularly with eyeglasses.

James Crabe, ASC

It is really tricky. I think it is really important that the cameraman on the movie makes sure that he sees the glasses people are going to wear before the picture starts. Maybe he could drop in a couple of words about hairstyles, too. Lots of times the hairstyle is so elaborate or wild that you cannot see the actress from a profile position.

Glasses can be a problem, particularly with big soft sources that are low and close to the lens. Almost all of these glasses are convex. I find that sometimes you can bend the glasses a tiny bit forward, or sometimes lift them off the ear just a little bit. It is of course a big pain to the actor and nobody has much sympathy with you at these moments when sud-denly there is a massive reflection in the glasses and the director wants to shoot. With Marlon Brando on The Formula, John Avildsen, who directed the picture and who was a cameraman himself in the past, had Marlon Brando there bending his glasses. Marlon was very cooperative about the glasses problem, but he asked Avildsen, How does Woody Allen make a movie? If you are working with a specular light, hard light, and the key is very high up or very far to the side, then you get shadows of the glasses itself on the eyes. You try to add eyelight and then, of course, it is right in the middle of the glass if it is near the camera lens. So I think that it is important to check those things in advance. In the old days you would take the glass out of the lens but nobody believes that anymore. Sometimes we

To create the harsh sunlight penetrating this darkish room, an arc was pointed through the window. A soft light was used as the key. *Frances*, **Laszlo Kovacs (ASC), cinematographer.**

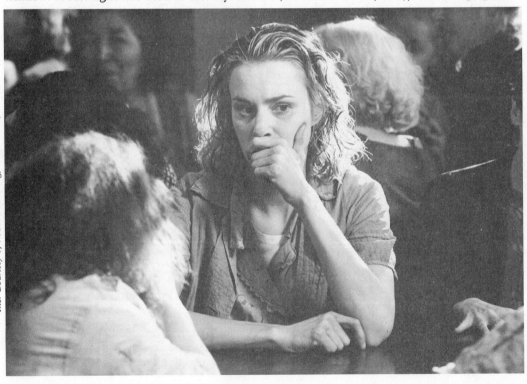

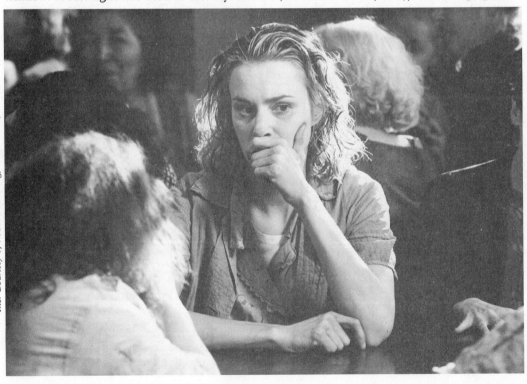

use flat glass. It gives you a little bit of a break because it does not reflect as large an area, but if you do go through the light then you really see it. The whole surface flashes on and off. It can be interesting. It is a difficult problem. The best that you can do is to get the key light as far up or as far around as you can get it without creating other problems. Sometimes glasses have to be pushed up to the face a little more or bent or played around with a little bit. I never tried anything like a Pola screen on the source and a Pola screen on the lens. You might be able to totally eliminate the reflections but of course that is not being realistic. Nobody has that kind of time anyway.

When a best compromise between the use of glasses and the most advantageous lighting has to be worked out, the production company will go to great lengths to provide the right glasses. Anything around the face can distract the eye.

Richmond Aguilar

On the last picture we had a glasses specialist. He had a kit full of glasses and he would shape them and bend them. They were flat and curved and had matching frames to work with. It may be as critical as that. If you are trying to make an actress look as pretty as possible, you want to put light in the most advantageous places. Glasses restrict the actor in relation to lighting because of all the reflections. But it gets to a point where worrying about glasses is not worth it if it restricts the actor too much. After three or four retakes of light reflections in the glasses, the actor loses his patience with it.

James Crabe, ASC

When you are doing close-ups of people, you see their hat, you see their collar, you see their tie, anything that comes within close proximity is very important to deal with. So often in films now the wardrobe person will come to a cameraman and say, Well, these new nurses' uniforms are all polyester and we cannot tech them down, we cannot gray them down. This happens all the time, so you say, okay, but it can be difficult, particularly if it encroaches on the face.

One solution to the problem is cutting a hole in the diffusion material to let more light through the middle. This brings up the face a little more than the light-colored dress.

EYELIGHT

The eyes are the windows of the soul, as the saying goes, and great care is taken to show the eyes of the protagonists. It is often necessary for the dramatics of the scene.

Caleb Deschanel, ASC

Sometimes you may not need to see the eyes to tell the story and then you may have other actors like the one I remember on The Black Stallion. We had this Italian actor in the poker game scene who came up to me and told me that he acted with his eyes. It was very important that we see his eyes. You do alter things to some extent based on the things you need to see. It is possible to use a hard light just to create a little dot in someone's eye, which brings out the eyes even if it does not create any exposure. You can bring the eye out of the darkness without increasing the exposure on the eye itself, because of the reflecting property of the eye.

Some lighting styles, like the overall soft light from above, will generally require eyelights more often. To obtain a clear sparkle in the eye, such light will usually be situated very close to the lens. But due to the curvature of the eye, some people's eyes will pick up an eyelight from the side as well. And some actors have to blink just before a take for more moisture in their eyes.

A small light mounted on the camera is traditionally known as an "Obie" light, because it was originally designed by the cinematographer Lucien Ballard for his actress wife, Merle Oberon. When this light is stronger, it can serve as a general fill light for a close-up, but often it is used at a very low intensity just to create glints in the eyes. Many times it will be a little Baby or an Inky Dink, with a lot of diffusion or scrims, or both.

Philip Lathrop, ASC

For an eyelight I use a little Inky Dink with a snoot on it. It is very soft. It does not fill the face. All it does is to reflect in the eye.

A sophisticated Panalite is often used. It is an eyelight made by Panavision with a 1000-watt quartz bulb. The intensity of Panalite can be varied by an ingenious reflector system which is made of metal rods half black and half white. When these rods are rotated, the amount of reflected light changes without affecting the color temperature which is the chief drawback with dimmers. This system is particularly useful when dollying in to a close-up and gradually diminishing the eyelight intensity. The only problem with Panalite is its tendency to jam when it overheats. It needs to be oiled. For an effect like cat's eyes in headlights, we can mount a 50 percent transmission front mirror at 45 degrees in front of the lens and shine a lamp into it. Light reflected by the mirror will hit the eye on the lens axis. By rigidly mounting the mirror and the lamp to the camera, we can execute pans and tilts with the light always staying on the optical axis of the lens. This

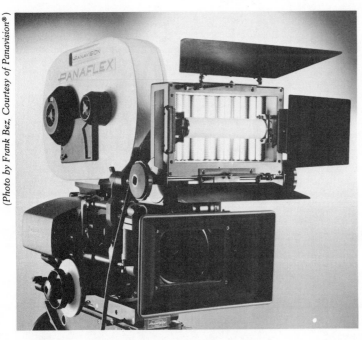

(Photo by Frank Bez, Courtesy of Panavision®)

Panalite. A sophisticated on-the-camera light with mechanical dimming which does not affect the color temperature of the light.

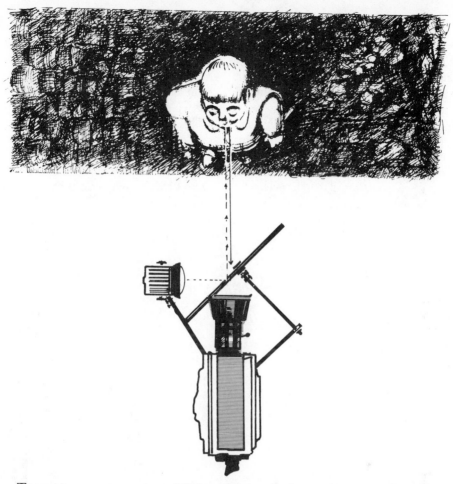

To create a very accentuated light reflection in the eye, the light must come on the optical axis of the lens. To obtain this condition a 50 percent surface mirror is mounted at a 45° angle in front of the lens, and an Inky lamp is pointed into it. A one-foot-square mirror and the lamp are rigidly mounted to the camera to remain in alignment during the camera moves.

method was used effectively by Jordan Cronenweth in *Blade Runner*.

The eyelight does not have to be circular. Using snoots and black masking tape, we can create other geometrical shapes. A strangely shaped eyelight can add a bizarre feeling to the scene. A special eyelight is of course superfluous if there is already a frontal fill light employed.

Richmond Aguilar

When you use a fill light close to the lens, it becomes your eyelight at the same time. With Laszlo Kovacs, we usually use a good size fill light. Usually a 2K, roughly 24 inches square, behind the camera and pretty close to the lens level. It puts a glint in the center of the eye.

Some cinematographers like to hand hold a reflector bulb with a barndoor attached to it as a fill/eyelight. This way they can obtain the exact position and angle and are able to move the light during the shot.

The traditional attitude of the Hollywood producers used to be that if you pay an actor big money, you want to see his eyes. Following this reasoning, the most expensive actors would be given the most elaborate eyelights. Happily this rather naive approach is nowadays often modified by the conceptual requirements of the story. It was rather revolutionary at the time to have Marlon Brando very dimly lit in some key scenes of *The Godfather*, photographed by Gordon Willis (ASC). Nevertheless, it became one of the cinematographic classics of our time. Once again, the thought expressed by many great cameramen comes to mind: What you *don't* light is often more important than what you *do* light.

CHAPTER Six

Lighting on Location

EVEN WHEN a film is shot primarily in the studio, the crew goes out to location for some of the filming. There are different kinds of locations presenting a wide range of problems.

The cinematographer has to cope with the weather and the changing light angles on a day exterior. He is often cramped in small spaces and faced with mixed light situations on interior locations. Night street scenes often call for low light levels to preserve the existing light ambience of shop windows and signs. And car interiors multiply all these problems by movement.

Many of these problems can be identified and solved ahead of time if the cinematographer is hired early enough to scout the locations and help to choose them. Director Robert Wise prefers to have his cameraman with him when scouting locations.

Robert Wise

I try to get a cinematographer at least three to four weeks ahead of the production if possible. If it is humanly possible, you should have your cameraman when you are looking for locations. At least he should visit the locations, talk them up thoroughly and discuss the shooting and the shooting continuity, how best to take advantage of the light in terms of the shooting.

As well as planning the logistics for shooting at the location, the cinematographer can make some aesthetic judgments in preproduction.

Caleb Deschanel, ASC

One of the reasons the cameraman should be involved early enough to go along and help to pick the locations is that he is the one who has to translate whatever those locations or sets are into the visual elements of the film. Usually stills are enough to document locations, but now I am getting into using video as well, because video can give you a sense of moving through a space.

One of the reasons you choose a location is because of what it is and you say, This is perfect, because of a certain mood or atmosphere that it has. I think that a lot of cameramen make the mistake of going into a location and having something that is absolutely perfect and then lighting it in a way that is the total antithesis of what that is, ruining what you had in the first place. I think that is a terrible mistake to make.

Apart from the aesthetic consideration, a cinematographer scouting a location should also investigate the logistics in depth. He should carry a compass with him to establish the arc of the sun even on an overcast day. He should investigate the power supply and the access and space for equipment. With today's economic considerations, the question of how much light is important; it will be related to the film stock to be used and to the action, which has to be established with the director. Once the action is discussed, the cameraman will be able to figure out how many hours it will take to light it.

LOCATION EXTERIOR

Leaving the predictability and comforts of a studio, one faces various challenges in terms of weather and logistics on exterior locations. At the same time they offer a rich palette of creative opportunities for the cinematographer.

DAYLIGHT

Film locations are infinitely varied and complex. Our chief interest here is the type of light encountered and used on locations. Let's start with daylight exteriors. Daylight is certainly the most exquisite source and its nuances are endless. It constitutes a great challenge and requires careful study. Great cinematographers never cease in this effort. The late James Wong Howe (ASC) described his preparations for exterior filming.

James Wong Howe, ASC

Before the shooting is scheduled I go there very early in the morning, before daybreak, and stay there all day 'till midnight to study how the light changes. I take still photographs on the same stock I use when filming. I take pictures every two or three hours from the same angle. I have positive transparencies made and project them on the screen.

Nowadays the cinematographer may not be given the time for such meticulous preparation but he should still be able to design the strategy of shooting the scene in relationship to the changing daylight. Unfortunately he is often at the mercy of the director and the schedule.

Vilmos Zsigmond, ASC

On exteriors it depends on the director, the budget, and the schedule. If I can convince the director that we will still finish the day's schedule and not pay all the big money for overtime, then he will let me shoot at the right time. But if it means a lot of money, they are not going to allow it. Then you just have to figure out how to make a scene look sunsety when you have to shoot at 2 P.M. You have this problem a lot of times. It is not easy but you just have to find ways of doing it.

The constant change in the character and quality of daylight causes many headaches for the cinematographer on location. There are several ways to tackle this problem.

Richard Hart

Daylight changes. What you try to do is to shoot your wide shots first and design them so the light is best for you in the overall condition. Then you shoot your coverage, your closer shots where there is more control, under the butterfly. You can alter your background. The saying in the old westerns was, A tree is a tree and a rock is a rock. If they went by this rock but now the light is gone there and there is another rock over here with light on it, that rock is the rock. Now, if there is architecture or another identifiable thing in the background, then you have other tools to try to work with. You cheat a little bit and still see some of the building or whatever. You scout the location and you take into consideration what you are shooting, and the time of the day you are going to be there. If you are going to be there all day, where does the sun come up in the morning and where does it go down? A lot of times they want to shoot the close-ups in the middle of the day. That way they can control the light with the silk over the top. Then they can light with additional lamps.

With the changing light and changing weather, day exterior shooting can be extremely challenging in the matching of shots. A scene may require a few days of shooting and over these days the light quality can be anything but constant. There are limits to what can be matched by skill and technology and it often becomes the problem of a production manager and other people involved in planning and scheduling. Nevertheless, a cinematographer with an ingenious and cooperative director can overcome considerable light changes by planning and staging the shots, and by the use of overheads and filters. For example, if a scene started in heavy smog and it is continued the next day in much lighter smog and the day after in clear air, the cameraman is likely to use a light low contrast or fog filter on the second day and increase the filter effect by using a heavy low contrast or fog on the third day. A scene may be started on an overcast day, but there is a good likelihood of the sun coming through later. The cinematographer can protect himself by creating a sunny effect with the arcs. If, on the other hand, the scene was started as cloudy and should continue as such, emerging sunshine can be blocked out in closer shots by a black solid overhead.

Often a skilled cinematographer can actually save time and money by creating lighting continuity in changing weather.

James Wong Howe, ASC

When actually shooting on an outside location, sometimes one has to create a sun effect when the sun is covered with clouds. For example, I had this experience when shooting a film with John Garfield in the desert in Palm Springs. We were shooting around a shed where they were packing dates. We lost the sunlight, so the production manager called the studio to tell them that we cannot continue shooting. The studio boss asked to speak to me and said, "Jimmy, I understand there is a problem there with the sun, but we don't know when that sun will be out again. Now I want you to try to finish it and come back to the studio so we can keep on schedule." I said, "Well, I can do it providing the director will let me pick the setups so that I don't have to make reverse shots shooting out towards the desert. I cannot light that desert up, but I can light the packing shed." He said, "Well, get the director on the phone." Naturally the director had to agree with this suggestion so I picked setups and had him plot the action so that we did not have to shoot the reverse shots. The packing shed was only about 50 feet across and I had 4 or 5 arcs. I could duplicate the sunlight and match it perfectly. Before we finished it started to rain. Fortunately with a light background (the packing shed was whitewashed) you could not see the rain coming down. We finished in time, packed up and went home. The next day we looked at the dailies and this scene matched perfectly together with the sunny part.

In the case outlined above, Howe used arcs, hard lights to create the impression of the sun, also a hard source. The soft light of the sky can also be augmented with the use of soft lights or bounced light. As Howe points out, however, this kind of "magic" can be used only in tight shots when matching to daylight. Long shots are the most difficult to doctor.

The long shots should be photographed within a reasonably short period of time so that they can be intercut without a noticeable light change. Close-ups can always be helped with proper staging and additional lighting. Especially in the late afternoon when the light is fading fast it is essential to get all the long shots in time. Another fact worth paying attention to is the ugliness of the very vertical sunlight between 11 A.M. and 2 P.M. in the summer. This depends of course on the latitude of the location. When the sun is high, the landscape looks more flat, woods and water look "dead." Once the scene is limited to a smaller area, we have much more control over the lighting. We can use large overhead frames with a variety of materials to modulate the sunlight. A black net (scrim) will cut its intensity, a white silk will soften it, or a black

solid will create a shadow. Depending on the size of these frames and the height at which they are set up, they will produce a stronger or weaker effect. The reason to use silk rather than plastic for the overheads is because the air goes through silk whereas plastic in a twelve by twelve foot frame acts like a sail and the wind can rip it right out.

Large overheads and flags allow for considerable modulation of the daylight.

Richmond Aguilar, who has worked as a gaffer with American cinematographers as well as European ones, feels that European cameramen tend to control the existing light rather than bringing in lighting units. For example, if an actor is standing under a porch in hot sun, a European might cut the light with a tree branch over the actor and fill him with a small unit, maybe a card or a small HMI. An American would probably use an arc to bring up the shade under the porch, to balance it better to the bright foreground. Another example of controlling the existing light rather than bringing in lighting units can be seen with an overcast situation.

Richmond Aguilar

On an overcast day there is a lot of top light. You can use a large flag, bring it down over the head, just enough to where it cuts down the top light. Now you have the light hitting the subject from the sides. Once you decide which side you want to be the key, you bring in another flag and ease it in on that opposite side to bring it down to the level where you want your fill light. Then you have a beautifully lit shot. People call it subtractive lighting, or negative lighting. It is taking light away instead of adding it. But you have to consider what your background is. If you are shooting against a wide open wheat field, and you are under the trees, you have this overcast situation. When you start taking this light off you may have f/2.8 in the shade but very hot elsewhere. Shooting into the dense greens in a backlit situation you can get away with a lot less fill light, because the backlight of the sun becomes just a rim on the shoulders and head and it can be way overexposed. It can be burned out. And you fill with enough exposure to balance them against the background which is dark backlit trees. Then you can use just bead boards, no lights at all, very little fill, and still you will balance it with your background. Now, if this whole situation was turned around, when the sun is hitting them in the face, now you have to bring out arcs to bring up the dark side of the face, because it is fully lit and the background is also fully lit. So if you have to shoot scenes without big equipment, you try to use backlight and fill minimally with the bounce boards. When you have to have one person in the sun and one backlit, usually it is the guy that suffers, the girl would have the backlight, a nice soft effect, and the guy will have a harsh high sun and lots of fill light. But you can cheat that around [have both people shot in the backlight] and get away with it.

Harsh lighting on the foreground can be either diffused by silk or broken up by shadow forming devices, such as a cucaloris.

Jordan Cronenweth, ASC

Foreground you can manipulate with nets, silks and solids. You can also use foliage effects and shadows. A silk between the light and the cucaloris will make the effect more subtle. Adjust the cucaloris and the silk moving it closer and farther away from the light and the subject. Silk allows you to have cucaloris closer to the subject and still soft. Otherwise, close to the lamp, it would give a gigantic shadow.

Another tool for using natural light is the reflector. Traditionally the film industry used silver reflectors called "shiny boards" with one side semimatte and the other bright and harder. Today they are rarely used to light faces, but are still useful.

Allen Daviau, ASC

Shiny boards are really wonderful for bushes and buildings. If you are shooting a backlit situation and you've got backrimmed people, the bushes and trees behind them will look like black holes. So you will use the shiny boards for this background and it will open up the greens, or you can shine a shiny board on a silk in such a way that the light will not travel directly through the silk, but it will light up the silk so it will glow and it will become the source, not the shiny board.

The older type of shiny board is covered with a fragile silver foil which needs frequent replacement. Today more durable plastic materials are available.

Ralph Woolsey, ASC

The silver fringes on reflectors do not soften the light, that is a myth. They are there because you have to overlap the squares of silver leaf when you glue them down. The advantage of silver is its reflective efficiency, and there are many degrees of reflectance available in materials today, many of which you can get in long rolls. But if you want something really soft, use a piece of foam-core clipped over a reflector. White reflectors, which produce very beautiful light, require working quite close to the subject, which you cannot do on long shots. For close-ups I often use a white card to redirect the light from a silver reflector, to create perhaps a backlight or sidelight effect in appropriate situations.

Sometimes, especially on exterior commercials, you may use a mirror to direct a narrow beam of light; for instance, in an outdoor luncheon scene where you want to get a special sparkle out of a glass of iced tea. You are working at a pretty high key light on a bright day, even through silk or other diffusion. So where ordinary lights are not bright enough or small enough to do it, I find that a fairly small, round, easily obtainable mirror is just the thing. It can throw a tremendous light for a long distance, and it can be fastened to a grip stand and adjusted.

Foam-core boards and silver reflectors can save on setup time and electricity in some special cases.

Michael D. Margulies, ASC

On a beach, if I have only one or two shots and the reflectors and foam-core boards can cover my needs, the electricians won't necessarily have to string 300 yards of cable or bring a battery pack down. It all depends on the circumstances. The big old reflectors can be used through silk. If you set up a six by six silk and a reflector in the back with a soft side, it will give you a very nice light. In commercials I have used a mirror to get a very fine pinpoint hot spot for example.

Daylight consists of a mixture of sun and blue sky. Yet, silver reflectors mainly reflect the sun, creating light which is often too yellow. For much cooler light, metallic blue surfaces can be used, or silver reflectors with a blue gel in front. On the other hand, golden reflectors will create more of a sunset effect.

Today, for lighting faces, white boards like the foam-core and white plastic sheets like Griffolyn are invariably preferred when reflected light is employed.

Allen Daviau, ASC

I like the white-on-white Griffolyn [G55], not the white-on-black [G65]. On an overcast day in winter the Griffolyn with no artificial light bouncing off it, just the skylight, will give half a stop on the faces, just using it as a big white bounce card. For people on horseback it is great because you have the upward angle reflecting the sky. Also as the daylight gets down we start bouncing our HMIs off it and getting just that little kiss of fill light to put the highlights in the eye and add a little detail into the face. What is beautiful about Griffolyn for the location pictures is that it folds up and stuffs into a bag just like silk. It is rugged, it can be rained on, you can wash it off with a hose.

All reflectors have their problems. They need to be continuously adjusted because of the moving sun, and they are easily upset by the wind. Lamps are much more dependable.

Among the lamps used in a daylight exterior situation, the arc remains the most sunlike, one shadow source, and projects its light the farthest distance. The most popular carbon arc is the 225 ampere Brute. For larger jobs a 350-amp Titan is sometimes employed. For a softer effect an arc light can be bounced off a white reflector or diffused. For a shorter throw HMI lights are easier to operate and more power efficient than the arc.

Various incandescent lights are used on an exterior location as well. The large clusters of sealed beam lights such as Nine Lights or Twelve Lights are very useful for general fill illumination or as a key light on an overcast day. They have to be filtered with blue gels unless they are equipped with FAY (daylight) bulbs. Both these alternatives have their drawbacks. The blue gels, such as Tough Blue 50 (TB5) or blue glass Macbeth filters, cut down the light output by more than half.

And the FAY bulbs are very expensive per hour of use. By comparison the 5600°K HMI lights are several times more efficient and actually less expensive to use. HMI lights may need some slight color correction as well. It is a good practice to check all the lamps in the morning with a color temperature meter and label the required gel corrections on each light.

Artificial light with correct color temperature for daylight will help to clean up a color cast created by an adjacent color, for example, the green lawn the actors are sitting on or a red fire engine near by. If this color cast is eliminated in the lab during printing, it will weaken the color in the background, that is, the lawn or the fire engine in our example. Lights used to bring up the light level on an overcast day or under an overhead are generally referred to as booster lights.

Sunlight is a harsh source and if we wish to use it as such without diffusion, then it is best used as three-quarter crosslight or direct backlight. A problem arises with a dialogue scene in full sunshine. Logically speaking, if one person is in a backlight, the other one should be facing the sun. Traditionally the one in full sun would most likely be protected by a silk or a scrim and the one in the shadow would be given light from one side to see the detail and this side would be balanced against the fill light. Being against the sun, his backlight would be stronger and you would usually cut it down with a net or silk. There is another way to handle such a scene when the background is not too obvious.

Vilmos Zsigmond, ASC

Just think of a situation when you are lighting people flat from the front and you are giving them full exposure. Now, you turn around for the reverse. Logically, actors in this reverse shot are backlit, the light is behind them. But

if you follow what the eye sees (what is correct in reality), the film would not cut. It would jump, from a very bright shot to a dark one. It would not match. Owen Roizman did a good job on this problem in Absence of Malice. He did exactly the same as Nestor Almendros does. He turned people so their backs were to the sun in both the master and the reverse shots. I would be very, very cautious with this approach. But it worked for Roizman. Everybody was always backlit. I could accept that, because if a scene is played around midday, the sun is very high in America so, in a way, everybody is backlit. In real life the midday sun casts an overly strong light on the nose, but that is where realistic photography differs from naturalistic. You do not have to follow nature that closely. You can change it so there is no harsh light on the nose and you can get away with it.

Sun, as a backlight or three-quarter crosslight, is also more interesting for the background. As James Wong Howe pointed out in an interview, one can introduce some smoke effect like burning green leaves in the woods or garden and use the sun as a backlight. It will give a marvellous three-dimensionality to the scene. The angle of the direct sunshine varies tremendously depending on the time of day and the geographical location. The high angle during the middle of the day produces a very unpleasant and unbecoming light, yet there are times when the story requires these conditions.

Vilmos Zsigmond, ASC

The final scene of High Noon had to be shot at high noon, even though light at that time is really horrible. Nobody likes to work at midday because the light is so bad, but since the story required it they had to shoot it in bad lighting whether the cameraman liked it or not. Sure, they could have shot it at sunset but it would be funny to call it High Noon.

When the story does not demand to be shot in the middle of the day, early morning and late afternoon are really the best for the long shots. The shadows are long and the textures are more accentuated.

Mornings tend to be more crisp, assuming that there is no fog. In late afternoons the air is more polluted, making the light softer and more orangy. This color shift is caused by the fact that the blue waves become more scattered by the impurities in the air and the light spectrum shifts toward red.

Around sunset the Kelvin rating of light goes down to the point when it is possible to remove the 85 filter and in this way gain two thirds of a stop. But if we do that, the photographed scene may be actually illuminated by 3200°K light and the effect of sunset will be gone. When an exaggerated sunset is asked for, the cinematographer may actually use two 85 filters to double the effect.

SUNSET

How to photograph a sunset really depends on several factors: the focal length of the lens, the clouds, the air pollution, the geographical location. Here are some comments on this subject from four cinematographers.

James Crabe, ASC

A smoggy day would help you. I've shot many commercials where the guys are standing against the sun, in fact, a Marlboro commercial where the guy is right inside the sun. Sometimes we used to do a lot of work with long lenses. We would have gel filters behind the lens and quite often they would just burn up in the camera from the sun. It is just like the microscope focusing all that light. But often I had shot at f/22 with maybe three stops of ND. Often the effects that we go for graphically in sunset situations are silhouettes, people silhouetted against the red sky. If the shot was pretty close to the sun, as on a 600mm lens, I think the sun would be about 50 percent of the frame height, more or less. Of course one hopes to be able to photograph the sun on the horizon. The lower the sun is in the sky, the more atmosphere you are shooting through and the more chance you've got of getting a reproduceable thing.

We have done stuff where we wanted to include the sun in a shot of a model, for example, where there is no sun. In this case we would take a great mirror and put it behind this person at a proper angle, and we can put the sun right behind her and the mirror probably doesn't even change the exposure. The mirror would have to fill the frame. It would be shot with a long lens so the sun would be very large compared to the subject's head for example. You can also put a big piece of a neutral density gel between the actress and the mirror, so you have a little bit of balance; you can take the sun down two stops. That has to be done pretty much by eye, because there are really no rules. But I can remember a lot of times shooting the sun with a 600mm lens stopped down to f/22 and then even a couple of stops over that corrected by ND as well. On wider shots I had sometimes looked at the sky and said, okay. What part of that sky should look like a flesh tone in density? Just take a reflected light reading from that part of the sky. Also I know that with an incident meter, lots of people feel that you turn this meter around and aim the bulb the 'wrong way' away from the sun, and that will give you a good sunset exposure.

Of course a good sunset exposure would be different from a good sunball exposure. Because in a good sunset exposure the sun might in fact be burned out, but still give you a nice gradation in the sky. I found that out just by intuition without making a lot of tests or bracketing exposures. The sun has generally been pretty cooperative. When it is blaring, blazing sun and totally undiffused sky, the color of the sun is not likely to be too pleasing either. If however you can shoot on a smoggy day then you've got a beautiful oriental painting where the sun is orange. If I was going to do any filtering at all in the usual sunlight situation, I would just throw in another 85.

Some of the fun we had on these Marlboro commercials in the old days, when a lot of them were done against the sun and the whole scene had to be shot in fifteen to twenty minutes, was trying to find a place where the sun was going down over a rolling hill. And we started at the bottom of the hill and as the sun comes down, we are coming up the hill, moving fast, shooting fast, grabbing the tripods, great fun. It was sometimes done with a 1000mm lens, when a cowboy comes into the middle of the sun. Here again the guy is in silhouette, we are not getting any detail out of him at all. And we also shot late in the day, so the sun was in fact photographed through a lot of atmosphere. It looked beautiful to the eye and it looked beautiful to the camera. It was usually exposed at f/22 with a couple of stops of ND in there.

Exposing sunset, like exposing anything else, involves an aesthetic judgment and the understanding how the exposure will affect the reproduction of the scene on film emulsion.

Caleb Deschanel, ASC

Basically everything moves around medium gray. Any reflected meter is going to give you medium gray, the middle of the scale. So if you take a spot meter and you read the sun, and it says f/22, well you obviously want it to be hot. What I do basically is I look at the scene and I try to make a judgment about what I am seeing. I say to myself, well, that is hotter than what I see as medium gray and therefore I should overexpose that a certain number of stops. You look at the color of the sun and you say to yourself, how much of the color do I want to preserve? If I overexpose the sun 4 stops, I am going to lose all that orange light. So I want to overexpose it, say 2 stops and I will still preserve some of that orange light. I just go within those ranges, but basically it is sunset. You can take a Weston meter and read the sky and get an accurate reading. What is a sunset? Sunset in a desert can be totally different than in a smoggy city where you can have it go down and in the last 30 minutes you get this huge orange ball which is not all that hot. Only maybe two stops hotter than the surrounding sky. If the sun is just small in frame you go for one exposure, and if it is a 500mm lens you would go for another exposure, because it is filling more of the frame. You can overexpose more if the sun is small in frame, because it is just going to be white anyway whether it is 8 stops overexposed or one stop overexposed. It is just small in the frame, so you certainly want to make sure that the sky is at a density that is hot. Because the sky is hot. It goes back again to the judgment of what you see. If I go to the desert and I look at a sunrise before the sun comes up, that is very hot and I think that you need to preserve that to some extent. You do not want to go more than say 3 or 4 stops over, or else it is going to blend in with the sun and you are not going to have any density but it's certainly got to be 2 stops hot or 1½ stops hot.

Another way to accentuate the sunset is by use of graduated filters. Usually the neutral density graduates are used but they come also in orange graduation for this purpose.

Richard Kline, ASC

I use graduated filters quite often in a sunset situation. More so than in a sunrise. It depends if there is a stratum of clouds. Then I have less need for any kind of filtration above. I also use color filters to enhance the sun. When you overexpose the sky to accommodate some objects in the foreground, you will lose all your color values, which I think you will want to retain. You can achieve it with graduate filters, neutral or color to darken the sky.

Sunrise lasts only 30 seconds. Sunsets last longer, although the last moment when it just goes behind the horizon is fast too. With sunrise there is the glow, then you start seeing it, and within 30 seconds the sun is up. And if there is no cloud formation it is a blast of light. Sunsets seem to go slower. Longitude and latitude of the location has a big bearing on that. I was in Finland last year, doing a picture, and we had a long sunrise, I mean it lay there forever and it was beautiful. In Africa and in California, it just comes and goes.

When shooting a sunrise or a sunset it is all judgment of what you want to see. If it is only the sun and not the terrain, then expose just for the sun. But if you want to still see something in detail, then you have to expose for that and tone down the sun, if you can do it. For sunrise and sunset I like the soft blend in the middle of the graduated filter. Attenuators are better for some landscapes.

Michael D. Margulies, ASC

For exposing a sunset bracketing your exposure would be a very safe and common way of doing it, if you have the luxury of available time. If you are lucky and have an Albuquerque sunset with beautiful big billowing storm clouds, then that detracts from the harshness

of a sunset. If the sky close to the sun would measure f/11, I would go one stop hotter and expose at f/8 because the sky is always hotter. In my filter box I have a two stops attenuator. I use it on a sunset, I use it on snow and I have used it sideways for a hot building, or a side of the street that is hot.

Unquestionably the most attractive light happens just after sunset, when the beautiful glow comes from an unrecognizable source. It is the so-called "magic hour," which may last only fifteen minutes in California and a few hours in Sweden. Shooting at this time of a day requires meticulous rehearsals and total concentration of everyone involved. As the light fades away, taking the 85 filter off extends the exposure for a short while. Finally one may keep cutting down the frames per second. This gives more exposure but it also speeds up the movement in the frame. To counteract it one has to instruct the actors to move slower and slower. Fading out light will be changing its color characteristic, but these variations can be corrected by the timer in the lab.

DAY-FOR-NIGHT

The technique of shooting night scenes during the day is one of the oldest tricks in Hollywood. There is no question that the most convincing night effects are shot at night proper. Yet, there are some valid reasons to shoot day-for-night. The most obvious is the need to see deep into the background. It is usually too expensive and often not feasible to light too far back into the distance. Another good reason is to avoid the inconvenience of working at night. Both actors and crew get tired faster and the quality may suffer. And the producers do not like paying people at the higher rate.

There is general agreement among cinematographers that the most successful day-for-night effect is photographed during the magic hour of dusk. When lights are used, electricians should have a good assortment of scrims to cut down their intensity as the daylight fades away. Checking the brightness of the sky with a spot meter indicates the dusk changes and the necessary light adjustments to keep the relationship between the sky and the close-up illumination in constant balance.

On the other hand, if we need only one master shot of the scene and intend to do close-ups later in artificial light, then every subsequent take of this master shot does not have to match the previous one. Under these circumstances as the sky light fades away we may want to add more fill light for the faces to keep the required exposure. Therefore in such situations we may start with several scrims on the lamps, and then as it gets darker we would take them off, to keep a constant light level on the faces.

James Wong Howe, ASC

When you are shooting in the city and do not want to lose the shape of the buildings you can shoot dusk-for-night to obtain a more realistic night effect. You still have a dark sky, which you can darken even more with a neutral density graduated filter. Of course this filter will limit your camera movements a little. In color you can use a polarizing filter but it works only with certain angles to the sky and again, if you start panning it will be visibly changing. Shots at dusk are limited to a very short period, so if it is possible more than one camera should be used. This way you will get at the same time the long shot, the medium shot and the close-up. Usually we start this type of shooting a little earlier than the "perfect" dusk and we shoot a few takes, first stopping the lens down a little more and per-haps putting an ND graduated filter over it. The next shot may be about perfect, so it should be the good one. But just to be on the safe side we will take another one this time opening the lens a little more to compensate for the diminishing light. The close range action will be a little "filled" with light and the task is to capture the right relationship between the foreground and the background which is getting progressively darker as the dusk time continues.

Approaching the day-for-night situation one should concentrate on the visual characteristics of moonlight. We observe that it is softer than sunlight and that objects do not seem as sharp as during the day. The main characteristic of night is the preponderance of dark areas. To obtain this effect during the day, we have to stage the scene in such a configuration that the sunlight comes as either a backlight or a crosslight. For this we need the cooperation of the director and the production manager, so that proper scheduling can meet our requirements.

Silver reflectors can be very useful in day-for-night shooting to redirect the sunlight.

Richard Hart

I worked with a cameraman a long time ago and I really liked his day-for-night stuff. He used mostly reflectors because there weren't any lights bright enough to use in the daytime. He would use the lead side of the reflector and the effect was fabulous. You print it down and the light looks like night. He used a lot of neutrals on the lens, so you could open up and then just use tons of light from reflectors. At night you do not want depth of field, it is the biggest giveaway in the world.

The technique described here by Richard Hart characterizes day-for-night lighting well.

The powerful amount of light on the foreground allows us to underexpose the background and still have the action area at a desirable level of illumination. At the same time we do not want to obtain the underexposure by stopping down the lens, as this would give us more depth of field, undesirable for the night effect. Instead, we use neutral density filters and keep the lens open. It all comes down to having the back- or crosslit foreground against a dark background, and a shallow depth of field. Together, all these elements give us the character of night.

After the light direction, next comes the problem of the sky. For all practical purposes it is much better when the sky is not visible. Therefore elevating the camera, or shooting against hills or mountains whenever possible is the best way. But obviously there will be many scenes when the sky will occupy part of the scene. In black-and-white photography, blue sky was made to look dark by the use of a red filter, usually #23A or #25. The only problem with these filters is that they render the faces chalk white. To bring faces back to normal, a green filter #56 was added. A typical combination for a day-for-night on black-and-white emulsion was 23A+56. Of course in color photography we have to deal with the sky differently. Polarizing filters will darken the sky, especially when the lighting comes from the side and when the sky is clear. Another filter for the job is the graduated one with neutral density in the upper part and clear glass below. The soft border dividing these two parts is matched with the horizon line. Finally there is also an attenuator, a filter which changes neutral density very gradually from top to bottom. Unfortunately all these filters limit camera movement. Polarization changes with the camera angle in relation to the sun, and graduated filters allow for a panoramic movement only if the horizon line is parallel to the frame line. As far as clouds are concerned, dark clouds will look darker when polarized, but white clouds will look whiter, so they should be avoided altogether.

A most convincing day-for-night effect can be produced by matting-in a black sky to replace the white one. This is done on an optical printer and due to the high cost of this operation, it is not very popular with producers. There is also the danger that any small inaccuracy in the optical printing will result in a fringe line separating the sky from the horizon. Vilmos Zsigmond, who used this method in the film *Deliverance*, advises a dark gray sky rather than a black one, which "would be like shooting against black velvet" *Dialog on Film* Volume 4, Number 1, October 1974, The American Film Institute).

Whether the sky is included in the frame or not, day-for-night effects require controlled underexposure. Cinematographers generally agree that the best results are achieved when underexposing two stops for the long shots and a stop and a quarter to a stop and a half for close-ups, so that we can see more details in the faces. Neutral density filter 0.6 cuts down the light by two stops, so it is convenient to use it without correcting an f-stop, to obtain the required underexposure.

One should generally pay more attention to the overall character of the night than to the clarity of the faces. Unless the facial details are very crucial, a more sketchy treatment better conveys the reality of the night.

On occasion a day-for-night situation will include a campfire. This is not an easy setup and it requires a well-shaded area.

Jordan Cronenweth, ASC

I am fond of shooting day-for-night in shadow. We once put the fire in among these trees where one could count for having shadow pretty much all day. We built the fire up so that it started to light the faces of the guys around the fire, and I shot it with an 81EF filter so that it went a little bluer than normal. I underexposed it a stop and a half and I shot this whole sequence just like that. We had gas pipes underneath to make the fire brighter. You could see the fire on their faces, you could feel the fire and the nice thing was that you could see all the trees in the background. But you don't want to see the sky.

To control the day-for-night effect it is important to be in charge of the timing. You will probably still want to print it down, so that the final print may be underexposed as much as three stops. Some cinematographers believe in starting with 2½ half stops underexposure to have very little detail on the film to start with, and then printing it down another stop.

Cameramen differ in their perceptions of the bluishness of night. It is a theatrical convention that night is supposed to be bluish. In the day-for-night situation the easiest way to achieve blue light is to remove the 85 filter from the lens. The less blue-oriented cinematographers replace it with an 81 EF filter that can be considered as only half as strong as 85 in its color correction. Of course any degree of bluishness can be introduced in the printing.

At the planning stage for the day-for-night scene, attention should be paid to the costumes which the actors will be wearing. Bright colors tend to give away the illusion of night. As we all know, at night our color perception diminishes considerably. In day-for-night a blue shirt will remain blue, perhaps only darker due to underexposure. (William Clothier [ASC], elaborated on this subject at the American Film Institute seminar, *American Cinematographer*, November 1977, p. 1161.)

NIGHT-FOR-NIGHT

In spite of the logistical and budgetary advantages of shooting night scenes during the day, day-for-night was never a very popular method among cinematographers. Today, when truly fast film emulsions are available it is even more desirable to shoot night-for-night.

A brightly lit urban street constitutes a lighting situation well within the exposure range of present day color negative stock. With skillful lighting of the foreground scene we are therefore able to utilize available light in the background and achieve a high degree of location realism. It is this character of night that makes night shooting so desirable if realism is what we are after.

The following remarks about street scenes at night were made by James Wong Howe several years ago, but in spite of the advances in lighting equipment and film emulsion since then, the basic principles are still the same.

James Wong Howe, ASC

In lighting streets I would have my lights coming from on high as if they were street lamps. That at least would give me a kind of light source. I would use the 3/4 backlighting principle and fill in, with the soft front light, the people closer to the camera, leaving the more distant players in semisilhouette. This light direction is also good for buildings at night. In certain places I may hide a lamp behind a lamp post and use that pool of light. As for types of lights, the best are spotlights slightly flooded out, and slightly diffused. They are better to control than big soft sources. Sometimes a bank of lights like a Maxi-Brute can be used, but coming from an established direction of a street lamp. If it is necessary, I add a little light in shop windows

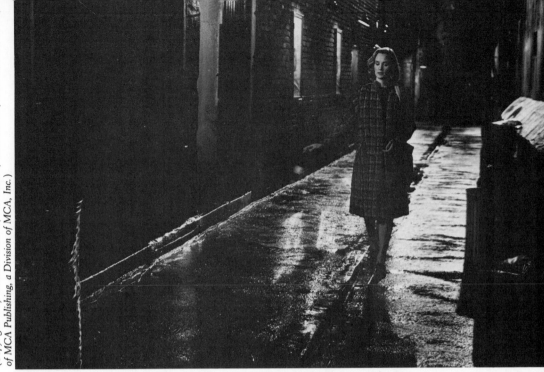

The key light in this shot comes from the back. It is generated by a 5K senior positioned on the fire escape as low as the frame line permits to get the long shadows and bright highlights. The frontal fill light is created by a small 1K soft light with an "egg crate" grid. This lamp simulates the lights illuminating the playbill posters on the left wall. *Frances*, Laszlo Kovacs (ASC), cinematographer.

when I intend to shoot into them and there is not enough light. This can be done with photofloods.

When shooting night-for-night in the streets, some cameramen insist on wetting the pavement to gain light reflections from it. I would not do it unless the story calls for it. Of course sometimes you want rain for an effect to indicate, for instance, the comfortable feeling of a fireplace with burning wood while the rain is falling outside the window. It is similar to the situation when there is no wind outside, but the director insists that the tree branches are slightly moving to add a bit of movement in an otherwise static background.

Our main objectives in an exterior night scene are to preserve the night character of light and

to create a feeling of depth. To achieve these objectives we need to scout locations at night and, if possible, to do the rigging preparation at night.

James Plannette

The best time to scout is at night. Then you will see how it is and how much you have to enhance it. And with fast film now, it is just a case of picking up the foreground. The thing to watch out for now is not to overlight it, because when you overlight it, you lose all the "free stuff" that you have in the background. If you can make the farthest background that you see bright, then you get a lot of depth and if somebody walks out of light at least you see him in silhouette against the background.

Generally you would use three-fourths back-light and fill light ideally would come from a showcard or Griffolyn. I would not underexpose the night. If you print down your blacks are very rich. I don't like lenses open more than f/2.3. Below that, focus is so shallow that it is distracting.

When one needs to light a whole city block or more, even with today's fast emulsions, the arc is still considered the best light source to use.

James Crabe, ASC

When you are talking about a point source and you want to have a lot of light that reaches out a long way and has punch even when it has gone a hundred feet, it is pretty hard to beat an arc. Maybe to light a whole city block with a little crosslight of moonlight, or something, you get a big arc and put it up on a ninety-five-foot scissors stand, or further up yet, and then you come close to being able to create your own moon.

For smaller areas, Master Lights or other units equipped with PAR 64 globes are good for reaching across the street or down the street because of their "punching" power. HMI lights are also excellent for such uses.
    The lighting should follow the logical light sources which in this case will be the street lamps and the store fronts. You can adjust your lighting to the street lights, you can overpower them, or you can cover them up.

Caleb Deschanel, ASC

Most of my ideas come from reality, from observing things. Using existing night street lights (practicals) you end up with mostly low pressure sodium vapor lamps. If they become pin sources and they burn out it doesn't make

that much difference, but if they really become your sources of light, then you have to start adjusting everything around them. You can let them go and overpower them in the foreground. Sometimes you may go daylight instead of tungsten. If you want to, you can totally adjust to it but unfortunately it is an incomplete spectrum, so you are really lacking in colors.

Richmond Aguilar

The mercury vapor street lights can be blacked out by simply covering them with a black cloth. They can be simulated by putting a Mighty Mole on two risers behind the post, 24 feet up. You do not see them in the frame but it gives the effect of the lamp and the spread. On New York, New York we had a scene when a musician is playing a saxophone underneath a street lamp. To help us out there with the effect on the sidewalk we had the pool of light painted on the pavement.

You may also paint the street darker if the backlight is showing too much. As always, the more you can test in advance, the better.

Jordan Cronenweth, ASC

On the street I would test how the available light looks, and then I would attempt to light the scene with the available light sources appearing to do the lighting. And I would work with the director in staging, to maybe have some interesting neon sign in the background, so you not only have a light effect, but one that has some of the environment in it in terms of color. And maybe establish some kind of overall ambient light, so that you see into some of the shadows. Ambient light comes from nowhere and everywhere. There is a reason for it. It not only looks good but you are letting the natural lighting do as much work as you can, so that hopefully you are buying the time to stay on schedule or to do something more unique somewhere else.

A street at night represents a rather high contrast scene. To bring the brightness range closer to what the film emulsion can handle we need to lower the excessive brightness of such elements as neons.

Haskell Wexler, ASC

On night exteriors in town one should be very careful not to overexpose the neons. If you do not wrap some net around it, it is likely to burn out to an extent that you cannot even read it. For night exterior shooting, one would often employ the fastest lenses on hand. The problem to watch out for, with the new fast lenses, is the phenomenon of double headlights when the light kicks them from a certain angle. You can avoid it to a certain extent when shooting at night by not having any glass filters in front of the lens.

Since this interview with Haskell Wexler took place, cinematographer Bill Fraker (ASC) requested that Panavision Corporation of California Ltd., develop a matte-box in which filters could be tilted back and forth. Now this Tilt Filter matte-box is available for use on Panaflex camera.

When the night exterior is not in town and the only logical source of light is the moon, lighting takes on quite a different character.

James Wong Howe, ASC

Of course when you are in the country where there are no street lamps, you have to light in such a way that you do not know where the light comes from. It is just kind of a general soft light that floods in. So the source of light is not obvious. You would use soft floodlights

for it. You can use Mini-Brutes or Maxi-Brutes with silk diffusers in front of them to scatter the light. You would have a normal exposure but print it down a little. When underexposed this type of lighting would result in a muddy picture on the print from your negative. If for a large area one has to use a 10K, I would put a diffuser screen in front of the lamp.

Not only the quality of light but also the angle of the light creates the night character. Usually a three-fourths back angle works well for such effect.

James Plannette

On E.T. we created moonlight with four 10Ks rigged on two cranes with arms extended 80 feet. We put those cranes on each side of the "landing site" as three-fourths backlights. With other 10Ks we lit the dark trees behind the 'landing site' and we took the direct light off the grass with solids [flags]. The ambient light which this very light grass picked up was enough to get a reading and yet it did not look lit. The site was about the size of a football field. The foreground action was filled with light reflected off a 12 x 12 Griffolyn. With Griffolyn you have a total control of the angle.

A very even moonlight can be created over a large area using the so-called Flying Moon, originally employed by Haskell Wexler. It consists of a 10-foot cube made of aluminum pipes and covered with bleached muslin. (The original Wexler Moon was shaped like a pyramid.) This cube, which houses four 2500-watt HMIs, is hoisted by an industrial crane to 80 to 120 feet. In this position it gives a usable ambient light level in a radius of a quarter mile. Apart from the high cost of the crane rental, another limitation is that

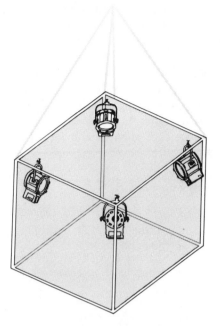

Flying Moon for an overall soft illumination
of a large area.

Flying Moon on an industrial crane, 80–120 feet high.

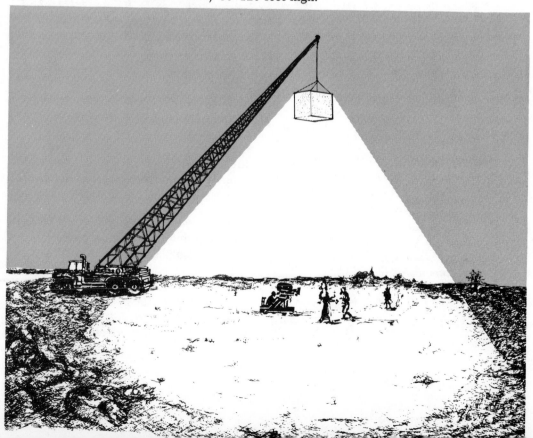

when there is a windy condition it swings. The Flying Moon can also be used on a high stage to simulate a night exterior.

The color of moonlight remains subject to interpretation.

James Crabe, ASC

Everyone has their own idea what moonlight is. I still believe moonlight to be kind of blue or bluish. Even though I know that time exposure by the moon will produce a photograph identical to sunlight, it won't be blue, it will be perfect. It is bounced sunlight off a white moon. When I go out to the desert to work on some commercial and I walk out from my room at night, from a room that has tungsten source, by comparison the moonlight seems blue. I generally would use a quarter to maybe a half blue gel. Sometimes you have to watch the electrical department a little bit. You would ask, Is that a white carbon or what filter is in that? If you are not careful you can overcorrect a lot. So if you are already putting a little warm light on for the interior or the fire, using maybe half MT2, which is pretty warm, and then add half blue on the other side, if you are not very careful, the printer can never make these two things work, because you are too far apart on your colors. It is one of those things you have to be very careful with, because when you are mixing lights within the scene, there is hardly any way you can get out of that dilemma. And of course moonlight, if it is in crosslight or backlight or glance light, then it is probably a little bit more believable than if it is very frontal. But that has been a sore point of cameramen and gaffers and other people for a long while, what color a moonlight should be.

The blue-oriented cinematographers may use just a white carbon arc with a Y-1 filter on it, or HMI lamps, that is, a daylight color temperature, at night. On some sequences when we do not see people, it is possible to shoot night scenes on black-and-white film and print them on color stock through a slightly blue filter. This technique gives an interesting result which should be tested to see how it will fit with the rest of the film.

On occasion a night location happens to be on the seashore. As we cannot illuminate the ocean, we have to create enough depth to indicate it.

Vilmos Zsigmond, ASC

Shoot the master shot as dusk for night, and try to shoot the coverage by using a few Brutes on the background.

This way the arcs will "rake" the white breakers of the surf.

Jordan Cronenweth, ASC

My preference is to try to find a location where there is a curved bay or a pier or a boat dock or something that gives you motivation for a light source, to give you halation in the water. And this applies to the ocean or to a lake or to a river. And you may be able to get by with just the available light, whatever is out there, and if there is none you can create it. You don't have to take the generator out there, you can have a battery pack and a string of lights, because you are not lighting as such, you are reflecting. You are creating practicals out there, to reflect in the water.

Another common night exterior is a campfire scene. Lighting people sitting around the fire can be accomplished in a variety of ways. Possibly the oldest device consists of pieces of white cloth hanging from a stick, which are moved in front of the light. Then came dimmers and finally a box with switches activated at random by a mercury blob moving around when the box is rocked by an electrician. The lights flickered by these devices can be positioned between the fire and the actors.

Vilmos Zsigmond, ASC

For a campfire effect there is a box with an automatic flicker device regulated for fast, slow, and so on. I am against overdoing the flicker effect. I would rather underdo it. You can hide some light behind the campfire. You may have a little dimming action. Too much flicker looks hokey, phony. The main thing is to determine your key. With a campfire you don't want to give people full exposure, it's better to have them a bit darker. They are usually sitting farther away from the fire and they should not be fully lit.

Another way to approach a campfire scene is to make the fire be the actual source of light. Auxiliary gas jets or gas pipes with many openings can be installed next to the fire, or next to the camera and the flow of propane gas is then regulated to create the flicker effect. This method was used by Nestor Al-mendros (ASC) ("Photographing *Days of Heaven,*" *American Cinematographer,* June 1979). To match the fire, incandescent lamps are usually gelled with MT-2 gelatin filters.

To create a delicate modulation of light for campfire scenes, cinematographer Harry Wolf (ASC), advises putting a smoke pot, like a trough, in front of a key light so that you get just a little bit of the flickering effect.

Another interesting effect was used in Kubrick's film, *The Shining.* John Alcott, who photographed this film, describes it in *American Cinematographer* (August 1980): "I wanted to get a full fire effect, a nice big glowing fire in the fireplace, but I didn't want to reduce the depth of field. So I shot the scene all the way through without the fire burning, then rewound the film, killed every light on the set, lit the fire, opened the lens up to T/1.4 and shot the fire by itself, which gave me a nice glowing fire."

To create the fire effect on people or sets, you can use an orange Mylar loosely stretched on a frame. You bounce the light off the Mylar, shaking the frame at the same time. The greatest danger is in overdoing this effect.

LOCATION INTERIOR

Location interiors vary from very confining spaces like bathrooms and elevators, to vast city halls and cathedrals. They also vary in the prevailing type of lighting—daylight, tungsten, fluorescent, or a mixture of all these. The amount of available working space will dictate the size and placement of the lighting instruments. Low ceilings and the lack of a grid forces the cameraman to place lights closer to the subjects. This creates two problems: Hiding the lights and achieving an even illumination. Whenever space permits, it is preferable to use a more powerful light from a greater distance in order to even out the light.

Nowadays fast film emulsions allow for much more use of bounced lighting and for the use of practicals properly arranged so that they are not too bright from the camera side. Often the practicals are augmented by hiding bulbs behind the existing light fixtures.

THE INTERIOR/EXTERIOR LOCATION

Daytime interiors often have a combination of daylight and artificial sources. The way in which each of these types of illumination is used will influence the atmosphere of the scene. Sunlight is often redirected into the interior. For example, standard silver reflectors positioned outside the building can reflect sunlight through the windows directly onto the ceiling off which the light again bounces to create a soft overall illumination in the room. Reflectors can also be used to provide a strong backlight coming from the outside.

Allen Daviau, ASC

Oftentimes you find that you can hide reflectors outside to give extra edges through the windows. It is amazing how the eye will forgive an edgelight, backlight coming in at an unusual angle. If you have a scene where there is one window way back across the room, and you have somebody sitting in the front, and it is obvious that in no way could that window be putting any light on this person, but if you direct edgelight on the person from the window side, the eye will accept it.

For a more specular redirection of light, mirrors can be used. Reflectors or mirrors positioned outdoors will require frequent manual adjustment because of the movement of the sun.

Ralph Woolsey, ASC

Years ago, particularly on westerns, some of the studios had heavy, reflector-size mirrors for bouncing sunlight. For a scene in a barn or a cave, you could direct a four-foot beam of light way in, and have reflectors inside to pick it up. Using two reflectors, you would lose some light even with the hard sides. But with a mirror to start, there is very little loss. Now it is possible to get lightweight mirrorlike plastic, but it must be stretched really tight and flat.

Location interior often requires lighting through windows. If the windows are visible in the frame, the light will have to come at an angle so that the lamps will not be seen. Watch out for overexposure of draperies, sometimes dyeing them will help in this respect.

When the exterior is too bright, neutral density gels will be placed on the windows. As an alternative to neutral density, some cinematographers like to use Roscoscrim, which resembles a black net. It cuts down the light by two stops. The general advantage of Roscoscrim over the ND gels is the fact that it does not reflect the light sources. Care has to be taken so that it is not in focus which would reveal its texture. To create an unobstructed path for the light generated by the lamps outside the windows, the gels or scrims are put at an angle, so that the light beam comes between them and the window. Neutral density gels and Roscoscrims are sufficient for sets illuminated with daylight-type lights, such as HMIs. For sets lit with tungsten light an 85 gel has to be added to the windows.

When the background brightness changes between shots, we have to keep changing the densities of the NDs on the windows so that the look of the whole scene will remain consistent. If we are using arcs to create a controlled sunlight coming through the windows, we will have to keep changing the intensity of these arcs to avoid inconsistencies between the brightness of the background and the amount of light coming through the window. For example, if the exterior gets darker and we exchange the neutral density gel for a lighter one (say from ND6 to ND3), we will have to scrim the arcs to bring less light through the window as our source. This way the intensity of the light patterns on the walls and floor will remain constant. When long scenes are scheduled to be filmed on such locations, frames should be prepared with gels

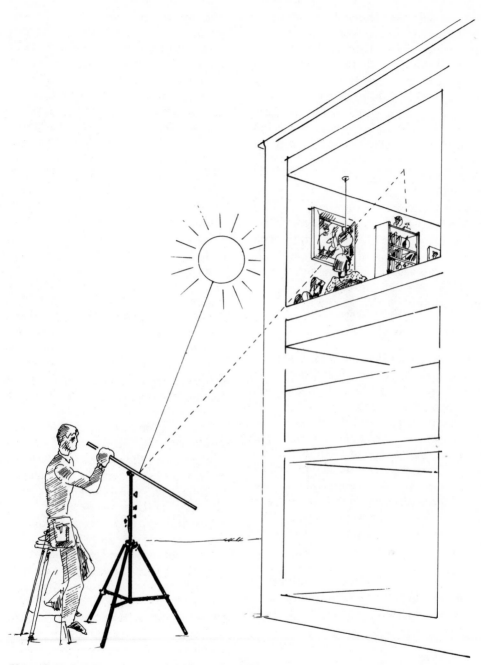

Shiny board reflectors are used here to bounce the sunlight into the building.

of various densities for all the windows, so that the gel changes between shots will not cause extensive delays. Particularly in the winter when the days are shorter, good planning is essential to maximize the use of the daylight. This type of lighting situation was used to obtain exquisite visual results in *Barry Lyndon*, photographed entirely on location by John Alcott ("Photographing Stanley Kubrick's *Barry Lyndon*," *American Cinematographer*, March 1976).

It is often desirable to have the exteriors slightly overexposed for the sunny, hot feeling, or actually bluish for a rather cold effect. A three-stop difference between the interior and exterior allows visibility of people on the outside. Here again the tests evaluating the latitude of a given film emulsion are extremely helpful.

Allen Daviau, ASC

Another thing that the cinematographer gets involved with is dressing the outside. Make sure that on location you have enough plant greens. Sometimes you can save what would be a disastrous shot by simply filling a piece of hot sky with one piece of green out there. And again, if it is out of focus it does not matter. There are some wonderful artificial greens available now, made of fabric. They are very expensive but they have this wonderful translucent, yellow-green quality. You can just roast them with light and you are not killing a real plant.

Window intensity can often be controlled by curtains or blinds. Jordan Cronenweth recalls using practical shades on the windows made of neutral density gels.

Jordan Cronenweth, ASC

You can filter the windows if you don't have somebody coming in and out through the doorway. If you have somebody coming in and out of the door, then you have to build a neutral density screen far enough back of the doorway so that they can get between the neutral and the door to make an entrance. Then you have problems with their shadows and you have problems with reflections in the neutrals. So, you have to build a black enclosure. It is one of those things that starts getting out of hand. The best thing to do is to go with nature as much as you can. Shoot the sequence late in the day if possible, light levels are then lower and you don't have to deal with such incredible differences.

There are all kinds of things that you can do to have the interior and exterior balanced. I had a scene in the last picture I did in a sales office overlooking the harbor. I had the set dresser and the art director make up neutral density shades that you could pull down, that looked like they were a part of the dressing. The kind of thing that people would pull over the windows during the heat of the day. So the camera was always looking on the exterior through the shades. And I left the 85 on the camera so the exterior looked neutral in color. In the situation like that, you have a conversation with the director and he is aware that you can shoot the entrances and exits later in the day, and you shoot the other angles when you don't look out through the door during the course of the day while you are waiting for the light to get ready to do the interior/exterior shots.

For continuity it is better to leave the 85 on the camera even if it is turning dark, but you are still creating an illusion of day.

Source lighting through the windows becomes much less complicated when the exterior does not have to be visible. Under these circumstances tracing paper is often used on the windows, and arcs can be substituted by large 6000-watt HMI lights, or nine-lights po-

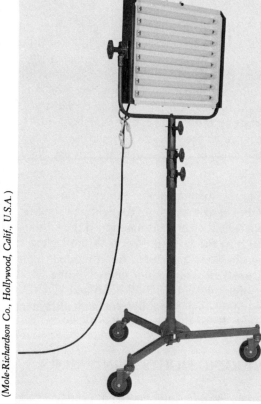

(Mole-Richardson Co., Hollywood, Calif., U.S.A.)

Eight-tube Molescent used as fill light when an overhead fluorescent illumination is used for lighting the scene.

sitioned just outside the windows. Such apparent daylight is fully controllable and stays the same all day long. The real daylight filtering in does not make much difference under these circumstances. The great advantages of lighting the inside with HMIs is the consistent daylight characteristic and the relatively cool temperature allowing for greater comfort.

FLUORESCENTS

Many location interiors are illuminated with fluorescent tubes. This poses several problems for the cinematographer.

Ralph Woolsey, ASC

Warm White Deluxe (WWX) is a standard fluorescent tube and generally available from large suppliers. It can be mixed with tungsten sources, as it is close to their color, plus a little added green. The plastic covers on many fixtures filter out most of this green. Cool White (CW) fluorescent is the most commonly found. It is daylight plus green, and can be converted to tungsten balance through an FLB filter on the lens. (This combines an 85 with a .30 magenta to take out the green.) If you can't afford the one-stop loss of the FLB, consider using at least a .20 or .30 CC magenta to remove the green and have the lab correct the rest. The results are somewhat better than a full fluorescent lab correction. This assumes that all sources of light are Cool Whites or the equivalent. If you have fluorescent lights visible in the shot and you cannot change them, or overpower them, then of course you have to match most other lights to the fluorescents. Then you may have a problem with the exterior, if you see out the windows. There are available several types of tubes which are true Daylight quality and they can be substituted if there is enough work scheduled to make it pay.

One of my problem situations was a large architect's office complex with over 600 Cool White Deluxe (CWX) tubes, which are half-way between tungsten and daylight, plus the usual green. There were also large windows all around. Ideally, a complete substitution with true daylight tubes was the answer, but only two days were scheduled there, and the cost would have been prohibitive. The solution was to use only HMIs, which we easily matched to the fluorescent, which was around 4000°K, plus green. The real trick was matching the windows, because inside we were now lined up with CWX. But my digital 3-color meter computed the needed correc-

LIGHTING ON LOCATION   169

tion and confirmed that YF101 material would do the job. This stuff is for correcting yellow-flame carbons and comes in rolls only 30 inches wide, so our windows used up a lot of it. Even if not in a shot, they were covered in order to convert the incoming daylight to the CWX inside. No added ND was needed as we had plenty of interior illumination with the converted HMIs. Since there was plenty of light, an 81EF filter on the lens plus a .20CC magenta inside the Panaflex converted the CWX illumination directly to 3200°K. When possible, I prefer to do the major correction this way during the initial photography, if for no other reason than to make the lab wonder how we did it without asking for their help.

On occasion mixing fluorescent with tungsten lights can add a certain documentary realism to the scene.

Richard Kline, ASC

If you have a mixture of fluorescent with daylight or with incandescent light, you have to figure out which way you want to go, because it is going to mix. Audiences are prepared now for a greenish look, so it is not as taboo as it was before. In fact I almost welcome a natural look, where you will blend a little bit. Where daylight is one thing, incandescent is something else and fluorescent is something else again. You have mercury vapor to work with and you have sodium. If it exists, I will use it as a source and then alter the lights with gels to fit it.

When we decide to use existing fluorescent light as our key illumination then we will need a portable frame of fluorescent tubes as fill light.

Richard Hart

I built large fluorescent fill lights which are three by four and they take eight 4-foot tubes and what we usually do is try to match whatever is there and then let the lab correct the color. Because it is usually low level you don't want to add FLB filters and all of that sort of thing on the camera and lose the light. I try to change all the tubes to Chroma 50, and then use daylight inside. Then you can use HMIs as well.

Several manufacturers produce fluorescent tubes closely matching daylight and tungsten sources. Richard hart mentioned the Chroma 50 tube for daylight. Warm White Deluxe is specified as matching the tungsten light. Duro-Test Corporation offers Optima 32 as compatible with 3200°K lights and Vita-Lite as simulating the full color and ultraviolet spectrum of sunlight.

RIGGING LIGHTS IN INTERIORS

Some location interiors require certain architectural adaptations to help hide the lamps. Often false beams will be spread across the ceiling, or false pillars along the walls. A false moulding along the corridor will hide the cables and even lights. When the ceiling is not visible in the shot a temporary lighting grid made of pipes or boards can be installed. Different room sizes require different lighting approaches.

Michael D. Margulies, ASC

To light a large interior like a dance hall takes prerigging. You need time to hang coffins or boxes or small coops. A large dance hall is best lit from the top. I like to work with ambient light, whatever the set is. Even at night.

Just a certain amount of ambient light and that is usually from the top. Sometimes I have it from the side if it is a night exterior. I always try to work with just a certain amount of ambient light to register on the film. Unless of course it calls for a closet door closing and then it is black so there is no reason to have the top of the clothes on a clothesrack still lit.

In practical locations if you cannot get a light where it is desirable in a given situation and in a short period of time, you have to compromise. The background may have to suffer. As far as the actor getting hotter when he is near the lamp, that is controlled as you would do with a hard light. You can put up doubles [scrims] for the hard light, whereas for soft light you can put up a solid [flag] and it will do about the same, because the light does bounce around. You can also bounce it from the ceiling and then when you get into a close-up or a two-shot you can clean it up.

INTERPRETIVE LIGHTING

Some location interiors incorporate very specific lighting. For example a theater during film projection. It is usually done as an interpretation of the visual atmosphere, rather than a realistic redition. In a real situation people are flatly lit by the light reflected from the screen. The projector beam does not backlight the audience, and there is almost no light spilling from the projection booth through the portholes. Yet, these are the effects which we usually try to incorporate. They are more realistic and justified in a small screening room like the scene from *Blow-Up* photographed by Vilmos Zsigmond.

Vilmos Zsigmond, ASC

When I was shooting toward the screen, the light source was the screen, so people were backlit, silhouetted against the screen. When I shot toward the projector I used a lot of backlight, as if it came from the projector and the booth. The booth was also lit.

I usually do not use the flickering effect on the people facing the screen because it looks phony. It also becomes very difficult to intercut. In real life a projection does not flicker. The flicker that you see in real life is caused by cuts where there is a light change, which is a lot less frequently than the phony flicker effect. Flicker from a television set also looks phony. I prefer to establish the light source near the TV and I do a few light changes which will give you an effect that you are watching television.

VEHICLES

A commonly encountered location interior is the car. Planes, trains, and other moving vehicles are also common. When planning such a scene an important decision is whether to shoot on location or on a sound stage setup with back projection. After the great love affair with location in the late sixties and early seventies, filmmakers tend to choose the comforts of a stage more often than not. Still, there are always many car, train or plane scenes shot on location.

Haskell Wexler, ASC

One of the things which I learned from working on the documentary on the bus, is that a lot of the equipment that we use when lighting inside cars is basically unnecessary to get good results. If you can control the intensity of the background with neutral density gels on the windows in the shot, it is possible to use the natural existing daylight in the car to make perfectly acceptable shots. This lighting may be further helped by bouncing some light into the people's faces. The only advantage of lighting inside the car is consistency. If you have a long scene which is supposed to look the same way for a long time, it is necessary to include your own sources of lighting, because you cannot count on the daylight or the direction of the road to help you.

Some of the problems of lighting daylight inside the car, when shooting through the windshield is getting sky reflections on the windshield. The way it is usually done in TV productions when they have to do it "fast and dirty," is to put a black tent over the top of the windshield and keep all the reflections out, and thereby going regardless of what the daylight is doing. In other words, the people inside the car are lit by a light that is coming from outside, either a nine-light or by an HMI hitting some paper reflector. The light that normally hits the windshield, which gives the reflections, is covered with an awning that goes from the top of the car, so what you see reflected in the windshield is the black cloth. If you like the audience to be conscious of the

A car scene with back projection. The effects of passing lights are produced by white reflecting boards rotating in front of the lamps and by a lamp moving up and down on a boom.

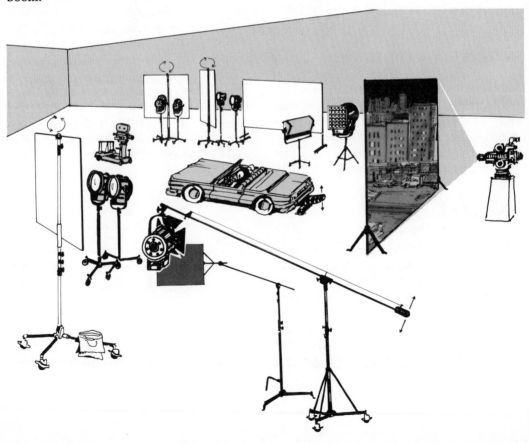

fact that there indeed is a windshield there, you have to drive on the road with an angle that does not cause the daylight to obscure people's image completely. An ideally suitable road would have trees hanging over it. Then you have a nice effect of shadows and light and movement on the windshield, like having a series of dissolves going on. Sometimes you can also use a Pola-screen to cut the reflection out.

There seems to be now a lot more use of rear projection for car scenes. I am certainly very much in favor of night shooting this way, for scenes of any duration, because you can get a perfect sound. Basically all that you can see out of the car at night are lights, so with good plates [back-projected footage] you can do a nice job.

Trains have different power than your lights, so you would probably take your battery packs with you. If you are just going to shoot for a few hours on the train, to do a small scene, I am sure that you can work with a light card and two or three HMI guns for the daytime. It is also good whenever you have a situation like that to have neutrals with you, so that if you have some windows which throw everything completely out of balance, you would be able to deal with it.

For the most convincing car photography, choosing a suitable road is as important as the lighting. Often artificial lighting can be minimized when proper shooting angles are established.

Vilmos Zsigmond, ASC

Many people use too much light [inside the car]. You make fewer mistakes having people in silhouette and having less light on them. It is more natural. Even when you use fiber optics there is a tendency to overlight.

Most of the car interiors are done in con-trolled situations like pulling the action car with a camera car equipped with batteries and lights. There is one angle in a car very difficult to light. That is when the people are sitting in the front seats and the camera is shooting from the back seat or through the rear window.

The most controlled situation is, of course, on the stage using rear projection. You can have rear projection combined with another projected image reflected on the windshield. One plate is prepared for the background and another plate is shot of the neons and street signs to project onto the windshield. It gives an extremely realistic look.

In an airplane, you can almost use only the existing light, or existing light augmented by a little bit of a bounced light, virtually available light. If you are shooting in a plane on the ground and you try to simulate flying, you can move a lamp up and down to create the illusion of the sunlight moving. You can float the camera up and down and sideways on two fluid heads joined together.

From these and the following statements we see how much thought and ingenuity goes into lighting the insides of vehicles to convey the realistic character of these confined spaces. However, in spite of the convenience of shooting using a back projection in the studio, many scenes are shot on location for a more realistic look.

James Crabe, ASC

Every picture nowadays has sequences with automobiles, so it is something you have to deal with. Sometimes you take a hand-held camera inside the car and do close-ups that way, but usually you are using such a short lens that it is not very flattering to people. Some camera cars can tow the subject car alongside, so that you can get a decent two-shot that way and it is much easier than putting rigs up. You also have the problems of reflections in the windshield which generally are to be preferred nowadays, ever since Polanski's Knife in the Water. Now everybody wants to have reflections in the windshield if one does not mind the fact that there is supposed to be glass between the speaking actor and the camera. Some directors feel that if you are shooting through glass you should not hear the people terribly clearly.

Car stuff is tedious. I am sure that there are people, grips and others who have fast ways of putting cameras on cars. But it always seems to be a major production. With the Panaflex it is now possible for an operator to lie on the roof of the car and bend the eyepiece straight up and look down. Of course, in car scenes people are leaning forward and leaning back and to keep that alignment so that they are not covering one another, and to figure out where you should place the focus takes some effort. Because usually there is not enough depth of field if it is a very tight two-shot to hold both subjects sufficiently in focus. So it is just a drag. If you are shooting at night and you want to see the street lights, in order to keep them in balance, you probably have to light your foreground characters at 12 footcandles or something very little in order that the background won't be wasted or so out of balance that it isn't doing you any good. I found in situations like that that sometimes a bounce card can be very effective. Of course this depends on whether or not the car is being towed or actually driven. If the car is being actually driven by an actor, as was the case in Save the Tiger with Jack Lemmon, who happens to be a very good driver, it is also quite dangerous, becuse you've got guys hanging on the car and you have a driver who has lights in his eyes and trying to drive at night. But we found that I could sit up on the hood of the car and just occasionally direct a

baby at the white cardboard and then take it off. The cardboard would be in front but not so much in front that he could not still see a little bit. Most people would not be able to do it. Jack is a really good driver.

I always thought that it would be wonderful to be able to do scenes where the sun is really so low that you can use the real sun coming in [the car] and hitting people, but if you are working in cities and streets where buildings abound, that just doesn't seem to happen a lot. And when it does, when you get those wonderful bursts of hot backlight that really comes in and pierces through the rest of the scene it is very believable and very realistic, even if it is several stops hotter than what you've got going on inside.

With process screen, no matter how you slice it, whether using front, rear or matte, the background becomes a generation farther away than the foreground. It works wonderfully if you are looking through windows that have a little dirt on them, or drops of water, or rain is going or some other effects.

I find, in commercials at least, one very handy thing that we carry with us all the time. It is a small surface mirror, a foot square. If we are doing a commercial and we want to see the guy smoking a cigarette and driving the truck, we just put that mirror with a piece of clay, stick it onto the dashboard and then take a hand-held camera and now you can be shooting through, past the gearshift, you can get shots you could not get any other way. We are shooting into the mirror. This has to be flopped, but in commercials almost everything is an optical anyway.

The direction of light for the car interior is not much of a problem during the day. After all, cars have windows all around. At night it becomes more problematic. The old-fashioned approach with a very bright dashboard is not quite realistic. Gaffers and cinematographers use various light units in various places to create believable lighting and the correct mood.

Richmond Aguilar

In a daytime situation we want the light to come through the window. The driver gets his primary light through the windshield and a little bit from the side, so you try to simulate it. You try to key him from the front if possible. A big FAY twelve-light with a diffusion on it will be rigged on the hood, near the camera, giving a big soft fill through the windshield. If you use two or three cameras for coverage, the light will be hemmed-in between them. It sounds very flat, but I think that if you get the intensity right, it looks like a very normal light coming through a windshield, its angle is justified and it always looks clean. With only one camera on the hood, you can put the light more to the side.

Lighting inside the car at night depends a lot on the scene. If the characters are a bunch of heavies, you might use the dashboard light coming up. There is, of course, the problem with the [shadow from the] steering wheel, and it always looks a little bit hokey. I use a long source rather than a small hard light.

There is the Lumeline light which looks like a fluorescent tube but has a filament running through it. They come in 12- and 18-inch lengths. This provides a long source of light, gives you enough light in the face, and when a hand moves in front of it, it does not burn up that bad and it does not give you a really hard shadow. These lamps are used in showcases. They are only one inch in diameter and you can literally tape them wherever you need them. The idea is that you have a big source from a little light. We sometimes use them up high, taped right onto the visor areas. It is far enough forward, high, and complementary to the people. It gives the ex-

posure, and you really do not know where it is coming from. It is soft since it runs laterally. These lights are 40 watt and 60 watt and they run on 120 volt from a battery pack. We put a dimmer on them, so you get exactly what you want. Color is not that important because at night you have all kinds of color. There is also an inverter available, from 12 volts DC to 120 volts AC. They made it mainly for mobile homes where you can run some appliances from your 12-volt battery. This inverter is good for 700 watts. Clip it on the battery and plug in your lights. The drainage will be about the same as your headlights.

For lighting people in the back, you may rig some lights from outside the windows, and turn lights on and off. And you will have a little fill light from the front. I have done it with little 12-volt bulbs, the ones used for the signal lights. They are fairly bright bulbs. I have very simple tin reflectors for them and you can plug them into your cigarette lighter. They can be taped to the backs of the front seats or on the window frames. They give enough exposure for the faces. You can do a nice job for a night car scene in the studio with a limbo black in the background and just lights flashing by.

The system that truly represents a technological advance in lighting the car interior at night is the fiber optic. With the lamp hidden in the trunk and the flexible fibers transmitting the beams, light can be conducted to the exact desired positions. Richard Hart developed his own fiber optics system that uses 3200°K light as a source.

Richard Hart

The difficulty is where to hide the light. The camera is usually mounted on the hood or through the side window on the raking two-shot, or something like that. You are very, very limited to where the light can come from. If you are lighting from inside the car, the lighting techniques up to now have been to hide some kind of a small unit, or an open globe diffused down, on the dashboard somewhere. Well, the problem comes with the hands in front of the light. If they are in the picture they are hot. If they are not in the picture you've got their shadow and the shadow of the steering wheel, and if you have any turns in it at all it just gets hard to lose that. So with the fiber optics you can literally take a tiny little light and move it around, hide it with tape.

Process projection is always a very time-consuming, very cumbersome way of doing something and if it is not really done well, you know that it is processed. Doing it in a natural environment with the new stock makes it so nice, because with fiber optics or anything else you can create a very small amount of ambient light in the car, and actually have the real street background coming in and out and creating those effects that are so desirable.

To simulate car movement when shooting a stationary car interior, Jordan Cronenweth suggests the use of a wind machine throwing water on the windshield and windows. It gives a very realistic effect especially in conjunction with light effects created by moving a cardboard with horizontal slots vertically in front of the lamp, to create a streaking light effect.

Whatever location we are going to use, we should approach it with open eyes and sensitivity. There is a great danger of coming to a location and changing its character through lighting. This often negates the primary reason for going there. Today's fast emulsions allow us to make good use of the existing, available lighting and therefore to preserve the unique character that each location offers. Under the best of circumstances our lights should just augment it and introduce the nuances required to achieve the mood desired for the scene.

CHAPTER *Seven*

Learning to Light

LEARNING FILM lighting must, by nature, follow a twofold path. We must know our tools but even more important we must learn to see. When I asked the British cinematographer Douglas Slocombe (BSC) what was the most important skill that he had learned over the years about lighting, his answer was, "The awareness of light; using one's own eyes. A child is aware of it; of light reflections in the bathtub, of the shine on the faucet, of a shaft of light under the door."

Although we all tend to lose the awareness of a child as we grow older, we can still develop our visual consciousness at almost any age. But we must try to see, to observe how light illuminates our reality, how it plays on things around us. What are the characteristics of the artificial light in a kitchen and in a bathroom? What pattern does the sunshine filtering through the curtains make on the living room furniture and the floor? How are people lit in our favorite restaurants? And how are they lit in church? Then we should

examine how other artists see the world. Cinematography did not evolve in a vacuum. We have to study the visual tradition of our medium.

Vilmos Zsigmond, ASC

We like to go back to painters. For cameramen, going to a museum is beyond entertainment. You can learn a lot from paintings. Your eyes see different kinds of lighting moods and it is a way to train your eyes and your feelings. You learn to see what painters do in certain situations, how they create mood, how they light, what kind of colors do they use. These are the primary sources to work with besides working in real life, keeping your eyes open and seeing things, or studying photographs. Still photographs are very good for us, actually, because they capture real life with certain color effects, certain moods, whether in color or in black and white. For feature film cameramen I think that painting is a more classical way to learn.

Looking at paintings and photographs allows us to linger. Watching movies, on the other hand, demands much faster observation. In this respect it helps to watch movies without sound. Finally we need to learn by doing. Traditionally, documentaries and commercials have been the training ground for many cinematographers.

Haskell Wexler, ASC

I find that I learn the most when working on documentaries. When the budget is minimal you are forced to look at light as you find it, and to make it look good. Fortunately with the modern fast films there is much less problem with exposure. In documentaries you are forced to observe very quickly, not just lighting but also framing because usually you are not able to tell people where to stand or where to walk. So you have to make framing decisions almost instantaneously. And you may have to be able to see right away that, for example, someone who is talking has a terrific mixture of light on his face: Perhaps a bluish kicker from the daylight and an overhead light from the warmer light above and a fill light bounced off the table.

Allen Daviau

I found that in commercials I could work with a variety of lighting styles as a lighting cinematographer and that this helped me to get closer to my goal which was feature motion pictures. And I found that I bet on a good thing, because the variety of experience that I got from commercials was very good.

Simultaneously with learning to see light we must develop a thorough knowledge of lighting tools. We must instinctively realize what a given light can do for us at a given distance and angle.

Vilmos Zsigmond, ASC

With time you learn to know your tools. You know your lights. When you turn a Baby Spot on, and you flood it halfway, you practically can guess what the exposure is. On exteriors at a given latitude, you know what the exposure will be, say at three in the afternoon, because of your experience. That is why many times you do not need your light meter. You can light with your eyes, you set the contrast and the mood with your eyes, you do not need a light meter for that.

A cinematographer needs to keep in touch with the constantly changing lighting technology. Manufacturers come up with new equipment and often his gaffer will alert him to those developments.

James Crabe, ASC

Every time I work, I am working with crew people who themselves are discovering new things. The gaffer might say to me, "Hey, listen, there is a new light . . . " and I will say, "Bring one, and we will see how we like it." I learn from the crew. No matter how you slice it, it is a very collaborative kind of thing, unlike the freedom that the still cameraman has to go out and be able to record pictures and just to show the ten out of two hundred that he took.

One of the significant ways that cinematography differs from still photography is in matching shots and sequences. This is the area where learning continues over the years. Matching shots is helped by timing the print, but balancing the various areas of one shot has to be done right the first time around. It requires an experienced eye and knowledge of film stock characteristics.

Vilmos Zsigmond, ASC

I think that most of the mistakes you make when learning, are in lighting. In balancing the light. Most overlighting and underlighting can be corrected with printing, but the balance between different areas of the room will not change in printing. For example when you establish sunshine coming through a window, it can be too much or it can be too little. But most mistakes are made in matching. You learn about matching one shot to another all of your life. The easy part of matching is interiors. On the stage you have all the control. The sun is not moving around, the clouds are not blocking the sun, so the interior is easier, you control everything, but it is still very difficult. What happens with exteriors when you lose the sun, and you have to use lamps to match the previous shots? Now, this becomes a problem of matching!

The more experienced you become with your lighting techniques the more flexible you can be.

John Alonzo, ASC

I am still learning about lighting. I am still learning that what works for one scene does not work for another scene. You sometimes have to become more inventive as to how you light a particular actor or actress. People are different. I am learning to be more and more flexible, so if it does not work I am not setting myself a rule that I must key somebody from this direction because that is the best. I become flexible and start finding other ways of lighting them. You start learning that you can do more sometimes with no light. I started learning how to use the newer lights that we have. I do not want to be pompous about it but it is like a painter. A painter never stops learning what he can do with color. He may become proficient at it and technically correct, but you never stop until you can make a full circle. Like a representational artist who finally makes the full circle to abstraction, who has got so much freedom that he just throws color everywhere and it looks good. That, I guess, is what most cameramen try to finally achieve, until you end up shooting and lighting in such a way that it is almost natural, that it does not look like it is lit. I watch actors, I look at how they talk, which way they move, whether they hold their chins up or down, what it is that they do, so that I don't say to them, you must look up because the light is over here.

A challenging aspect of film lighting is that after we learn all our tools and become familiar with the most often-encountered situations, the unexpected is bound to happen and we will be asked to improvise. The late James Wong Howe described two interesting improvisations from his long and fascinating career.

James Wong Howe, ASC

It happens sometimes that you have to improvise your lighting equipment in the most unexpected situations. I will give you an example.

Many years ago we were making a Zane Grey western down in Arizona and in those days we did not have electric generators out on location. We had to light everything with reflectors. On this particular occasion the director wanted to go up the side of the mountain to get a full-figure shot of an actor on horseback looking down into the valley. He said to me, "Jimmy, leave the reflectors here, we will just get a long shot silhouetted against the sky. We will take only the camera and our lunches up there. So we did. We went with a reduced crew and we shot the silhouette of the rider. But the director said, "Oh, Jimmy, I am sorry, but I've got to have a close-up of him and a shot of the valley where he is looking. It wasn't in the script but action dictates it." So I said, "Well, look, we left all the reflectors down there and I don't have any lights." "Will it take long to get them up here?" he asked. I said, "Yes, we have to send the men down and the reflectors are very heavy to carry up. Do you have to have this close-up?" He said "Yes, I have to have it." I suggested that we could shoot the close-up later somewhere else, but the director insisted on having it done up there.

This was in the days before we had paper cups and there were a lot of tin cups in which we were drinking coffee. This gave me an idea. I asked [one of the crew], "Vic, how many tin cups can you pick up and hold in your hand?" "Oh," he said, "I can hold maybe four or five." I said, "Fine, see if you can hold eight or ten cups and reflect the sun on the face. And I need about four or five fellows over here with cups doing the same thing."

They couldn't hold the cups still but it was all right, and on the screen it looked like the sunlight was coming through the leaves and giving an unsteady broken pattern.

Another time I was doing the picture Air Force. This was a story of sending nine B-17 bombers to Hawaii. They got halfway there when they heard over the radio that the Japanese had just bombed Pearl Harbor. But as it was a routine flight they had just enough gas to get there. So they had to land although the tower told them that the field had been bombed.

We were down in Florida. We duplicated the field and I had my lights all set up. We expected nine B-17s to come in about quarter of seven. Two or three hours before that time we were ready to photograph. I asked my electrician to start the generator and light up

to see if everything was going to be all right, as these B-17s were to land only once. Well, the generator broke down. I have no lights. I go to my director who is Howard Hawks, and say, "Howard, we are in trouble." He says, "What?" so I explain, "The generator broke down." He says, "What do you mean, 'we are in trouble,' that's your problem. I am not the photographer, I am just directing this picture."

So I went to my special effects man. I always had him carry flares for emergencies. I asked him how many flares he had. He said, "Oh, Jimmy, I have two or three boxes of three minute and one minute flares." So where I had my lights set, I took the reflectors out of them and mounted the reflectors on stands. In front of them I had sticks in the ground with a flare on each of them. I then had them all wired up and we tried one out. When we hit the switch it ignited the flare. At quarter of seven the B-17s came in. Just when they were close enough I gave the signal, the man hit the switch and all the flares lit up. They flickered and the smoke came through, and you could see the B-17s with their headlights penetrating through the smoke. The flickering flares reflected on their wings and fusilages. Of course, the airfield was supposed to be bombed and on fire, so it all fitted beautifully. It was much more effective than if I had the electric lights. They would have been too steady. Well, we saw it on the screen. Hawks said, "Jimmy, this is great! Now we can send the generator back home. We can save a lot of money and we don't need the damn thing, because it is breaking down and we will finish the picture here with flares!"

Such unexpected improvisation helps us to keep fresh and open to new things. But even without such emergencies we should try to start every picture with the benefit of our past experience and still with a very fresh and inventive attitude.

Conrad Hall, ASC

After you have done a picture you forget everything you have ever known, so that you become a child again, or an infant or a void into which the new pictures creates a whole new evolvement, a whole new growth, a whole new development, so that you do not have to keep doing the same thing all over again. In other words you take yourself back to ground zero. Of course you cannot unlearn what your brain knows. But I mean it emotionally, I mean that you just become scared again, as if you do not know anything. Instead of having a sense of arrogance that makes you feel you are the master, you feel like the opposite. I never felt on top of it. I never felt that I knew so much that I could sit back with a cup of coffee and it would all turn out wonderful. I always felt that unless I work really hard at it and pay really close attention to it every second of the way, that I may not end up with something that somebody would like.

When we are learning the tools and training the eyes we must not lose sight of the reason we are learning all these things: to communicate.

Allen Daviau, ASC

When reading scripts you have to be true to yourself and ask the question, Do I really want to have my name on that?

This last question is perhaps the most important question that a cinematographer can ask himself or herself. It is a question about the ultimate self-esteem of an artist. Let us never forget that our talents and our skills can be used to convey base values as well as noble ones. The choice is ours.

Notes on the Contributors

Richmond ("Aggie") Aguilar. Gaffer.
Works with such cinematographers as James Crabe, Laszlo Kovacs, Sven Nykvist, and Billy Williams. Some of his credits as gaffer include: *Easy Rider*, 1969, *Paper Moon*, 1973, *Shampoo*, 1975, *New York, New York*, 1977, *The Postman Always Rings Twice*, 1980, *On Golden Pond*, 1981, *Frances*, 1982, and *Star 80*, 1983.

John Alonzo, ASC. Cinematographer.
Some of his credits include: *Harold and Maude*, 1971, *Sounder*, 1971, *Lady Sings the Blues*, 1971, *Chinatown*, 1974, *Farewell My Lovely*, 1975, *Norma Rae*, 1979, *Cross Creek* and *Scarface*, 1983. Alonzo's directorial credits include *FM* and several TV movies that he also photographed.

James Crabe, ASC. Cinematographer.
Some of his credits include: *Save the Tiger*, 1972, *Rocky*, 1976, *Sextette*, 1976, *The China Syndrome*, 1979, *The Formula*, 1980 (Academy Award Nomination), *Night Shift*, 1982, *The Karate Kid*, 1984, and several TV movies such as "The Letter," 1982 (Emmy Award winner), and also Emmy Award nominations for "The Entertainer," 1976, and "Eleanor and Franklin: The White House Years," 1977.

Jordan Cronenweth, ASC.
Cinematographer.
Some of his credits include: *Play It as It Lays*, 1972, *Gable and Lombard*, 1976, *Altered States*, 1980, *Cutter's Way*, 1981, *Blade Runner*, 1982 (British Academy Award winner), and *Best Friends*, 1982.

Allen Daviau, ASC. Cinematographer.
Some of his credits include: *E.T. the Extra-Terrestrial*, 1982 (Academy Award nomination), *The Falcon and the Snowman*, 1984, *The Color Purple*, 1985 (Academy Award nomination), and such TV movies as "The

Streets of L.A.," 1979, and "The Rage," 1980.

Thomas Denove. Cinematographer.
His credits include over twenty features and 200 commercials. He is a lighting consultant for LTM Corporation of America, a college lecturer on cinematography and the developer of the Cinemeter® exposure meter system.

Caleb Deschanel, ASC. Cinematographer.
Some of his credits include: *The Black Stallion*, 1979, *Being There*, 1979, *More American Graffiti*, 1979, *The Right Stuff*, 1983, and *The Natural*, 1984, (Academy Award nomination). Deschanel's directorial credits include *The Escape Artist*, 1982.

Conrad Hall, ASC. Cinematographer.
Some of his credits include: *The Professionals*, 1966, *In Cold Blood*, 1967, *Hell in the Pacific*, 1969, *Butch Cassidy and the Sundance Kid*, 1969 (Academy Award winner), *Tell Them Willie Boy is Here*, 1969, *Fat City*, 1972, and *The Day of the Locust*, 1975.

Richard Hart. Gaffer.
Works with such cinematographers as John Alonzo, Jordan Cronenweth, Sven Nykvist, and Haskell Wexler. Some of his credits as gaffer include: *Lady Sings the Blues*, 1971, *Sounder*, 1971, *Harold and Maude*, 1971, *Cutter's Way*, 1981, *Blade Runner*, 1982, and *The Man Who Loved Women*, 1983. Hart also works as a cinematographer, mostly in TV commercials.

Adam Holender, ASC. Cinematographer.
Some of his credits include: *Midnight Cowboy*, 1969, *Panic in Needle Park*, 1974, *Man on a Swing*, 1976, *The Seduction of Joe*

Tynan, 1979, *Promises in the Dark*, 1979, *Simon*, 1979, and *The Idolmaker*, 1980.

James Wong Howe, ASC. Cinematographer from 1922 to 1974.
Among his nearly 120 feature credits, some of the most memorable are: *Air Force*, 1943, *Body and Soul*, 1947, *The Rose Tattoo*, 1955 (Academy Award winner), *Picnic*, 1955, *Sweet Smell of Success*, 1957, *The Old Man and the Sea*, 1957, *Hud*, 1963 (Academy Award winner), *Hombre*, 1967, *The Molly Maguires*, 1970, and *Funny Lady*, 1974 (Academy Award nomination).

Richard Kline, ASC. Cinematographer.
Some of his credits include: *Camelot*, 1967 (Academy Award nomination), *The Boston Strangler*, 1968, *The Andromeda Strain*, 1971, *Soylent Green*, 1973, *The Terminal Man*, 1974, *King Kong*, 1976 (Academy Award nomination), *Star Trek, The Motion Picture*, 1979, and *Body Heat*, 1981. *All of Me*, 1984.

Philip Lathrop, ASC. Cinematographer.
Some of his credits include: *Days of Wine and Roses*, 1962, *The Cincinnati Kid*, 1965, *They Shoot Horses, Don't They?*, 1969, *Portnoy's Complaint*, 1971, *Airport '77*, 1977, *The Driver*, 1977, *A Change of Seasons*, 1980.

Alexander Mackendrick. Director.
Particularly known for the following films: *Whisky Galore (Tight Little Island* in U.S), 1948, *The Man in the White Suit*, 1951, *The Ladykillers*, 1955, *Sweet Smell of Success*, 1957, *A High Wind in Jamaica*, 1965.

Michael D. Margulies, ASC.
Cinematographer.
Some of his credits include: *Minnie and*

Moskowitz, 1971, *My Bodyguard*, 1980, *Six Weeks* 1982, *Police Academy*, 1984, and such TV movies as "The Blue Knight," 1973, (Emmy Award winner), "The Law," 1974 (Emmy Award winner), "Robert Kennedy and His Times," 1984.

James Plannette. Gaffer.
Works with such directors as John Alonzo, Allen Daviau, Laszlo Kovacs, Sven Nykvist, and Vilmos Zsigmond. Some of his credits as gaffer include: *Young Frankenstein*, 1974, *The Cheap Detective*, 1978, *Flesh and Blood*, 1979, *Inside Moves*, 1980, *Cannery Row*, 1982, *E. T. the ExtraTerrestrial*, 1982.

Haskell Wexler, ASC. Cinematographer.
Some of his credits include: *Who's Afraid of Virginia Woolf?*, 1966 (Academy Award winner), *The Loved One*, 1966, *In the Heat of the Night*, 1967, *The Thomas Crown Affair*, 1968, *Bound for Glory*, 1976 (Academy Award winner), *Coming Home*, 1978, and *The Man Who Loved Women*, 1983. Wexler's directorial credits include *Medium Cool, Latino*, and several political documentaries.

Robert Wise. Director.
Among his dozens of films, some of the best known are: *West Side Story*, 1961, *The Sound of Music*, 1965, *The Andromeda*

Strain, 1971, *The Hindenberg*, 1975, *Audrey Rose*, 1977, *Star Trek, The Motion Picture*, 1979.

Harry Wolf, ASC. Cinematographer.
President of the ASC in 1982. Some of his credits include: "Baretta" and "Through the Eye of a Sparrow," 1975 (Emmy Award winner), "Colombo" and "Any Old Port in a Storm," 1973 (Emmy Award winner), and Emmy nominations for "Brave New World," 1980, and "Little House, A New Beginning," 1983.

Ralph Woolsey, ASC. Cinematographer.
President of the ASC in 1983. Some of his credits include: *Little Fauss and Big Halsy*, 1970, *The New Centurions*, 1972, *The Iceman Cometh*, 1973, *Lifeguard*, 1976, *Mother, Jugs, and Speed*, 1976, *The Great Santini*, 1979, *Oh, God! Book II*, 1980.

Vilmos Zsigmond, ASC. Cinematographer.
Some of his credits include: *McCabe and Mrs. Miller*, 1971, *Deliverance*, 1972, *Images*, 1972, *The Long Goodbye*, 1973, *Sugarland Express*, 1974, *Close Encounters of the Third Kind*, 1977 (Academy Award winner), *The Deer Hunter*, 1978 (Academy Award nomination), *The Rose*, 1979, *Blow Out*, 1981, and *The River*, 1984 (Academy Award nomination).

Glossary

Answer Print (Trial Composite Print). A print used to identify scenes or shots that require further correction in color, density and sound quality. The final composite print has all the corrections accomplished.

ASA Speed (now Exposure Index, or E.I.). Film sensitivity to light as rated in numbers; established originally by the American Standard Association.

ASC. American Society of Cinematographers

Attenuator. A filter with a continuous gradual change from a specific density to clear glass, or from heavier to lighter density. Sometimes used to designate a Graduated Filter.

Baby Spot. Focusable studio lamp with a Fresnel lens and a 500-watt to 1000-watt bulb.

Backing. Painted or photographed background used behind set windows and doors.

Barndoor. Two or four metal shields hinged in front of a lamp to limit and shape the pattern of light.

Best Boy. Electrician who is second in line of command after the gaffer.

Blocking. Staging the actors in relation to the camera and establishing the camera movements for a given shot.

Booster Light. Usually a carbon arc, an HMI, or cluster quartz lamps used on exterior locations for augmenting the daylight, especially when filling the shadows.

Brightness. Ability of a surface to reflect or emit light in the direction of the camera. Also referred to as luminance.

Broad. A single or double lamp designed to provide even illumination over a relatively wide area. Used as a general fill light.

Brute. A type of arc lamp that uses 225 amps.

Butterfly. A net stretched on a frame and supported by one stand. Used over an outdoor scene to soften the sunlight.

CC Filters. Color-compensating filters. A series of filters in yellow, cyan, magenta, blue, green and red, increasing in density by small steps. Used for correcting and modifying the color of a scene either when shooting or printing.

Candela. A unit of light intensity. The luminance of a light source is often expressed in candelas per square meter.

Century Stand. A metal stand for positioning a lighting accessory such as a flag, cookie, or scrim. Also called C-stand.

Coffin Light. An overhead light consisting of a

boxlike frame with a few rows of bulbs which either point up toward a reflective surface, or down toward a diffusing screen, thus producing soft light.

Color Temperature. A system for evaluating the color of a light source by comparing it to a theoretically perfect temperature radiator called a *black body*. At lower teemperatures a black body emits reddish light, and when heated to high temperatures its light changes to bluish. Color temperature is measured in degrees Kelvin. A degree Kelvin is the same as degree Centigrade, but the two scales have different starting points. ($0°K = -273°$ Centigrade).

Complementary Colors. Colors obtained by filtering out from the visible spectrum three primary colors, in turn. Yellow filter (minus blue) subtracts blue, but allows green and red pass through resulting in yellow light. Magenta filter (minus green) subtracts green light, transmitting blue and red seen as magenta. Cyan filter (minus red) subtracts red light, transmitting blue and green seen as cyan.

Converter. A general name for electrical devices that serve certain functions in changing electrical characteristics such as conversion from AC to DC or vice versa, voltage conversion (transformer), or frequency conversion.

Cookie. Also called *cucaloris*. An irregularly perforated shadow-forming flag, opaque or translucent, made of plywood or plastic.

Cool Lights. Lights designed to dissipate heat toward the rear of the lamp, through the reflector, allowing for a more comfortable temperature in front of the light.

Coop, Chicken Coop. An overhead, boxlike light with a cluster of six, usually 100-watt globes, for top lighting of sets.

Coverage. All the footage shot from all the angles that is foreseen as necessary for the editor.

Croniecone. A device developed by Jordan Cronenweth for mounting a diffusion screen directly onto the light. It protrudes from the lamp as a widening cone so that light will not spill to the side and the diffusion screen will be a few feet wide.

Cutter. A shadow-forming device, usually rectangular in shape; a type of flag.

Cyclorama (Cyc). A sound stage background, usually white, with rounded corners, to create a limbo or sky effect. Made of plaster or stretched plastic.

Cyc-Strip. A lighting instrument shaped like a trough with up to 12 bulbs for even illumination of a cyclorama.

Dailies. Also called *rushes*. The first print from original footage, with or without synchronous sound tracks, delivered from the lab daily during the shooting period, for viewing by the director, cinematographer, and other members of the production.

Density. The thickness of the silver deposit, or color dyes on the film, which affects the amount of light projected onto the screen.

Depth of Field. The distance through which objects will appear sharp in front of and behind the point at which the camera is focused.

Desaturation. Lowering the degree of hue in a given color.

Dichroic Filter. A filter used on tungsten lamps to convert their color temperature to that of daylight. The filter reflects excessive red and transmits light that is bluer.

Diffusers. For lenses: Fine nets, granulated or grooved glass, petroleum jelly or glycerine smeared on glass, positioned in front of the lens to soften the photographed image. For lamps: Diffusing materials like tight nets, spun glass, frosted plastic, and so forth, placed in front of the lamp.

Dimmer. An instrument used to change the voltage of lights on the set to regulate their intensity. Not always useful for color cinematography, as the color temperature of the lights will also change.

Dot. Shadow-forming device in the form of a small round scrim.

Drop. Curtain or screen of black cloth hung vertically over the set to control the passage of light. For example, blocking the backlight from unwanted areas. Also known as a teaser.

EV (Exposure Values). Units used in calibrating modern reflected light meters. As with f/stops each whole number increase is equivalent to twice the brightness. For example E.V.6 means twice the light of E.V.5.

Fay. Lamp letter code designation for a 650-watt PAR bulb of a daylight color temperature.

FC. See Footcandles.

Fiber Optics. A technique that makes it possible to put light in difficult places. It uses glass or plastic fibers through which light can travel even when they are bent. A very useful device in delivering illumination to cramped spaces, such as car interiors.

Fill Light. Light shining on the scene from a point near the camera and illuminating the shadows caused by the key light.

Finger. Narrow rectangular shadow-casting device. See also flag.

Flag (or Gobo). Shadow-casting device made of cloth stretched on a metal frame. Specific types of flags include the cutter, finger, target, and teaser.

Flashing. A laboratory procedure for lowering the image contrast by exposing the film, before development, to a very weak light. This introduces a slight overall fog, which is more noticeable in the shadows than in the highlights, and makes the shadow details more marked.

FLB Filter. Camera filter used to color correct a scene illuminated by a "cool-white" fluorescent tube, to a type *B* (tungsten) film stock.

Floater. A light, a flag or a net moved intentionally during the shot.

Flying Moon. A lighting contraption in the shape of a cube made of aluminum pipes and covered with bleached muslin. It houses four 25,000-watt HMIs and is hoisted by an industrial crane to 80 to 120 feet. Used to create artificial moonlight.

Foam-Core Board. A white cardboard with soft styrofoam inner layer. Fomecore is the brand name for this product. Used to bounce light.

Footcandle. International unit of illumination. The intensity of light falling on a sphere placed one foot away from a source of light of one candlepower, also, one candela.

Forcing. Also known as *pushing*. A laboratory procedure of overdeveloping the film to compensate for underexposure.

Fresnel Lens. A type of lens used on spotlights. The convex surface is reduced to concentric ridges, to avoid overheating and to reduce weight. Lamps equipped with this lens are called Fresnels in popular ι age.

Frost. The term used for the plastic diffusion material which resembles a shower curtain in weight and tracing paper in appearance.

f/Stop. A number obtained by dividing the focal length of lens by its effective aperture (the opening through which light passes within the lens). f/stop represents the light transmitting capability of the lens at any given setting.

Gaffer. The chief electrician on the film crew.

Gimmick Bulb. A small bulb, like the FEV globe used in Inkies or a "peanut" bulb, used for hiding in confined spaces.

Glow Light. A very weak light source that creates a slight glow in the actor's face, usually directed onto the face from one side.

Gobo. See Flag.

Graduated Filter. A filter with neutral density or color covering only a certain portion of the glass. There is a gradual transition between the dense and the clear part of the filter. This *bleed line* may vary depending on the purpose of the given filter. See also Attenuator.

Gray Scale. Chart showing tones of gray from white to black.

Griffolyn. The brand name of a plastic material used for large reflecting screens.

Grip. A member of a film crew responsible for laying camera tracks, erecting scaffolds, and positioning flags and diffusion screens.

Hair Light. A light source positioned specifically to light the actor's hair.

High Key. A lighting style in which the majority of the scene is in highlights. Usually enhanced by bright costumes and sets. A low ratio of key light to fill light lowers the contrast, helping to obtain this effect.

HMI. Hydrargyum Medium Arc-Length Iodide, a metal halide discharge lamp constituting, in effect, a mercury arc enclosed in a glass envelope. Gives off color temperature equivalent to daylight.

Honeycomb. A grid used on soft lights to control the lighting pattern and direction. It is shallower than the egg crate grid.

Hue. A scientific term for color.

Incandescent Light. Electric light produced by

the glowing of a metallic filament such as tungsten. Modern quartz lamps, more accurately called tungsten-halogen lamps, are incandescent.

Incident Light. Light coming directly from the source onto the object and the light meter, as opposed to light reflected from the photographed subject into the light meter.

Inky-Dink. The smallest focusable studio lamp with a Fresnel lens and a bulb up to 250 watts.

Insert Car. A vehicle used for towing the action car (target vehicle) during certain moving car shots. Camera and lights are often mounted on the insert car.

Inverter. An electric device converting direct current (DC) to alternating current (AC).

Japanese Lantern (Chinese Lantern). A large lightweight light made of paper, silk, or other translucent materials, housing a Photoflood bulb and producing a very soft illumination. Due to its light weight, a Japanese lantern can be easily hung in the desired part of the set.

Junior. A focusable, studio lamp with Fresnel lens and 2000-watt bulb. Perhaps the most common studio lighting instrument.

Kelvin Degrees. See Color Temperature.

Key Light. The main source used to light the subject. Its direction and ratio to fill light establishes the mood of the illumination.

Kicker. A light source positioned approximately three-fourths back of the subject, usually on the side opposite the key light. Used to separate subjects from background.

Latitude. An emulsion's ability to accommodate a certain range of exposures and produce satisfactory pictures. Also called Exposure Latitude.

Low Contrast (LC) Filters. Screens used on the lens to reduce the image contrast.

Liner. A light source to one side of the subject that produces a rim of light that will help to create a three-dimensional effect.

Low Key. A lighting style in which the majority of a scene is lit sparingly. It is usually enhanced by dark costumes and sets. A high ratio of key light to fill light is employed for this effect.

Luminaires. The term used in the film industry for lighting instruments (lights) of different designs. Sometimes they are popularly called *lamps*, but strictly speaking, a lamp is just the electric bulb in the lighting instrument.

Master Light®. A popular light using the PAR 64, 1000-watt bulb which can be boosted to higher voltage and subsequently higher color temperature, by means of an autotransformer. Manufactured by Leonetti Cine Rentals Inc. Hollywood, Calif.

Master Shot. The widest angle on a scene that establishes the characters in relation to their environment and to each other.

Matte. A mask used on the camera or an optical printer to protect certain parts of the frame from exposure, which will later be exposed to a different scene, for example, substituting a different background.

Maxi-Brute. A cluster of 1000-watt PAR lamps (manufactured by Colortran).

Meat Axe. A colloquial term for a small flag.

Midget. A small but sturdy light (up to 250 watt) with a Fresnel lens, made by Mole-Richardson.

Mini-Mole. A small Inky Dink light (up to 250 watt) with a Fresnel lens, made by Mole-Richardson, but not as sturdy as the Midget.

Neutral Density (ND) Filters. Colorless filters of graduated densities, used to cut down the amount of light entering the lens. They can be employed on either the camera or on windows. They are used when light is too intense for a given film or required f/stop.

Nooklite. An open-ended lamp with narrow housing designed primarily to fit into wall and ceiling corners but often used in studio-built overhead coffin lights.

Original. Negative or Reversal film stock that was exposed in the camera and processed to produce either a negative or a reversal picture.

Overhead. A large frame, supported by two stands or ropes, with white silk or black cloth, to diffuse or block out the direct sunlight on an exterior scene.

PAR (Parabolic Aluminized Reflector). A lamp designation for a bulb with a self-contained reflector and lens, similar to the automobile headlight.

Peanut Bulb. A small bulb used for hiding in confined areas. GE 6S6 is one example of such a bulb.

Photo flood. A type of light bulb in which the light output and color temperature are higher than that of a comparable household bulb but with a shorter life.

Plate. A film material shot for front or back projection.

Practical. A lamp on the set that is rigged to be operational as a luminaire during the scene action.

Primary Colors. Blue, Green and Red. See also Complementary Colors.

Printer Light Scale (Printing Lights). A graduated scale of printing light intensity, allowing one to print the original images brighter or darker to obtain an evenly exposed print from an original with uneven exposures. The light scale is also used when executing optical effects such as fades and dissolves.

Process Shot. A technique of filming live action staged in front of the screen on which the background view is projected. This background plate can be projected either from behind the translucent screen (back projection), or from the front on a highly reflective screen (front projection).

Pushing. See Forcing.

Raking Shot, Raking Two Shot. A shot of usually two people taken from one side, with the foreground head in profile. Example: A shot through the side window of a car with one or both persons in profile.

Riser. The extending part of a lamp stand or century stand.

Scoop. A studio lamp with a soft, wide round throw of 500 to 2000 watts.

Scrim. A lighting accessory of wire mesh or net, positioned in front of a light source when attenuation of light is required.

Senior. A focusable studio lamp with a Fresnel lens and 5000-watt bulb.

Skypan (Skylite). A nonfocusable studio lamp with a 5000-watt to 10,000-watt bulb providing illumination over a broad area, such as set backings.

Snoot. A funnel-shaped light-controlling device used on lamps in place of barndoors for a more exact light-beam pattern.

Spun Glass. A diffusion material made from glass fibers. Extremely heat resistant but like fiberglass it irritates the skin and eyes. It is generally replaced now by Tough Spun which is nonirritating.

Storyboard. A series of drawings used as visual representation of the shooting script. The sketches represent the key situations (shots) in the scripted scenes. They indicate the framing, camera angle, blocking, gross character movement in the frame and basic props and sets. Dialogue, effects, and so on, appear below the pictures.

Target. A solid or net disc, up to 10 inches in diameter, used to control the lamp beam and create desirable shadows. A type of flag or scrim.

Teaser. A large black cloth screen for controlling soft light, often put on stands or hung over a set.

Teching Down. The method of treating costumes and draperies to better accommodate them to reproduction on color film. For example, rinsing white fabric in weak tea lowers the highlighting tendency of pure white. The term comes from the process originated by Technicolor.

Tener. A focusable lamp with Fresnel lens and 10,000-watt bulb.

Timing (Grading). A lab operation before printing to select printer lights and color filters to improve the densities and color rendition of the original footage and thus obtain a more visually satisfactory print. The technician in charge is called a timer (in Britain, grader).

Tough Spun. A diffusing material made of synthetic fibers. Highly heat resistant.

Translite Backing. Backing for windows and doors prepared from large photographic enlargements and lit from the back for a desired effect.

T/Stop. Calibration of the lens light-transmitting power arrived at by an actual measurement of the transmitted light for each lens and each stop individually. T/stops are considered more accurate than f/stops.

Variac. Trade name of a popular variable transformer for manual AC voltage regulation.

Wild Wall, Wild Ceilings. Walls and ceilings made to be moved at will, even during the shot.

Zinger. Any directional light source used to highlight a scene predominantly lit with soft light.

"Zip" Softlight. A narrow, 8" x 17½" soft light with 2000-watt bulb, made by Mole-Richardson®. Useful in a low ceiling situation.

Index

Interiors, shooting, 165–76
  See also specific subject headings
Interpretive light, 171
  specific lighting requirements, 171

Keylights, use in image manipulation, 54
Kline, Richard, 14, 55–56, 70, 73, 85–86, 95, 156, 170
Kovacs, Laszlo, 31, 94, 145

Laboratories, film manipulation in, 70 *et seq.*
  See also Image manipulation
Lathrop, Philip, 65, 71, 108, 138, 144
Learning to light, 177–81
  awareness of light, need for, 177
  balancing light, need to understand, 179
  commercials, from, 178
  crew, learning from, 178–79
  documentaries, from, 178
  matching one shot to another, 179
  painters, studying, 177–78
  visual traditions of cinematography, learning, 177–78
Lensless lights, 27
Lightflex system, 68–69
Light, generally
  See also specific subject headings
  accessories to control, 39–48
  battery operated, 36, 39
  character of, 83
  cinematographer's role. *See* Cinematographer, role of
  compact lights, 37–39
  composition of movement and. *See* Composition of movement
  daily life, changes in light during, 1
  equipment. *See* Lighting equipment
  experience, flexibility in re lighting techniques and, 179–180
  gaffer, role of, 19–20
  improving equipment and, 179–180
  improvisation and, 180
  intensity, controlling, 39
  Lowel-Light system, 37
  measuring and evaluating. *See* Image manipulation
  power supply, 48–50
  scene coverage, planning for, 13

Light (*continued*)
  sources of, cinematographer's role in deciding, 93–96
  strategic lighting. *See* Strategic lighting
  studio, advantages of shooting in, 98
  styles of lighting reflecting certain periods or film studios, 2
Lighting equipment
  cinematographer's role in developing, 22
  development over the years, 22
  gaffer's role in developing, 22
  light sources, uses, 22
Location, lighting on, 147–176
  aesthetic judgments in preproduction, need for, 147–48
  best time for shooting daylight scenes, 154
    See also Daylight, shooting in
  diffusion; cucaloris, use of, 151
  exterior shots, problems as to, 148–70
    See also Daylight, shooting in; Day-for-night exteriors, shooting; Night-for-night scenes; Night interiors; Sunset scenes, shooting
  identifying problems in preproduction, 147
  interiors, shooting, 165–176
  preproduction preparation, 147–48

Mackendrick, Alexander, 2, 3, 8, 10–11, 15, 16, 17, 18
Makeup artist, working with, 11–12
Margulies, Michael D., 20, 66, 67, 106, 122, 138, 141, 152, 156, 170
Mixing, need for practical experience, 85
Movement, composition of. *See* Composition of movement

Nets, use as diffusion filters, 65–66
Night-for-night exteriors, shooting, 159–65
  arc lights, use, 161, 164
  bluish light, achieving, 164
  campfire effect, achieving, 165
  city/country exteriors, 161–62
  color gels, use, 164–65
  contrasts of, 162
  desirability of, 159
  existing street lights, use, 161
  fast film emulsion affecting, 159–61
  fire effects, achieving, 165
  main objectives of, 160

Timing and printing the film, 71–78
  See also Image manipulation, subhead: printing and timing
Tone values from light to dark, effectiveness, 52
Trusell, Hal, 123
Tungsten incandescent bulbs, 22–23

Vehicles, shooting interior locations in, 171–76
  buses, 171–72
  cars as most common location, 175
  fiber optics, use and effect, 175–76
  location shooting for realism, 173
  planes, 171
  simulating movement, 171
  trains, 171

Video transfers, 78–82
  Flying Spot Scanner, effect of use, 79–80
  quality requirements, 79
Von Sternberg, Joseph, 140

Walls, treatment of, 117–118
Wide screen ratios, 17
Windows as source of light, 100
Wexler, Haskell, 6–7, 10, 16–17, 18, 21, 27, 65, 85, 94, 96, 118, 162, 171–73, 178
Wise, Robert, 3, 10, 12, 17, 67, 147
Wolf, Harry, 35, 53, 56, 118, 123, 165
Woolsey, Ralph, 33, 57, 58, 63, 64, 108–109, 110, 113, 127, 137, 151, 166, 169

Zsigmond, Vilmos, 18–19, 36, 55, 58, 63–66, 70, 72–74, 85, 93–95, 96, 121, 148, 153, 164, 165, 171, 173, 177, 179

994-4
75-74
C